ENGLISH MANTRA

ENGLISH MANTRA

Spoken English, ELT Activities and Job Grooming

JANARDAN MISHRA

PARTRIDGE

A Penguin Random House Company

To order additional copies of this book, contact
Partridge India
000 800 10062 62
www.partridgepublishing.com/india
orders.india@partridgepublishing.com

This maiden work on ELT by the author is dedicated to
Prof. Dr. D. K. Ray, a known name in the academic circle of Odisha,
for his guidance to bring out the book successfully.

CONTENTS

FOREWORD

English Mantra by Janardan Mishra fills in a much acknowledged gap in the area of practice material to develop various communication skills in English. The book is not theory laden but uses an activity oriented approach, which is well graded to develop both accuracy and fluency in using English in different contexts. Starting with pronunciation, the activities move towards conversational skills winding up with higher level GD and presentation skills.

The materials offer commonly used English expressions for daily communication and conversation in informal and formal situations. Learning these expressions will help the users sound more natural and polite. The activities are structured and paced keeping in mind the practical aspects of learning. Another commendable aspect regarding the book is its dual focus. It can be used as a self learning material by any enthusiastic learner. It can also be used as classroom teaching material under the guidance of the teacher.

It is a laudable maiden attempt on the part of the author that will go a long way in fulfilling the communication requirement of students from undergraduate level upwards.

Kalyani Samantray
Reader, PG Department of English
Utkal University, Bhubaneswar, Odisha

PREFACE

The basic assumption of this book is that there should be special teaching courses on 'communication and fluency' for the ESL students at school and college levels. With the advent of globalisation, there has been an enormous increase in the number and size of professional organisations and English communication plays a vital role in the smooth functioning of those organisations. A realisation of this need by the authorities of different educational institutions has led to the introduction of special courses on oral communication (Spoken English) in all premier institutions to enable the students to compete in the globalised world with more confidence and better communicative skills. The main aim of this book is to provide assistance to the students in acquiring proficiency of a higher level for their command of good English.

Spoken English or English communication has become an integral part of any curriculum at school and college levels. "English Mantra" is a bold attempt in this regard specially designed for the teachers and the students to develop their English language fluency through different language speaking activities. These activities can be conducted in classrooms with ESL students for improving their English Speaking skills in different situations. Some of these activities will also develop confidence of the learners to face the audience and speak in a group and remove their stage fright. These speaking activities include On the Spot, Short Prepared Speech, Interactive Stories, Micro Presentation, Role Play, Story-Building and Retelling, Debating, Crossfire, Dumb Charade, Press Conference, Public Speaking, Extempore, Instant Translation, Teaching for Better Fluency, Forum, Descriptions, Telephonic Conversation, Body Language, Group Discussion, Case Study, Personal Interview, SWOT Analysis, Situation Reaction Test, Brainstorming, Mock Seminar, Picture Reading, etc.

The outstanding feature of this book is that it contains specially designed curricula for different levels of students and guidelines for teachers to adopt those curricula. Now-a-days the teachers are not getting proper curriculum or syllabus for teaching Spoken (Communicative) English in schools and colleges. They are also keenly interested in different types of ELT activities for their students. I am sure this book will be very helpful for them. The book contains three types of curricula for Secondary, Higher-Secondary and Advanced students. Many students of all these levels of study face the problem of good communication in English. The book will serve as a good and useful guide for them.

This impressive manual will also enable the readers to improve their English pronunciation and acquire the correct patterns of accent, rhythm, and intonation. A very long chapter of the book is dedicated for this purpose. It contains all the forty-four English sounds including short vowel sounds, long vowel sounds, diphthongs, consonant and other sounds. The mechanism for properly producing those sounds is also given with suitable examples. The rules to get the number of syllables in a word, stress pattern of those words, etc. are also provided with much lucidity.

One part of the book contains special chapters on job grooming. Chapters like Group Discussion, Personal Interview, SWOT Analysis, Situation Reaction Test, and Writing Resumes will be very convenient for the students preparing for jobs and higher studies.

Grammar is a necessary part of English language learning. Of course, one need not complete a whole grammar course for speaking English better. Therefore, the book contains simple grammar items like Tense, Sentence Patterns, Uses of Tense, etc. It also contains many grammar-based conversations which will be very much essential for the students of different age groups. The class-room teachers would certainly get examples of patterns of good English sentences to which they can refer and improve further by initiating practice by students in a variety of ways.

Well, the book is a single panacea for the whole problem of communication.

—Janardan Mishra

ACKNOWLEDGEMENT

I am indebted to thousands of my students, particularly the students of Ravenshaw University who have inspired me to give a shape to my classroom teaching by writing this book. They are the real stake-holders of the success of this book. I sincerely acknowledge their contribution to the teaching-learning situation. Credit also goes to the teachers who have attended my teacher-training sessions. They have always appreciated and inspired my effort to develop materials for the ESL learners.

An international brand name, i.e. Partridge India, a Penguin Company, has taken the trouble of adding value to this work by bringing it out and making it available worldwide for the ESL learners. I sincerely appreciate the effort of all the members of staff of the company behind the achievement of getting this book published.

Finally, I gracefully acknowledge the comments, suggestions and recommendations of my colleagues in different colleges and universities where I have been working as a freelancer to develop the fluency of the students and make them employable. All suggestions for incorporating new materials for further improvement of this book will be greatly acknowledged.

—Janardan Mishra

CHAPTER 1

COMMUNICATION—PROCESS AND TYPES

COMMUNICATION:

Communication means to exchange or share ideas with other individuals in the society. Decide one day not to communicate with anyone and see how difficult life is. Our days begin with exchanging greetings. We smile at people and receive smiles. These are examples of communication. However, it is not that we communicate only with others. Often we sit silently and contemplate. At that time we actually communicate with ourselves. Thus, communication is inevitable and it has unparalleled utility and significance in the wake of an age of globalization.

THE PROCESS OF COMMUNICATION:

Communication is a process that involves a sender who sends the message, which is then carried via the communication channel to the receiver who receives the message, processes the information and sends an appropriate reply to the sender (feedback) via the same communication channel. Figure 1 shows a simple communication model.

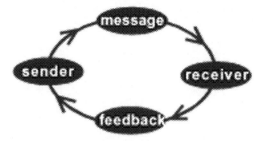

(Fig. 1—A Simple Communication Model)

Types of Communication

⇨ **Verbal Communication**

Verbal communication means written or oral communication. Written communication can be either via mail or email. The oral communication refers to the spoken words.

⇨ **Nonverbal Communication**

Non-verbal communication includes the overall body language like postures, gestures, overall body movements, the facial expressions, etc. It also includes gestures like a handshake, a smile or a hug. Non verbal communication can also be in the form of pictorial representations, signboards or even photographs, sketches and paintings.

⇨ **Group Communication**

Group Communication includes many senders and many receivers. A group discussion or a meeting can be the best example of a group communication.

⇨ **Inter-Communication**

Inter-Communication basically involves two people, a sender and a receiver. Most of the communication in the world belongs to this category. Figure 1 shows the process of inter-communication.

⇨ **Intra-Communication**

The term 'intra' means 'one'. So intra-communication includes only one person. He is the sender and he is the receiver. It may sound nonsense. But it is possible. You might have seen people talking to themselves aloud. That is a very good example of intra-communication. Most people are bathroom singers. In this case, the singer himself is the sender as well as the receiver in the process of communication.

1.1 The Uses of Language

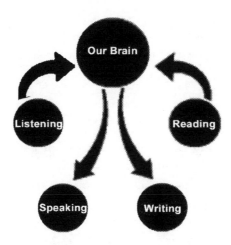

(Fig. 2—Uses of Language)

Language has four uses. These are 'listening', 'speaking', 'reading', and 'writing'. While 'listening' and 'reading' are inputs of brain, 'speaking' and 'writing' are outputs. If there is no input, there is no output. Therefore, listening and reading activities are very important to speak and write effectively. Many people are not fluent in a particular language because they do not listen a lot of that language. Figure 2 illustrates the different uses of a particular language.

1.2 Methods to Learn a Language

Basically there are three methods to learn a language. These are "Parents Method", "Force Method" and "Use Method".

⇨ **Parents Method**

Have you ever asked yourself: "How did I learn my own language?" In fact, you never really "learned" it at all—you just started speaking it. One day, when you were about two or three years old, you started speaking your language—a few words at first, not full sentences. But you spoke. It was like magic! But it wasn't magic. It was the result of listening. For two to three years, words went IN to your head. Then words came OUT of your head! As "listening" is an input and "speaking" is an output, more listening means more speaking. Most of the people learn their native language by this method.

⇨ **Force Method**

Have you ever asked yourself: "How can a little student of the public school (English Medium School) speak so fluently at such an early age??" Well, the school environment forces the child to speak. He is nervous at the beginning. Even he does not speak at all on the first day. He finds himself alone among the students speaking English words and chunks (short terms or sentences). Slowly he also tries to do that and succeeds. Nobody looks at his grammar or pronunciation at that stage. He goes on speaking from words to phrases and from phrases to sentences.

⇨ **Use Method**

Have you ever asked yourself: "What happens in a spoken English class?" Here the learner gets a lot of practice in speaking fluently and accurately. Nobody cares about any mistakes at the beginning. The trainers motivate the trainees to use the language under different situations like Role Play, Extempore, etc. and the trainees become confident to speak in the long run. It's like handling a cell-phone without going through the manual seriously.

1.3 Tips to Speak English Better

⇨ **Start thinking everything in English and don't translate.**

Always think in English and speak spontaneously. Talk to yourself. Think a lot in English (Intra-Communication). This will help you to improve your fluency. Also don't try to speak sentences translated from other languages. It is because Translation will make the thinking-speaking process longer and also you may not find the exact English terms of certain words used in your native language. That will always put you in trouble.

➩ **Use Chunks (short expressions) at the beginning.**

This helps the beginners particularly. Chunks are phrases or groups of words which can be learnt as a unit by one who is learning a language. Examples of chunks are 'Good morning sir' and 'Pleased to meet you', etc. Chunks reduce the pressure of speaking sentences with grammar. It is very important to use words together to speak. Chunks help you do so.

➩ **Observe mouth movements of good English speakers.**

Observe the mouth movements of the speakers. Repeat what they are saying, imitating the sounds, accent and intonation of their speech.

➩ **Don't worry about Starting Trouble and grammatical mistakes.**

Even native speakers of English find it difficult to get started. So, don't let the starting trouble disturb you. Using discourse markers (a word or phrase that organizes spoken language into different parts, for example 'Well . . .' or 'On the other hand . . .') is a good idea in handling starting trouble. Okay, all right, right then, well, hmm', you know, like, etc., are all examples of discourse markers used in conversation. They are employed to give the speaker a second to think about what he wants to say. At the beginning don't speak fast. Being fluent does NOT mean speaking quickly. It is better to speak slowly and clearly at the beginning than quickly and incoherently.

➩ **Read aloud for 20 to 30 minutes every day.**

When somebody reads aloud, he uses the language in three ways—he reads, he listens and he speaks. Thus he gets both the inputs of brain that are helpful to get the output that is speaking. Reading also helps to learn new words or to use words that you have already known. But you should read something with active vocabulary.

➩ **Listen to the English music and dialogues every day.**

As listening is an input of brain, it is very much essential to listen a lot to speak. Listening native speakers helps in developing proper pronunciation of words.

➩ **Develop your Active Vocabulary (daily used words).**

There are three types of words in every language—Active, Passive and Slang. While active words are daily used, simple words, passive words are basically bookish. Slang is dirty and used to hurt others. Active vocabulary is required for fluent and comfortable speech.

⇨ **Record and listen your own voice for more perfection.**
Record your own voice (if possible) and listen for pronunciation and grammar mistakes.

⇨ **Do not follow written English style and don't mug up.**
Don't try to follow a formal written English style or don't make deliberate attempts to speak full and complete sentences as in written English.

⇨ **Find a partner for making conversations.**
Conversation requires two agents. If you are alone, you are helpless. But intra-communication (thinking and talking to yourself) will help you a lot.

1.4 Assessment of Speaking Activities by the Teacher

When a student writes an essay, the teachers award marks for the same, that is, 8 out of 10 or 5 out of 10, etc. But when somebody speaks, it is difficult to award mark. It is because 'speaking' involves many factors like the body language of a person, the accuracy and correctness of his language, the content of his speech (subject matter), etc. It is difficult to award marks for all the above areas which are subjective by nature. Therefore, a formula can be devised for assessing the performance of the speaker. This is called the BLT FORMULA. BLT stands for Body Language, Language and Topic.
All these areas are graded. For example one can assign C grade for Very Poor, B grade for Poor, B+ grade for Average, A grade for Good, A+ grade for Very Good and O grade for Excellent performance. Let us explain in details.

⇨ **Body Language**
It includes eye-contact, proper position and movements of different parts of the body, facial appearance, confidence level, etc. It is because 'speaking' is not a word process, it is a people process. Like an actor or an actress let the speaker's face, eyes, shoulders, hands, tone, all channels help in getting his message across. Body language also includes the capacity to handle the pressure of being on the stage.

⇨ **Language (with Delivery)**

It includes appropriate wordings, proper inflection or grammatical function, correctness and clarity of enunciation (pronunciation of words or sounds), audibility, naturalness, rate of speech (fast, slow or varied), etc.

⇨ **Topic (Content)**

Here we should consider the subject matter of the topic including facts and figures, logical arrangement of facts, proper argument for or against the subject, etc. It also includes proper introduction, and conclusion.

⇨ **Group Behaviour**

It includes certain criteria like the level of cooperation and conflict inside the group, commitment to group-objective, group knowledge (knowledge of one group member about the other members), handling crises jointly, etc.

In classroom condition, a student is supposed to go through different speaking activities and continuously develop the skills related to all the areas discussed above. Both the teacher and the student should maintain a record card of this development. The teacher can give his remarks on the performance of the student after each class. This card is shown in **Figure 3**.

ASSESSMENT RECORD-CARD OF SPEAKING ACTIVITIES

●C = Very Poor ●B = Poor ●B+ = Average ●A = Good ●A+ = Very Good ●O = Excellent

CLASS NO.	BODY LANGUAGE	LANGUAGE	TEXT	GROUP BEHAVIOUR	TEACHER'S REMARK
Sample	A	B+	C	X	no eye-contact / pauses / grammatical mistakes
Class 1					
Class 2					
Class 3					
Class 4					
Class 5					
Class 6					
Class 7					
Class 8					
Class 9					
Class 10					
Class 11					
Class 12					
Class 13					
Class 14					
Class 15					
Class 16					
Class 17					
Class 18					
Class 19					
Class 20					
Class 21					
Class 22					
Class 23					
Class 24					
Class 25					
Class 26					
Class 27					
Class 28					
Class 29					
Class 30					
Class 31					
Class 32					
Class 33					

(Fig. 3—The Assessment Record Card of Speaking Activities)

1.5 The Aim Card for Developing Fluency

An 'Aim Card' is a check list for the daily reading and listening habits of a student which is ultimately monitored by the teacher. Here are certain instructions to maintain the Aim Card by the students and an illustration of the Aim Card (Figure 4).

INSTRUCTIONS

⇨ READ aloud and LISTEN English for half an hour daily.

⇨ Choose the text for reading with Active Vocabulary. Story books and newspapers are preferable.

⇨ It is better if you can listen the native speakers.

⇨ Start all these activities with short prayers for better concentration. In case of irregularities, bounce back.

⇨ Maintain a record of these activities using the following table. If you have completed the reading assignment on one particular day put a tick mark, otherwise put a cross. This is only to maintain a continuity of practice. Get the table checked by your teacher.

⇨ Do all these activities at a fixed time daily. Have patience, you will get the best result.

AIM CARD

→W D↓	SUN R	SUN L	MON R	MON L	TUE R	TUE L	WED R	WED L	THU R	THU L	FRI R	FRI L	SAT R	SAT L	Trainer's Sign
W-1	✓	✗	✓												
W-2															
W-3															
W-4															
W-5															
W-6															
W-7															
W-8															
W-9															
W-10															
W-11															
W-12															
W-13															
W-14															
W-15															
W-16															
W-17															
W-18															
W-19															
W-20															
W-21															
W-22															
W-23															
W-24															

(Fig. 4—The Aim Card)

1.6 Self Assessment of LSRW Activities

How well do you listen?

"He understands me," we say with elation when someone perceptively listens to us; "Oh, forget it," we say in frustration when others don't listen or understand. How are you as a listener? What are your beliefs about listening? Look at the following questions. Indicate whether you agree or disagree with the following keys:

(1. Strongly Disagree   2. Disagree   3. Undecided   4. Agree   5. Strongly Agree)

1. An effective listener pays attention both to what a person is saying and what she or he is not saying. (1/2/3/4/5)
2. We can understand another person well even if we don't 'hear' their feelings. (1/2/3/4/5)
3. I can listen better to my subordinates if we have worked through our expectations of one another. (1/2/3/4/5)
4. Words fully express what a person feels. (1/2/3/4/5)
5. We tend to hear things which support our prejudices and not hear things which counteract them. (1/2/3/4/5)
6. Listening with understanding to another means agreeing with him or her. (1/2/3/4/5)
7. Persons who listen with understanding run the danger of being changed themselves. (1/2/3/4/5)
8. Our very natural tendency to evaluate is a help to effective listening. (1/2/3/4/5)
9. Some things can only be said with the leap of the listener. (1/2/3/4/5)
10. Listening is primarily a word process, not a people process. (1/2/3/4/5)
11. As I listen, I should be aware of my own feelings. (1/2/3/4/5)
12. It is more important that the other be given a chance to talk than that he or she be understood. (1/2/3/4/5)
13. Advice giving or dogmatic statements tend to superiorize the one who makes them. (1/2/3/4/5)
14. Silence is not communicative. (1/2/3/4/5)

Scoring: Many psychologists would agree with the odd numbers and disagree with the even numbers.

HOW WELL DO YOU SPEAK?

The following is a checklist for your speaking practices. Check the following answer keysthat best fit your habitual practice.

Always (1)   Usually (2)   Sometimes (3) Rarely (4)   Never (5)

1. Before speaking my first words, I take an easy breath, wait for silence, pick out a face on the left, centre, and right of the audience, pause and then begin. (1/2/3/4/5)
2. Even if there is little time for preparation, I think, at least, of how I will begin and how I will end my talk. (1/2/3/4/5)
3. As far as time and opportunity allow, I try to get data on my audience before I begin work on my speech. (1/2/3/4/5)
4. I do not use a microphone unless it is quite necessary. (1/2/3/4/5)
5. If possible, I prefer to stand on the same level as my audience rather than on a platform above them. (1/2/3/4/5)
6. At the beginning of my talk I check whether those in the rear can hear me. (1/2/3/4/5)
7. I use, as a rough estimate of the effectiveness of my talk, the amount of discussion it generates. (1/2/3/4/5)
8. I am conscious that there is a point of diminishing returns in speaking and end my talk swiftly when I've made my point. (1/2/3/4/5)
9. Even if I do not write out my speech ahead of time, I will at least have a half-page systematic outline of it. (1/2/3/4/5)
10. I stand erect, yet relaxed, being careful neither to lean on anything nor to cross my legs. (1/2/3/4/5)
11. I fill my talk with comparisons, vivid illustrations, and striking statements or questions. (1/2/3/4/5)
12. I go through my speech to cut out abstract, picture-less sentences, especially where they occur consecutively. (1/2/3/4/5)
13. I am conscious that I speak to the audience through many channels other than my voice: my eyes, my facial expression, my arms, shoulders and whole body. (1/2/3/4/5)
14. I am aware that it is most important in the beginning to set up a warm relationship with the audience. (1/2/3/4/5)
15. While I am concerned about my message, I am even more concerned about the audience. (1/2/3/4/5)

Scoring: The more checks you have on the 'left', the more you are 'in the right'. Areas checked 'rarely' or never' are those where you need to improve.

How well do you read?

How efficient are you as a reader? The following questions will give you an idea. Be honest. Check the column that best describes your actual practice.

Always (1)   Usually (2)   Sometimes (3)   Rarely (4)   Never (5)

1. I adjust my speed to the type of reading material. (1/2/3/4/5)
2. I avoid moving my lips when I read. (1/2/3/4/5)
3. I try to see the relations between title, headings, and sub-headings. (1/2/3/4/5)
4. I pay great attention to words in italics. (1/2/3/4/5)
5. I read to answer questions I pose to myself. (1/2/3/4/5)
6. I talk about my reading with others. (1/2/3/4/5)
7. I read the preface, contents, and introduction. (1/2/3/4/5)
8. I pay attention to the first sentence in a paragraph. (1/2/3/4/5)
9. I avoid backward glances and re-reading words. (1/2/3/4/5)
10. I have a fixed place for serious study, another for light reading. (1/2/3/4/5)
11. I begin by reading summaries at the end of chapters. (1/2/3/4/5)
12. I concentrate on meaning, not on words. (1/2/3/4/5)

Scoring: The more checks you have on the 'left', the more you are 'in the right'. Areas checked 'rarely' or 'never' are those where you need to improve.

How well do you write?

The following statements provide a checklist for your writing habits. Check the column that best describes your actual practice.

Always (5)   Usually (4)   Sometimes (3)   Rarely (2)   Never (1)

1. I prefer vivid picture words to abstract words. (5/4/3/2/1)
2. I prefer one-syllable words to two-syllable words. (5/4/3/2/1)
3. I picture the reader clearly in my mind. (5/4/3/2/1)
4. I write in terms of the experience of the reader. (5/4/3/2/1)
5. I prefer the active to the passive voice. (5/4/3/2/1)
6. I ask myself: "Just what do I want to say" before beginning. (5/4/3/2/1)

7. I have one thought only in each paragraph. (5/4/3/2/1)
8. I avoid the use of qualifiers, e.g. 'very', 'little', etc. (5/4/3/2/1)
9. I try to avoid beginning sentences with 'however', 'and', 'or', 'but' or 'nor'. (5/4/3/2/1)
10. My style is informal, punchy and image-filled. (5/4/3/2/1)
11. I keep my average sentence length short.   (5/4/3/2/1)
12. I go back over my writing to see which words I can cut out. (5/4/3/2/1)

Scoring: Add up your score by using numbers at bottom of columns. Good: 48 and above; below 40, some practices need attention.

1.7 Curriculum for Different Levels of Students

School-Level (Secondary)

Duration   :   100 hours (over 3 to 4 months)
Objective   :   Developing LSRW
Participants   :   School-going Students (Poor in LSRW)
Methodology :   Repetitive—75% and Participatory—25%

Activities
1. Introduction + Voice Recording
2. LSRW Test (The teacher will take a test of the students to assess their competency on listening, speaking, reading and writing activities. After the test, the teacher will put the students in different groups according to their competencies.
3. Daily Expressions (The teacher may take 'n' number of classes according to the standard of the students and make them understand the uses of "Daily Expressions". He/ She should not quit unless the students are not good in expressing themselves under formal and informal situations. All the students should be able to use short expressions like 'good morning', 'Sit down, please,' etc.
4. Prepared Speech (Topics should be chosen according to the standard of the students.)
5. Seminar (Don't make the students speak with grammar-free English. Let them speak whatever they like at this stage. 'Communication' is more important than 'Correct English' at this stage.

6. Interactive Stories (Follow the rules strictly.)
7. Descriptions (Give the topics from the immediate surroundings of the students.)
8. Story Telling (Let the students tell any story. They can tell any story of their choice. If the students fail to express themselves in English, they can be allowed to tell the story in their native language. Then they should be encouraged to speak in English.)
9. Role Play (Let the students manage with very simple situations like 'asking permission from the teacher to go out of the classes', 'asking for the correct way to the traffic police', etc.)
10. Instant Translation (Follow the KISS—Keep It Short and Simple way.

Note: As a teacher, repeat these activities until you find the students confident enough to communicate. These students are secondary learners of the foreign language. The teacher should reassure them at every stage of the language learning. Most importantly the teacher should be involved with all the activities personally. The approach should be trying to develop all the LSRW skills, not just 'Speaking'. Besides, more and more Listening Activities should be given utmost importance.

Higher Secondary (Intermediate)

Duration	:	80 hours (over 3 to 4 months)
Objective	:	Developing LSR
Participants	:	People from any age group (Poor in LSR)
Methodology	:	Repetitive—50% and Participatory—50%

Activities
1. Introduction + Voice Recording
2. Tips to Speak English/SRT
3. Tips to Speak English/Picture Reading
4. Grammar + Vocabulary
5. Role Play + Grammar
6. Interactive Stories + Vocabulary
7. On the Spot + Grammar
8. Prepared Speech + Vocabulary
9. Micro Presentations + Grammar
10. Debating + Vocabulary
11. Press Conference + Grammar
12. Story Building + Vocabulary

13. Crossfire + Grammar
14. Dumb Charade + Vocabulary
15. GD + Grammar
16. PI + Vocabulary
17. Public Speaking + Grammar
18. Telephonic Conversation + Grammar
19. Feedback + Voice Recording

Note: As a teacher, repeat these activities until you find the students confident enough to communicate. These students are higher secondary learners of the foreign language. The teacher should reassure them at every stage of the language learning. Most importantly the teacher should be involved with all the activities personally. The approach should be trying to develop all the LSR skills, not just 'Speaking'. Writing Assignments should be avoided at this stage as the students always want to write something and speak. Besides, more and more Listening Activities should also be given utmost importance.

Advanced (Job Grooming)

Duration	:	50 hours (over 1 to 2 months)
Objective	:	Developing Speaking
Participants	:	People from any age group (Poor in Speaking English)
Methodology	:	Repetitive—0% and Participatory—100%

Activities
1. Introduction + Voice Recording
2. Role Play- 1
3. Role Play- 2
4. Role Play- 3
5. Role Play- 4
6. PI—1 (Individual)
7. PI—2 (Individual)
8. PI—1 (Panel)
9. PI—2 (Panel)
10. PI—3 (Panel)
11. Micro Presentation—1
12. Micro Presentation—2
13. GD—1
14. GD—2

15. GD—3
16. GD—4
17. GD—5
18. Crossfire
19. Forum

Note: These students are advanced learners of the foreign language. Therefore, the teacher should not give importance on 'vocabulary' or 'grammar'. The approach should be trying to develop confidence among all the students to develop 'Speaking Skills'. Writing Assignments should be avoided at this stage as the students always want to write something and speak. Besides, more and more stage exposure should also be given utmost importance.

"You can change your world by changing your words . . . Remember, death and life are in the power of the tongue."

– Joel Osteen

CHAPTER 2

ENGLISH PRONUNCIATION

2.1 The 44 English Sounds

There are 26 letters in English alphabet, 5 vowel and 21 consonants. But there are 44 sounds. Out of them 7 are short vowel sounds, 5 long vowel sounds, 8 diphthongs, 8 voiced consonants, 8 voiceless consonants and 8 other consonant sounds. Every sound is represented by a symbol as given below:

7 Short Vowel Sounds

/ɪ/	as in k<u>i</u>t, b<u>i</u>d and m<u>i</u>n<u>u</u>te
/ʊ/	as in f<u>oo</u>t, p<u>u</u>t and g<u>oo</u>d
/ʌ/	as in m<u>u</u>d, l<u>o</u>ve and bl<u>oo</u>d
/ɒ/	as in l<u>o</u>t, <u>o</u>dd and w<u>a</u>sh
/ə/	as in <u>a</u>bout, butt<u>er</u> and <u>a</u>bove
/e/	as in dr<u>e</u>ss, b<u>e</u>d and h<u>ea</u>d
/æ/	as in tr<u>a</u>p, st<u>a</u>mp and b<u>a</u>d

5 Long Vowel Sounds

/iː/	as in f<u>ee</u>l, r<u>ea</u>d and mach<u>i</u>ne
/uː/	as in tw<u>o</u>, bl<u>ue</u> and gr<u>ou</u>p
/ɑː/	as in f<u>a</u>ther, st<u>ar</u>t and h<u>ar</u>d
/ɔː/	as in l<u>aw</u>, n<u>or</u>th and w<u>ar</u>
/ɜː/	as in st<u>ir</u>, n<u>ur</u>se and l<u>ear</u>n

8 Diphthong Sounds

/ɪə/	as in n<u>ear</u>, h<u>ere</u> and w<u>ear</u>y

/ʊə/   as in t<u>our</u>, j<u>u</u>ry and c<u>u</u>re
/aɪ/   as in pr<u>i</u>ce, h<u>igh</u> and tr<u>y</u>
/ɔɪ/   as in n<u>oi</u>se, b<u>oy</u> and b<u>oi</u>ler
/əʊ/   as in g<u>oa</u>t, sh<u>ow</u> and n<u>o</u>
/eə/   as in f<u>air</u>, squ<u>are</u> and v<u>a</u>rious
/aʊ/   as in m<u>ou</u>th, n<u>ow</u> and f<u>ow</u>l
/eɪ/   as in f<u>a</u>ce, d<u>ay</u> and br<u>ea</u>k

8 Voiced Consonant Sounds
/b/   as in <u>b</u>ack, <u>b</u>a<u>b</u>y and jo<u>b</u>
/d/   as in <u>d</u>ay, la<u>dd</u>er and o<u>dd</u>
/dʒ/   as in ju<u>dg</u>e, a<u>g</u>e and sol<u>di</u>er
/g/   as in <u>g</u>et, <u>g</u>i<u>gg</u>le and <u>gh</u>ost
/v/   as in <u>v</u>iew, hea<u>v</u>y and mo<u>v</u>e
/ð/   as in <u>th</u>is, o<u>th</u>er and smoo<u>th</u>
/z/   as in <u>z</u>ero, mu<u>s</u>ic and bu<u>zz</u>
/ʒ/   as in plea<u>s</u>ure, lei<u>s</u>ure and vi<u>s</u>ion

8 Voiceless Consonant Sounds
/p/   as in <u>p</u>en, co<u>p</u>y and ha<u>pp</u>en
/t/   as in <u>t</u>ea, <u>t</u>igh<u>t</u> and bu<u>tt</u>on
/tʃ/   as in <u>ch</u>urch, ma<u>tch</u> and na<u>t</u>ure
/k/   as in <u>k</u>ey, <u>c</u>lo<u>ck</u> and s<u>ch</u>ool
/f/   as in <u>f</u>at, co<u>ff</u>ee and rou<u>gh</u>
/θ/   as in <u>th</u>ing, au<u>th</u>or and pa<u>th</u>
/s/   as in <u>s</u>oon, <u>ce</u>ase and <u>s</u>ister
/ʃ/   as in <u>sh</u>ip, <u>s</u>ure and na<u>ti</u>onal

8 Other Consonant Sounds
/m/   as in <u>m</u>ore, ha<u>mm</u>er and su<u>m</u>
/n/   as in <u>n</u>ice, k<u>n</u>ow and fu<u>nn</u>y
/ŋ/   as in ri<u>ng</u>, a<u>n</u>ger and tha<u>n</u>ks
/h/   as in <u>h</u>ot, <u>wh</u>ole and a<u>h</u>ead
/l/   as in <u>l</u>ight, va<u>ll</u>ey and fee<u>l</u>
/r/   as in <u>r</u>ight, <u>wr</u>ong and so<u>rr</u>y
/w/   as in <u>w</u>et, <u>o</u>ne and <u>wh</u>en
/j/   as in <u>y</u>et, <u>u</u>se and f_ew

MORE ON ENGLISH SOUNDS

Consider for a moment people within your own circle who speak English. What do you observe about them? What do they have in common? English is not everybody's cup of tea. Some of them are seriously wrong. Here are some more examples on English sounds.

SHORT VOWELS

1. /i/ (Vowel Spelling: i, y)
/i/is a short vowel. The mouth is held slightly open and in a lateral or smile position. The tongue tip is slightly raised and held flat and rests in the middle of the inside back of the lower front teeth. The rest of the tongue is held flat and moves down slightly as the sound is said. There is an extra air puff pushed out from the throat at the end.

'i'—words: hit, is, miss, this, gym, live, igloo, mint, ink, initial, insist, print, it, ill, pill, trip, bin, list, admit, little.

'i'—sentences:
Which city is good to live in?
Will you fit this in?
His fin is pretty.
I insist that you sit on the tin.
The pig is licking the rubbish bin.
The little ticket is for the cricket.
It 's inside the difficult puzzle.
Nick put the pin in the string.
Little Linda hit the ball over the hill.
He insisted they invite Lily to the institute.

2. /oo/—foot (Vowel Spelling: oo, u, ou)
/oo/ is a short vowel. The lips are protruded with a small opening between them, and the lip muscles are held tight. The tongue is flat and elevated at the front so that the tip is raised a little above the bottom teeth. The tongue

is held flat at the back. The sound is resonated in the throat and sent up towards the top of the mouth.

'oo '—words: foot, could, put, would, soot, should, book bull, good pull, wood, look, hood, rule, full, cruel, took, shook, hook, brook.

'oo'—sentences:
That is a good book.
Pull it apart and put it on the wood.
He took a rest when he could.
It was a cruel rule.
You should look under the hood.
The fireplace was full of wood.
The bull shook the hook hard.
They saw that the little running brook ran crookedly into the river.
Please push the sugar bowl to me.

3.   /u/ (Vowel Spelling: u, o, ou)

/u/is a short vowel. The mouth is held half open, and the lips are held flattish against the teeth. The tongue is held flat and the tip is just touching where the bottom teeth meet the gum inside the mouth. Resonance is at the back of the mouth.

'u'—words: up, love, run, country, tough, butter, but, brother, other, done, fun, us, mud, hunt, young, funny, lunch, cup, money.

'u'—sentences:
They love to have fun playing in the mud.
My younger brother likes to act rough and tough.
Mrs. Summers is like another mother to us.
His lunch was under the funny coloured cloth.
Cut some cloth from around the buttons, but don't cut too much.
Please come and visit us on Sunday for lunch.
Sometimes in summer we get off the bus and run home to jump in the pool.
On Monday he had such trouble wrapping the bundle of papers.
He struck the drum so loudly that they came out to see what he had done.
You can come under the umbrella to keep dry.

If you undo the strap it will become uncomfortable.

4. /o/ (Vowel Spelling: o)

/o/is a short vowel. The mouth is held quite rounded and the lips are held quite forward. The tongue tip is pulled back about one third away from the front teeth and raised up. The rest of the tongue is flat and the voice is switched on.

'o'—words: hot, dog, cost, stop, clock, cotton, pot, golf, bottom, wrong, octopus, spot, orange, on, lost, off, lock, rock, lot, sock.

'o'—sentences:
He lost the lock at the bottom of the pond.
John wanted to stop when he got too hot.
How much does the clock in the box cost?
The orange sign was on the wrong office door.
Oliver dropped the hot cooking pot.
She tossed the rock into the pond.
The drain on top of the roof was blocked.
They continued to run in the competition even though it rained.
His cotton socks fell onto the golf stick.
He got a frog and a dog from the pet shop.

5. /u/ or /e/ (Vowel Spelling: u, o, ou)—To some extent similar to /u/ Vowel Spelling: u, o, ou

u or e—words: about, backward, problem, liberty, terrible, observe, effort, famous.

6. /e/ Vowel Spelling: e, ea

The /e/vowel is a short vowel. The mouth is held in a much wider lateral or smile position than for /i/ and the bottom jaw is held slightly further open (down), and moves up slightly at the end of the /e/. The tongue is held in the same position as for /i/. There is also an extra puff of air pushed out from the throat at the end of the production of this sound.

'e'—words: bed, spend, send, kettle, ten, elephant, then, direction, bread, let, enemy, gentle, arrest, every, wet, endless, ready, echo, went, tread.

'e'—sentences:
The bed is ready for anybody to come and rest.
They met when they went to the festival.
Send the letter in September.
The men arrested the enemy.
Every pen in the case was yellow.
Let's send ten gentle hens.
The ferry went in the wrong direction.
Lenny's pet was wet.
Can you lend me a metal kettle?
His presentation ended when the money was collected.

7. /a/ (Vowel Spelling:a)

/a/is a short vowel. To make the /a/sound the mouth is open, but not as much as for /u/.The lips are lateralised (pulled as in a smile position), slightly. The tongue tip is slightly raised and the rest of the tongue is held flattish but slightly off the bottom of the mouth. The tip touches in the middle of the bottom teeth inside the mouth. The voice is switched on, and the sound is 'resonated' at the back of the mouth.

'a'—words: bag, happy, black, Saturday, sack, have, thank, anchor, man, apple, handsome, had, plan, am, pack, pan, and, land, can, answer,

'a'—sentences:
Can you hand me that black bag please?
He has to have his apple after the ham.
Andy planned his adventure and then packed his knapsack.
The man ran down the long track until he reached the sand.
I am at band classes on Saturday
His answer made the man happy
What happened when the cans fell out?
Please add these numbers in your Math exam.
The application form had a pattern on it.
They found the candle handy when the lights blacked out.

LONG VOWELS

8. /ee/ (Vowel Spelling: e, ee, ea, ie, ei, ey)
/ee/is a long vowel that is made by moving the lips into a wide smile/lateral position. The tongue is slightly raised and the tip is resting and touching just in the middle of the back of the front bottom teeth. The sound resonates toward the throat, and the back of the tongue is slightly raised near the throat.

'ee'—words: see, receive, seem, he, real, sheet, key, read, sheep, peel, feet, she, repeat, easy, seal, cheese, piece, neat, lead, meet.

'ee'—sentences:
I feel as if I need to sleep.
Keep the key near your feet.
It's easy to eat meat.
I see sheep in the country.
The sheet was on me
We really need to heat the room.
Keith is sitting on the seat.
Can you reach the piece of cheese?
Peter's street is painted green.
She previewed the screening of the cheapest movie in the East district.

Tip: Try these contrasting long and short vowel words. Make the 'ee' slightly longer than normal so you hear and feel the difference. Try saying the list both ways, that is say the 'ee' words then the 'i' words and then reverse the process.(sheep-ship; ship-sheep).You might want to tape yourself saying the above contrasting words and hear if you are making them right.

sheep—ship, heap—hip, leap—lip, meet—mit, feet—fit, steel—still, green—grin, been—bin.

Set yourself a mental note to notice and make sure you keep the 'ee' long in everyday situations till it becomes automatic.

9. /oo/—(Vowel Spelling: oo, o, ou, ough, ew, ui)
/oo/ is a long vowel. The lips are forward but flattish (as if to whistle), and there is a slight opening between them. The tongue tip is slightly raised at the front and lifted slightly above the top edge of the bottom front teeth. The tongue is bunched in towards the midline. The sound resonates from the back and travels around the tongue towards the front.

'oo'—words: food, to, soup, group, spoon, do, through, shoe, boot, grew, flew, moon, fruit, new, lose, bruise, flute, drew, room, you.

'oo'—sentences:
Who first flew to the moon?
How do you do?
She bought boots at the new shoe shop.
How could you lose your flute in your room?
He threw the ball through the hoop and it landed in the pool.
Where is my soup spoon?
The groom ate fruit after his soup.
The cute boy in blue grew quickly.
The detective knew the bruise was not enough proof of the crime.
It was true that the crew knew how to fly the plane to New York.

10. /ar/ (Vowel Spelling: ar, a)
/ar/is a long vowel. The mouth is quite open so the bottom jaw is dropped down quite a bit. The tongue tip is pulled back from the bottom teeth very slightly. The tongue tip is flat but not touching the bottom of the mouth-it is slightly raised off the floor of the mouth.

The back of the tongue is flattened down towards the bottom of the mouth. Again resonance is more from the throat/back of mouth. Again the /r/sound is not pronounced in British English.

'ar'—words: park, glass, card, garden, alarm, past, father, harder, bath, staff, army, bark, laugh, darling, fast, after, heart, bar, star, class.

'ar'—sentences:
His father was a sergeant in the army.
His heart beat fast in the park.
The fire alarm started to ring in the bar.

The card fell in the bath.
They laughed in the garden.
He finished building the last part of the car.
The class can't fit in your apartment.
A dog's bark can't harm.
There was a large star shape printed after the newspaper article.
The partnership finished after they argued.

11. /or/ (Vowel Spelling: aw, or, au, ough)
This is a medium length vowel. The lips are held quite forward and rounded so that the circle formed between the lips is quite small. The lip muscles are held quite tightly. The tongue tip is pulled back quite a bit and relaxed. The muscles of the middle and tip of the tongue are contracted or pulled in towards the midline of the tongue-the tongue is bunched in towards the midline. The /r/sound is not pronounced in 'or ' in British English pronunciation.

'or'—words: saw, more, alter, door, before, caught, call, story, important, thought, straw, orchestra, fall, reward, prawn, law, torn, floor, brought, fought, autumn.

'or'—sentences:
It was important for Paul to hear more of the orchestra.
This morning I saw a story about a new law.
The workman repaired the floor near the door before he left.
He caught his shorts on a wire fence and noticed they were torn.
The mother ordered a new car horn when the baby was born.
She sorted four more corn bags for her work in the store.
He couldn't see the ball when it went over the tall wall.
They formed a corporate portfolio for their business.
He thought he would travel to the nearby port after the autumn winds stopped.
After the carpenter installed the door, he altered the handle as well.

12. /er/ (Vowel Spelling: er, ir, ur, wor, ear)
The /er/vowel is a short to medium length vowel. For this sound the lips are quite rounded and forward. The front one third of the tongue is scooped up and the tip is raised up but stays behind the bottom teeth. The back of the tongue is slightly raised at the back. In British English the /r/sound in 'er' is not pronounced.

'er'—words:

bird, search, first, nurse, word, turn, her, person, learn, work, thirsty, pearl, worm, dirty, germ, curtain, heard, fern, fur, certain.

'er'—sentences:

At first he got to work early.
The bird was searching for worms.
The girl curled her hair.
She heard from the nurse that Burnie was thirsty.
Turn the curtain around so we can see the fern.
His first birthday was on Saturday.
They rehearsed and learnt their lines on Thursday.
Are you certain the pearl is perfect?
She purchased the purple purse herself.
He burnt the certificate by accident.

DIPHTHONGS

13. /eer/ (Vowel Spelling: eer, ear, ere, ier, ea)

This sound, to some extent, is similar to /ee/ Vowel Spelling. The /eer/ vowel is a diphthong. For this sound the 'e' is accented and then comes 'r'.

'eer'—words:

period, here, serious, mere, zero, severe, cheer, fierce, deer, idea, dear, near, ear, real, fear, theatre, hear.

14. /our/ (Vowel Spelling: our, ur)

The /our/ vowel is a diphthong. For this sound the lips are weakly rounded at the beginning and neutral at the end.

'our'—words: sure, tour, jury, cure

15. /ie/ (Vowel Spelling: I, ie, igh, y)

/ie/ is a medium length vowel. The mouth is held open slightly and the lips are pulled laterally (smile position) a little. The jaw moves up from an open position towards the top teeth, but stays open a little.

The tongue is flat and the tip is resting slightly on top of the bottom teeth. As the sound finishes, the tongue naturally retracts (goes back)very slightly. This sound is also a diphthong and the mouth moves quickly from an /ar/ sound to an /ee/sound.

'ie'—words:
pie, my, mind, fire, Hi, night, mine, bright, find, cry, line, crime, by, sigh, tie, lie, light, behind, tight, blind.

'ie'—sentences:
They might buy a pie for dinner.
We changed our mind and decided to find a new night club.
He stood behind the white line.
After crying, he had red eyes.
He drove for nine miles to get to the building site.
He might have nine bicycles to fix.
He couldn't write because the light was too bright.
They had to identify the tin mine without a proper sign post.
He felt fine, but still went to lie down.
The kind man walked by our house.

16. /oy/ (Vowel Spelling: oy, oi)
/oy/is a medium-long vowel. The lips are rounded and forward for the /o/ position and then quickly move back to a smile position for the /ee/ sound. This is also a diphthong.

'oy'—words:
boy, boil, toy, toil, oil, loyal, join, soil, enjoy, coil, royal, alloy, annoy, ointment, oyster, point, coin, spoil.

'oy'—sentences:
The boy enjoyed playing with his toys.
The singers were annoyed by the noise in the audience.
The royal advisers were loyal.
Please eat the oysters now before they become spoiled.
She dropped the coins into the hole in the soil.
They asked him to point to the right ointment to heal their rash.
Don't leave the oil to boil, please.
He joined the broken toy back together with glue.

The rag was oily.

17. /oe/(Vowel Spelling: o, oe, oa, ow, ough)

/oe/is a medium vowel (held on for a medium amount of time).It is made by moving the mouth quickly from one position to another. It is a diphthong. The lips are rounded and quite open at first, and then the jaw is brought forward and the lips move into a smaller circle configuration. As the jaw moves forward, the tongue moves with it and the space between the tongue and the bottom of the mouth becomes less. The tongue generally starts out with the tip pulled back about a third of the way and is slightly raised. The rest of the tongue is flat. It is made by moving the mouth quickly from the /o/sound to the /oo/ (long as in food) sound.

'oe'—words:

nose, over, boat, drove, toes, low, road, load, go, slow, show, moan, though, hose, phone, grow, soap, no, pony, flow.

'oe'—sentences:

Don't phone before you go to the pony show.
You left your coat in the boat.
Even though he knows the code he had to show his pass.
I suppose he goes up the road often.
She hoped that he froze the fish before he came over to visit.
His toe was caught in the hose.
Were you home alone?
The proposal was to close the old cold storage factory.
He drove slowly because he was carrying a heavy load.
She said no when asked for a new stove.

18. /ai/ (Vowel Spelling: air, ar, ear)

/ai/is a diphthong. It is made by making the lips neutral.

'ai'—words:

air, fair, chair, various, pair, low, square, care, bear, prayer, rear, their.

19. /ow/ (Vowel Spelling: ou, ow, ough)

/ow/is a long vowel. It is made by quickly saying the /a/and /oo/ vowels in sequence.

'ow'—words:

now, mouth, out, bow, loud, town, crowd, sound, down, crown, shower, ground, house, how, bough, clown, mouse, about, brown, trout.

'or'—sentences:

The brown mouse found another house.
The largest bough on the tree fell to the ground.
How many sounds can the machine make?
It sounds like the shower is still on.
The trout tasted so good in his mouth.
Mother read a story about how they found the king's crown.
Now he is going out.
She was not allowed to make a loud sound.
The fountain showered water all over the round shaped clown.

20. /ay/ (Vowel Spelling: a, ay, ai, eigh, ei, a-e)

The /ay/vowel is a medium length vowel and is also made by moving the mouth from one position to another. It is made by moving the mouth quickly from /a/to /ee/.

'ay'—words:

rain, bake, day, pain, eight, ray, plane, came, face, date, stay, reign, straight, make, ate, rail, wake, paper, mail, navy.

'ay'—sentences:

On a rainy day it's good to stay indoors.
His face showed his pain.
The train came to the main station.
He took a break from work at eight o 'clock.
They went straight to see the play.
Take the plate and make her a great steak.
They train for the race every day
She was late so she ate after the plane took off.
Don't complain about the stain on the paper.
How long does it take for the mail to arrive from the Navy?

VOICED CONSONANTS

21. /b/ (Consonant Spelling: b)

/b/is a consonant made the same way in your mouth as /p/, except that you add voice from your throat at the same time. That is, you gently close your lips together and pop the lips open by pushing air out between the lips while voicing from the throat at the same time. It is a voiced sound. Lips need to be popped or pushed open quickly and lightly.

'b'—words:

back, able, describe, borrow, labour, labor, cube, beneath, above, tub, baby, hobby, job, buy, February, rub, boat, neighbour, neighbor, club, bean, rubbish, pub, biscuit, rubbing, web, business, vegetable, tube, boil, maybe, crab

'b'—sentences:

The baby bounced on the board.
Please begin rubbing the blue spot.
Somebody was able to break the rubber part.
The book was beautiful.
They ate baked beans, bananas, biscuits and crab.
Before they went to the night club, they went to the pub.
The boy had a job aboard a boat.
What number is the neighbour's/neighbor's house?
He bought a cupboard in November.
She broke the brand new blue blind last February

22. /d/ (Consonant Spelling: d)

/d/is a consonant that is made the same way in your mouth as /t/, but said as a voiced sound. You hold the front part of your tongue flat and lift it up to touch or tap on the area just behind your two front top teeth. You tap or touch your tongue up to this area and then drop it quickly. The movement is light and quick—not held in the lifted position.

'd'—words:

decide, radio, wanted, different, understand, second, door, radish, carried, do, shadow, bad, describe, undo, hard, disappear, reading, kind, doll, order, road, dad, Sunday, had, dog, introduce, outside, dinosaur, ladder, feed.

'd'—sentences:
Dad decided to shut the outside door.
The dog carried a doughnut/donut.
Debbie had a different card.
The wedding is on Tuesday in that building.
She made some hard dolls.
They followed the red bird into the shade.
David drove down the second road.
I don't understand.
The director said he would divide the introduction into two parts.

23. /j/ (Consonant Spelling: j, g, dge)

The sound /j/is the minimal pair of /ch/.It is made in exactly the same way except that it is a voiced consonant. /j/is made by closing the teeth together gently, or almost closing the teeth together. The tongue blade (front 1/8th of the tongue), is placed flat on the gum ridge behind the front top teeth and then moved back and down slightly as the sound is made. Let air pressure build up in the mouth and release as the tongue moves slightly down and back. /j/is a voiced consonant. Note: when the letter 'g ' is followed by an e, I or y most of the time it says / j /

"j"—words:
joke, engineer, page, judge, vegetables, George, jump, pager, badge, jazz, agent, wage, jewel, magic, average, journey, reject, large, gentle, oranges, package, gym, legend, courage, jog, agile, manage, giant, manager, luggage.

"j"—sentences:
The engineer joked and opened the package.
George likes ginger with his vegetables.
My manager wore a badge.
The courageous gymnast jumped over the burning cage.
They took refuge on the other side of the bridge.
There were many packages and some luggage in the train carriage.
She earned an average wage.
The food judge rejected the juiciest oranges.
We jogged around the jeep.
Just don't drop the jar.

24. /g/ (Consonant Spelling: g)

/g/is a consonant. It is the voiced minimal pair of the /k/sound. That is, it is made the same way but voicing is added./g/is made by lifting the back of the tongue up towards the top of your mouth at the back of the mouth. Bunch the back of your tongue in from the sides at the same time, and release the tongue down suddenly while switching on your voice at the same time.

'g'—words:

groceries, negative, handbag, gather, bags, fog, gorgeous, sugar, drag, ground, bargain, big, glass, forgive, dog, go, figure, flag, get, forget, dig, goal, logo, bag, gate, bigger, frog, give, angry, leg.

'g'—sentences:

The girl with the groceries forgot the bag.
He had a gorgeous garden behind the gate.
The big bug gathered gum.
The girl got a bargain at the great sale.
Don't begin until I get there.
They grew gold flowers in the big, green, glass house.
Can you guess why she is giggling?
The dog dragged the rag on the ground.
We were given a catalogue/catalog in August.
The magazine was much bigger this month.

25. /v/ (Consonant Spelling: v)

/v/is made exactly the same way as /f/, but is a voiced consonant. Place the top front teeth on the middle of the bottom lip (as if gently biting your bottom lip), and gently blow air out of the mouth over the bottom lip while switching on the voice at the same time.

/v/—words:

vacant, even, nerve, vegetables, conversation, active, value, festival, remove, vanish, advantage, arrive, vision, forever, stove, village, envelope, dive, very, lively, love, video, November, drive, vase, over, move, valley, river, give.

/v/—sentences:

Leave the stove over near the vacuum cleaner.
The vegetable soup was full of flavour/flavor.
He's moving to live in the valley.

Please cover every avocado over there.
They removed the furniture from the vacant apartment.
Several elevators were giving trouble.
They found primitive drawings when they discovered the cave.
The vet received a valuable video.
Every day is a new adventure.
After the festival the conversation was very lively.

26. /th/ (Consonant Spelling: th)

This is the voiced pair of these two minimal pair consonants and is therefore produced with the same mouth positioning. There is no separate letter symbol for this voiced sound. This sound is made by sticking your tongue out a little between the top and bottom teeth so that the front top teeth touch the top surface of your tongue. That is, as if you are gently biting your tongue. At the same time you gently blow a little air over your tongue as you also produce voice from your vocal cords. As you do this you feel the part of your tongue that is between your teeth tingle or vibrate a little.

'th'—words:

this, breathing, breathe, these,   clothing, clothe, those, mother, soothe, that, father, loathe, then, brother, them, other, the, bother, there, weather, though, leather, their, feather.

'th'—sentences:

Their mother and brother came.
The man didn't know whether the other book was there.
These are the leather ones.
It was smoother than their one.
This one goes on that.
His father checked the weather.
Don't bother getting another one.
You can either have a feather or this ribbon.
Though his clothing was wet, he still went further.
I would rather gather the bigger feathers although the smaller ones are better.

27. /z/ (Consonant Spelling: z, s, x)

/z/is the voiced minimal pair consonant to /s/.It is made with the teeth gently closed together and the lips are pulled sideways into a smile position.

The tongue may be placed up on the ridge behind the front top teeth or just at the back of where the top and bottom teeth meet inside the mouth. A little bit of air is then forced out over the centre (center) of the tongue while switching on voice in the throat at the same time. This is a voiced consonant.

'z'—words:

zero, dozen, exercise, zinc, design, apologise, apologize, zone, business, prize, zip, horizon, organise, organize, xerox, visitor, papers, xylophone, cousin, roses, zoo, amazing, buzz, zoom, houses, rise, zipper, closing, froze, zebra, supposed, cheese.

'z'—sentences:

The zoo does have amazing animals.
The visitor was organised/ organized well.
He collected his prize after his exercise.
My cousin doesn't have a hose.
I suppose it is closed.
Please choose dessert.
She couldn't resist the dazzling design.
I wasn't teasing you.
Isn't the zipper closing?
He was late because he had to memorise/memorize his lines.

28. /zh/ (Consonant Spelling: si, su)

/zh/is the voiced minimal pair consonant of 'sh'. It is therefore made the same way in the mouth. The teeth are almost closed together. The lips are pushed forward. Lift the tongue tip slightly towards the roof of the mouth and allow the sides of the tongue to touch the inside of the side teeth. Blow a little air over the tip of the tongue while switching on voice (sound in the throat), at the same time.

'zh'—words:

Asia, Malaysia, vision, treasure, pleasure, occasion, measure, rouge, Indonesia, beige, division, mirage, television, camouflage, Australasia, prestige.

'zh'—sentences:

It was a pleasure to go to Asia.
His vision was to find treasure.
I saw how he measured the erosion on the television show.

The invasion created division among the people.
There was a collision and an explosion.
We painted the garage beige.
She made a decision to stay at a lodge in Malaysia.
While the student did some revision for his exam, he watched television.
It was a happy occasion.
They had problems with their vision when they saw the mirage in the desert.

VOICELESS CONSONANTS

29. /p/ (Consonant Spelling: p)

/p/is a consonant made by closing the lips together with gentle to medium pressure, and then popping the lips open by pushing air out between the lips. The /p/sound has no voicing at the throat level. It is a quiet, unvoiced sound. It is made lightly.

'p'—words:

pie, apartment, envelope, party, apple, hope, people, open, ripe, pocket, opposite, hop, pub, paper, tap, plenty, copy, map, positive, happen, stop, popular, zipper, keep, possible, puppy, pup, pen, tapping, tip.

'p'—sentences:

Please pass the pepper.
The people dropped the rope in the park.
Don't open the soap in the supermarket.
The popular group played music at the pub.
I put the map in my pocket.
Put that piece on top.
We went for supper at the restaurant that was painted purple.
She placed pumpkin, chips, peas, plums and pizza on the plate.
Perhaps you could stop wiping and help to sweep the mess.
Is it possible to see the apartment opposite this one?

30. /t/ (Consonant Spelling: t)

/t/is a consonant that involves the front part of your tongue held flat and lifted up to touch or tap in the middle of the area (ridge) just behind your two front top teeth. You tap your tongue in this position and drop it quickly. It is a quiet or unvoiced sound, and is produced lightly and quickly. For English spoken in the United States of America: When the /t/ is said between two vowels, most of the time, it changes and is not a definite /t/ sound. It becomes more like a soft /d/sound e.g., letter, writer, etc.

't'—words:
total, later, fat, telephone, bottom, late, today, letter, plate, Tuesday, certain, diet, towel, container, favourite, favorite, toward, fantastic, appointment, taste, capital, right, tap, continue, cat, ten, daughter, paint, two, water, hat.

't'—sentences:
She started talking on the telephone after dinner.
Are you certain today is Tuesday?
Yesterday I made an appointment at the doctors.
The tea is at the bottom of the container.
Don't sit on the wet towel.
He can't put it on the teak table.
Please get the two tickets and meet me at the last gate.
The pilot jumped out of his seat.
Wait a minute, please.
He entered the computer technology development area where there was a large amount of security.

31. /ch/ (Consonant Spelling: ch, tch)
/ch/is a sound made by closing the teeth together gently, or almost closing them together. The tongue blade (front 1/8th of tongue), is placed flat on the gum ridge behind the front top teeth and then moved back and down slightly as the sound is made. Let air pressure build up and release as the tongue moves slightly down and back. 'ch' is a quiet or unvoiced consonant. The 'sound' is from the air being pushed out of the mouth.

'ch'—words:
chair, matches, match, chain, kitchen, fetch, chalk, butcher, much, chocolate, crutches, such, church, teacher, March, cheerful, Manchester, touch, chess, Rachel, which, cheese, Richard, branch, Chinese, achievement, bench, chew, beaches, sandwich

'ch'—sentences:

Please put the cheese and chocolate on the bench in the kitchen.

The butcher chose two thick chops for me

They will build the church in March.

Watch out for Rachel's teacher.

Please choose carefully as it can't be changed.

The catcher chose matching pictures for the coach.

The birch wood couch was a natural colour/color.

A colourful/colorful bird was perched on a branch.

We can munch on a sandwich for lunch at the beach.

He had achieved a high level in his Chinese studies.

32. /k/ (Consonant Spelling: c, k, ck,-que, qu, ch)

/k/is a consonant. You lift the back of your tongue up towards the top of your mouth at the back, bunch the back of your tongue in from the sides at the same time, and release the tongue down suddenly. Do not use voice. This is a non-voiced sound.

'k'—words:

kind, market, headache, chemist, kicking, earthquake, keep, making, cork, kangaroo, pocket, track, kennel, marked, ink, cat, baker, ink, kitchen, barking, crack, kindergarten, soccer, cheque, check, close, packet, take, come, rocket, rock.

'k'—sentences:

Keep the cheque/check in your pocket.

Can my cousin pick the colour/color?

Park the cream coloured/colored car outside the kitchen.

He knocks on the locked back door every day.

Please cut the cake in the packet.

I took the sock out of the bucket.

The computer cord is in my coat pocket.

Cover the cat with a blanket and close the cupboard.

They are concerned about his comfort.

He occasionally cued the choir director when he became distracted.

33. /f/ (Consonant Spelling: f, ph, gh)

/f/is a consonant made by putting the top front teeth on the middle of the bottom lip (as if gently biting the bottom lip), and blowing air out of the mouth gently at the same time over the bottom lip. This is an unvoiced or quiet sound.

'f'—words:

furniture, offer, laugh, forward, difference, tough, further, official, enough, favourite, favorite, effort, half, family, traffic, knife, flavour, flavor, coffee, cough, photo, definite, rough, fright, afterward, giraffe, finish, prefer, leaf, fan, laughing, roof

'f'—sentences:

My family laughed and drank coffee.
He was definite that he could finish all the food.
She found her favourite/favorite photographer.
Fred fell off the first roof.
After fishing on the wharf they went surfing.
They ate roast beef and meat loaf for dinner.
The fireman found a waterproof fireplace.
She felt funny in the new office.
Follow me after the game has finished.
The furniture on the first floor was comfortable.

34. /th/ (Consonant Spelling: th)

/th/is a consonant made by sticking your tongue out just a little between the top and bottom teeth so that the front top teeth touch the top surface of your tongue. That is, as if gently biting your tongue. While your tongue is in this position you gently blow air out of your mouth over your tongue. This is an unvoiced, quiet sound. Just air is heard.

'th'—words:

theatre, theater, nothing, fourth, thank, anything, fifth, thunder, everything, sixth, thorn, author, seventh, thin, arithmetic, path, thigh, bathtub, both, thought, healthy, mouth, theme, wealthy, beneath, third, Athens, earth, three, birthday, tooth.

'th'—sentences:

Mathew found his birthday present beneath the table.
I think he threw the ball through the window.
He had nothing in his mouth.

They went down the third path to the theatre/theater.
The thief found a toothbrush on the tablecloth.
Something thick fell in the bathtub.
The teacher measured the length with both hands.
Take the three o 'clock train north to Athens.
He felt thirsty without a drink.
She thought the toothpaste without sugar was healthier.

Tip: Feel the air cool your tongue as you make the sound. Try holding the teeth on your tongue position for a second or two longer than usual allowing you to move more effectively (and control the movement),and easily to the next sound in the word. (You can hold slightly longer for the voiced 'th' as well.)

35. /s/ (Consonant Spelling: s, c)

/s/is made by gently closing the teeth together and the lips are pulled sideways in a smile position. The tongue tip may be placed up on the ridge behind the front top teeth or just at the back of where the top and bottom teeth meet inside the mouth. The air is forced out over the centre (center) of the tongue out of the mouth to make a hissing or snake sound.
The tongue does not stick out for this sound but stays behind the teeth. This is a non-voiced consonant the sound being made by the air stream coming out of the mouth.

Note: When the letter 'c' is followed by an 'e', 'I' or 'y' it always says /s/.

's'—words:
September, passing, piece, string, somebody, understand, generous, stop, syllable, passenger, circus, space, session, disappear, sauce, smile, sock, sausage, yes, small, see, saucer, house, snow, sun, racing, price, slowly, sail, loosen, glass, sleep, soft, parcel, race, sky, silver, kissed, nice, scrape.

's'—sentences:
We celebrate the anniversary next September.
Some people eat sausages with sauce.
The socks have sand in them.
My surprise parcel disappeared.
What is the price of that house?

Of course summer is a hot season.
They stopped to see the circus in the small town centre/center.
After he dressed he had to loosen his pants.
Yes, most of my business is in that office.
That's just the box for my books.

36. /sh/ (Consonant Spelling: sh, ti, ci, si, ch)

/sh/is a consonant made by almost closing the teeth together. The lips are pushed forward. Lift the tongue tip slightly toward the roof of the mouth and allow the sides of the tongue to touch the inside edge of the side teeth. Blow air out over the tip of the tongue. It is the sound we make when telling someone to be quiet. This is an unvoiced sound with no voicing involved.

'sh'—words:

shade, bishop, English, shampoo, worship, smash, chivalry, nation, foolish, chef, facial, radish, sharp, session, selfish, sheet, Russia, wash, shelf, machine, fresh, shine, station, rubbish, shock, addition, bush, short, fashion, cash, should, washing, push, shut, cushion, dash, shrink, shrub, shrewd, shrill, shrivel.

'sh'—sentences:

Show me the shop she owns.
He put the smashed shell in the rubbish.
The ship came into shore.
The chef sat at the station and ate a fresh radish.
When she washed the shirt and shorts they shrank.
They rushed to the national convention.
The shiny machine was crushed.
Those cushions are in fashion.
Can you push the fish into the ocean?
I wish the shrimp meal was fresh.
The chef was passionate about the delicious shark soup.

OTHER CONSONANTS

37. /m/ (Consonant Spelling: m)
The lips are closed together and kept together for this sound, therefore the sound made is resonated in the nose while simultaneously voicing (making sound), in the throat. This is a voiced consonant.

'm'—words:
market, swimming, dream, meat, lemon, storm, music, lamp, overcome, malaria, September, fame, management, woman, ice cream, mango, ambulance, William, marriage, amplifier, drum, make, coming, jam, mile, embarrassed, farm, mate, camera, come.

'm'—sentences:
My family and I went camping on a farm last summer.
We dreamed of swimming in September.
William makes many frames.
The woman is coming to meet the musician.
Some men came to eat ice cream.
The famous mailman might hum a tune.
It was too humid for most animals.
Please remove the name from the poem.
He sometimes eats lamb and ham
They were embarrassed in front of the camera.
Come home with him.

Tip: For those who confuse /n/for /m/at the end of words, remind yourself to feel your lips close together at the end. Say these aloud and try feeling and hearing the difference:

hone—home (come home)
cane—came (he came out)
nane—name (my name is)
sane—same (it's the same one)
han—ham (ham sandwich)
cuns—comes (he comes today)

38. /n/ (Consonant Spelling: n, kn, gn, pn)

To make the /n/sound lift the blade of the tongue (front 1/8 th of tongue) held flat, up to the centre (center) of the ridge behind the front top teeth. The sides of the tongue around the middle part of the tongue touch the sides of the teeth inside the mouth.

Open the mouth slightly and push the tongue blade up and let the sound come out (resonate), of your nose. Use voice at the same time. This is a voiced consonant.

'n'—words:

news, bananas, brain, neighbour, neighbor, China, flown, national, many, nine, nothing, container, common, knock, find, spoon, pneumonia, channel, information, gnaw, constant, section, kneel, animal, curtain, not, mountain, pin, nose, into, sign.

'n'—sentences:

That's not the information channel.
We can't find the container.
The candle blew in the wind.
Knock on the door next to the number nine.
None of the nephews were noisy.
Don't bend the needle.
Send the pianist a sign when he needs to stop.
The generous founder of the institute was funny.
I know that is mine.
They couldn't find the tin mine.

39. /ng/ (Consonant Spelling: ng)

To make this sound raise the back part of your tongue up towards the soft back part of your palate. Open the mouth slightly. Resonate the sound from your nose and allow voicing at the same time. This is a voiced consonant.
Note: The /g/sound is not pronounced when saying this sound.

'ng'—words:

belong, singing, twinkle, sing, hanging, ankle, sang, ringing, drink, song, singer, blanket, bring, hanger, single, wing, longing, angry, ring, swinging, hunger, bang, belonging, angle, long.

'ng'—sentences:
The singer sang a moving song.
The hanger was hanging on the metal ring.
Don't bang the gong.
He was covered with a long blanket.
The dog's tongue was hanging out.
They were buying a single frying pan to cook the chicken wings.
My uncle hurt his ankle.
She was looking angry after the boat sank.
The ingredients for the drink were under the sink.
Even though he was trying, he was losing the game.

40. /h/ (Consonant Spelling: h)

To make the /h/sound, open the mouth slightly and force the air out as if sighing. This is an unvoiced, quiet vowel. The 'sound' is just that of the air 'sighing' out. The air flow is soft, not constricted.

'h'—words:
holiday, ahead, hear, pothole, hold, inhabit, hide, exhale, help, inhale, hurt, coherent, height, behind, huge, unheard, human, somehow, humour, humor, Hugo.

'h'—sentences:
He heard her talking behind the house.
The hunter found a huge horse up ahead.
His headache hurt.
He wanted his friend to help him.
Somehow Harry held onto the hat.
How did she inhale the dust?
How many has she got?
Have you hit the nail with that hammer?
They had half a hot hamburger each.
The horse was happy to have a hazelnut.

41. /l/ (Consonant Spelling: l)

To make the /l/sound, lift and push the tongue tip up to the middle of the ridge just behind the two front top teeth while switching on voice. This is a voiced consonant.

'l'—words:

late, colour, color, nail, blue, cloud, leaf, melon, camel, black, climb, lion, pillow, shell, planet, glad, lazy, lollypop, little, pleasant, glue, loud, telephone, metal, place, glass, limp, loudly, control, fly, line, koala, ball, floor, light, television, full, slow, lunch, hello, tail, sleep, lose, toilet, mail, clean.

'l'—sentences:

Lyn will telephone a little later.
Lions like to laze in the sun.
He lay on the pillow and looked at the television.
Will you lend me the little ball?
Emily coloured/colored the palace black, blue and yellow.
They cleaned the toilet loudly.
The pleasant lady said hello.
He was glad that the well was full.
Please stop pulling my sleeve and gloves.
Let's land the plane and have lunch.

Tip: For clearer production of words ending in /l/ : While the tongue is not held in the position for as long as when saying it at the beginning of words, make sure you still raise the tongue tip up to the /l/position briefly to finish saying the word.

Practising these, saying them out loud and making sure you listen to and feel for the difference in your mouth:

wi	—	will (will go)
fee	—	feel (feel well)
fa	—	fall (fall down)
spi	—	spill (spill it-said as: spi-lit)
sti	—	still (still home)

42. /r/ (Consonant Spelling: r, wr)

To make the /r/sound lift the tongue up as if to touch the highest point of your palate or roof of your mouth, but leave a little space between tip of your tongue and the high point of your palate. While your tongue is in this position, contract the muscles at the front part of the tongue near the tip-this means, make the sides at the front of the tongue curl in towards the mid line a bit-and switch on voice (sound in the throat). This is a voiced consonant.

Note: In Australian English this sound is said more 'weakly' than in American English.

In Australian and British English the /r/ sound is not pronounced if it occurs at the end of a word, e.g., car, pair. It is also not pronounced when it occurs in the 'er ' combinations—er (her), ir (first),ur (burn),wor (word),ear (learn)-and not pronounced in, or (form, or), and ar (barn).

In American English (from the United States), the /r/ sound is pronounced at the end of words and when it occurs in—or, ir, ur, wor, er, ar,-car, pair, her, first, burn, word, learn, form, or, barn.

'r'—words:

radio, carry, break, dry, great, read, very, brown, drink, screw, really, hurry, breath, from, scrape, write, memory, practise, free, screen, ring, material, proud, friend, sprout, round, garage, produce, credit, spring, road, arrow, train, cry, spray, record, pirate, tree, cricket, street, wrap, paragraph, trade, green, strong, wrist, parrot, dream, grow, strip.

'r'—sentences:

The road went around the rocks.
When the radio fell it broke.
The first pirate had a parrot.
Ron carried a green sack of carrots to the car.
Mark wrapped the material around a really narrow tree.
He read the paragraph to her for a while.
Her friend was frightened and ran up the road.
You can have a pair of rings or the rest of the radios that are left here.
Tomorrow the ferry drivers will go on strike.
They were worried about the cracks in the railing.

Tip: For those having difficulty distinguishing production of /l/ and /r/ try practising the words that follow. Remember /l/ is produced with tongue raised at the front of the mouth (see /l/ section), and for /r/ the tongue is up in the middle of the mouth.

Say these aloud and listen to and feel the difference in your mouth. Hold the /l/ or /r/ sound on longer than usual to gain control and awareness then glide on to the vowel.

lie	—	rye
lip	—	rip
light	—	right
last	—	rast (not a real word)
leaf	—	reef
lice	—	rice
long	—	wrong

43. /w/ (Consonant Spelling: w, wh)

Put the lips forward (as if to kiss someone), and have the lips slightly open. Then release the lips to a more open mouth position by dropping the bottom jaw a bit-the lips are still slightly rounded-while voicing at the same time. This is a voiced consonant.

Note: If you say /v/for /w/, you will need to make sure you put your lips forward to pronounce the /w/at the beginning of words.

'w'—words:

weather, away, twin, wheel, however, twice, why, toward, when, allowance, whale, Edward, weapon, between, water, bowing, winner, beware, west, cobweb, want, twenty.

'w'—sentences:

The whale swam toward the tower.
The woman was swimming between the flags.
What time is the wedding?
He wanted water when he finished the race.
Why do you want the wood?
He was rowing quickly away from the waves.
I'm going to lower the weapon twice.
Beware of the wild waterfall.
He didn't know whether the weather would be wintry
Whatever you do, you must wait for her to finish twirling.

44. /y/ (Consonant Spelling: y)

/y/is a voiced consonant./y/is made by holding the tip of your tongue against the middle of the back of your bottom front teeth. At the same time, raise the middle part of your tongue and make the sides at the middle part of your tongue touch the inside of your bottom teeth. As you switch on the voice you drop the raised middle part of your tongue a little towards the floor of your mouth.

Another way to make this sound is to make a short /ee/sound and move on quickly to the /u/(as in up)sound. You must move from one sound to the next very quickly and not make the /ee/as long as usual for this to work.

Note: For U.S. English speakers the words—wire, fire and tire should not be included in your practise.

'y'—words:
yacht, mayor, yellow, billiards, year, higher, yesterday, wire, yen, fire, yard, tire, yourself, yoyo, you, canyon, your, paying, young, lying.

'y'—sentences:
Yesterday, the mayor played billiards in the yard.
The millionaire tied his yacht to your yacht.
Don't yell in the yellow canyon.
The junior sailor couldn't use a kayak yet.
The lawyer yawned as he paid the bill.
It was unusual yoghurt.
Many young children have yoyos.
This year they will eat egg yolks.
He was tired from fighting the fire as it became higher yesterday.

2.2 Pronunciation, Stress and Intonation

While thinking of 'pronunciation' one need to practise the sounds of words and accent the syllables properly. When we speak, we divide the words into syllables and pronounce them. A syllable is a unit of one vowel sound with a consonant before or after it. Take the word 'pen'. There are three sounds p-e-n. The vowel sound is central to the syllable. The consonant sounds are placed before and after the vowel sound. The word 'pen' has one syllable. The word 'always' has two syllables. Some syllables are more prominent than the others. Such prominent syllables are said to receive the accent or stress. While pronouncing them, we place more emphasis on them. In the word 'always', the first syllable 'al'—gets the stress. And then one should follow correct intonation. Intonation is the rise and fall of the pitch of the voice in speaking. For instance, when you put a Yes-No question, you use the rising intonation. *Do you get it? Is it clear?* When you make a statement, you use the falling intonation. *I get it. It is clear.*

Features to Note while Speaking English by Indian Background Speakers:

It is very important that you notice and practise using the correct rhythm and pitch pattern when speaking English. This feature is a difficult feature to write about and you must listen and notice this.

⇨ The pitch is not as up and down as when speaking an Indian language. While English is not spoken as a monotone it doesn't have as much difference between the 'up and down ' within words and between words in a sentence.

⇨ It is important to also notice the rhythm or timing of the words—are they said quickly together, are they spaced out evenly—what is the beat of English.

⇨ Stress and intonation are also elements that must be noticed and practised and kept in mind when speaking English. Together these form the speech melody. Together they make use of the following vocal features.

Pitch   -   the rise and fall of your voice
Loudness   -   how loud you make your voice in different places
Length   -   how long you hold a sound or syllable
Vowel quality   -   how a vowel is simplified (or stressed—that is lengthened) in connected speech.

⇨ In English the 'th' sound ((both voiced and unvoiced),is made with the tongue definitely between the teeth and held on more, rather than made as plosives ('exploded ' sounding)).

⇨ Voice resonance generally is more from the throat and does not involve chest resonance as much.

⇨ Indian background speakers need to notice which syllable/s of multisyllabic (word with more than one syllable) words are stressed (the vowel is made slightly longer and hence clearer).

⇨ English is not spoken as quickly as the Indian languages and so it is very important to slow down when speaking English. You will not sound strange and you will be understood more easily.

⇨ It is important to note that there is no /u/sound added to final consonants in words in English. That is, the last sound in words is not said heavily or held on.

For example:
dedicated (/d/said lightly and not held on), not 'dedicate du'
big (/g/said lightly and not held on), not 'bi gu'

BASIC SYLLABLE RULES

1. **To find the number of syllables:**
   ⇨ Count the vowels in the word.
   ⇨ Subtract any silent vowels (like the silent "e" at the end of a word or the second vowel when two vowels a together in a syllable).
   ⇨ Subtract one vowel from every diphthong. (Diphthongs only count as one vowel sound.)
   ⇨ The number of vowel sounds left is the same as the number of syllables.

   The number of syllables that you hear when you pronounce a word is the same as the number of vowels sounds heard. For example the word "came" has 2 vowels, but the "e" is silent, leaving one vowel sound and one syllable. The word "outside" has 4 vowels, but the "e" is silent and the "ou" is a diphthong which counts as only one sound, so this word has only two vowels sounds and therefore, two syllables.

2. Divide between two middle consonants. Split up words that have two middle consonants.

   For example, hap/pen, bas/ket, let/ter, sup/per, din/ner, and Den/nis. The only exceptions are the consonant digraphs. Never split up consonant digraphs as they really represent only one sound. The exceptions are "th", "sh", "ph", "th", "ch", and "wh".

3. Usually divide before a single middle consonant. When there is only one syllable, you usually divide in front of it, as in "o/pen", "i/tem", "e/vil",

and "re/port". The only exceptions are those times when the first syllable has an obvious short sound, as in "cab/in".

4. Divide before the consonant before an "-le" syllable. When you have a word that has the old-style spelling in which the "-le" sounds like "-el", divide before the consonant before the "-le". For example: "a/ble", "fum/ble", "rub/ble" "mum/ble" and "this/tle". The only exception to this are: "ckle" words like "tick/le".

5. Divide off any compound words, prefixes, suffixes and roots which have vowel sounds. Split off the parts of compound words like "sports/car" and "house/boat". Divide off prefixes such at "un/happy", "pre/paid", or "re/write". Also divide off suffixes as in the words "farm/er", "teach/er", "hope/less" and "care/ful". In the word "stop/ping", the suffix is actually "-ping" because this word follows the rule that when you add "-ing" to a word with one syllable, you double the last consonant and add the "-ing".

ACCENT RULES

When a word has more than one syllable, one of the syllables is always a little louder than the others. The syllable with the louder stress is the accented syllable. It may seem that the placement of accents in words is often random or accidental, but these are some rules that usually work.

1. Accents are often on the first syllable. Examples: ba'/sic, pro'/gram.
2. In words that have suffixes or prefixes, the accent is usually on the main root word. Examples: box'/es, un/tie'.
3. If de-, re-, ex-, in-,po-, pro-, or a- is the first syllable in a word, it is usually not accented. Examples: de/lay', ex/plore'.
4. Two vowel letters together in the last syllable of a word often indicates an accented last syllable. Examples: com/plain', con/ceal'.
5. When there are two like consonant letters within a word, the syllable before the double consonants is usually accented. Examples: be/gin'/ner, let'/ter.
6. The accent is usually on the syllable before the suffixes -ion, ity, -ic, -ical, -ian, -ial, or -ious, and on the second syllable before the suffix -ate. Examples: af/fec/ta'/tion, dif/fer/en'/ti/ate.

7. In words of three or more syllables, one of the first two syllables is usually accented. Examples: ac'/ci/dent, de/ter'/mine.

STRESS PATTERNS

In this segment the discussion is on stress patterns in English words. English is a stress-timed language. Indian languages are syllable-timed.

In stress timing certain syllables receive greater emphasis and are heard more prominently than others in a sequence of words. Within a word, stressing is fixed in the sense that the stress always falls on a particular syllable in that word. However, stress in English words is not tied to any given position in a word. We cannot say, for instance, that the first or the second or the last syllable in a word will always be stressed in English. For different words the syllable to be stressed is different.

Points to Remember about Stressing:

1. The very first requirement for any native-like English accent is the acquisition of stress-timing.
2. To acquire stress-timing one has to pay close attention to vowels, both to their quality and to their relative emphasis.
3. Stress is the extra emphasis placed on a syllable. In English, stress determines both pace and rhythm.
4. Stress is a matter of greater prominence and greater audibility.
5. If the stressed vowel is shorter than the unstressed vowel, (eg. HOS-tile, IN-voice) care should be taken to articulate the stressed syllable with greater breath effort.
6. If a word has two syllables and both vowels are short, (eg. EX-it, EN-try, COV-ert, PRE-face), a contrast in breath effort should be maintained by consciously emphasizing the stressed syllable.
7. Indians, by and large, have difficulty with word-initial stresses. The tendency, among Indians, is to emphasize the final syllable in a word. Thus, English words in which the stress falls on the last syllable do not pose any problems to Indian learners.

MORE ON STRESS

Words with TWO SYLLABLES (Stress on the <u>First</u> Syllable)
AD-vent
FOR-ay
MO-bile
VI-rile
OUT-rage
RE-vel
IN-voice
A-vid
SUR-face
EF-fort
FER-vent
IN-come
VAC-cine
O-ver
AD-verb
CA-vil
PRE-face
HOS-tile
BAN-dit
IM-pulse
FRA-gile
UM-pire
PUR-pose
PRO-file
DIF-fer
NE-ver
FOR-feit
FU-tile
ES-sence
PRO-gramme
UN-der
A-lien
DO-nate
RES-cue
WIN-dow
COM-ment

NA-tive
A-gile
THIR-ty
CHA-os
CHI-cken
OUT-line
SUR-feit
FER-tile
GRO-vel
CARE-ful
ENG-lish
CRAY-on
LI-sten
GLU-cose
CON-scious
NA-zi
GLOUCES-ter
EX-ile
BI-got
DE-mon
Exit
CO-vet
FOR-tune
FA-cile
FOOL-some
PRES-tine
IN-stinct
PE-trol
GES-ture
MA-nger
PRE-cious
HOUSE-wife
EX-pert
NO-tice
SO-cial
FOR-head
AS-thma
STA-tus
ER-sazts,

E-poch
DA-tum

You must be careful with words like virile, fragile, umpire, facile, glucose in which the second syllable contains the long vowel or a glide. Indians tend to emphasize this second vowel instead of the first.

Words with TWO SYLLABLES (Stress on the <u>Second</u> Syllable)

In words such as event and machine Indians tend to place too much emphasis on the first syllable. In general in a two syllable word, make sure that the stress is properly on either the first or second syllable and not evenly distributed between both.

De-LIGHT
Dis-CREET
e-LITE
des-PAIR
ca-SHIER
ca-BAL
dis-CUSS
ca-PRICE
in-FER
fi-NESSE
ab-SURD
de-MURE
e-XULT
cha-RADE
la-TRINE
ma-RINE
pre-TEND
re-SENT
e-RECT
ma-LIGN
bi-ZARRE
ra-VINE
pres-TIGE
a-LIVE
de-FER

o-PAQUE
dis-EASE
es-CHEW
a-NON
de-TAIN
na-IVE
ef-FECT
de-MUR
in-ANE
pre-FER
e-VENT
ma-CHINE
a-WRY
an-TIQUE
pa-TROL
in-DICT
nu-ANCE
in-SANE
ma-TURE
dis-STRESS
rout-TINE
de-TER
bur-LESQUE
re-BUFF

Words with THREE-SYLLABLES (with the stress on the <u>First</u> Syllable)
QUAN-tity
IN-nocence
BA-chelor
PE-digree
CA-taract
CA-pital
AL-lergy
SE-perate
DIS-parate
CON-template
TEM-poral
TE-lephone
E-nergy

IN-valid (sick)
IM-petus
EX-igent
PUR-posive
A-trophy
IN-terest
IL-lustrate
IN-tegral
TE-legraph
CIR-cumstanc
AL-titude
E-nervate
GAS-oline
AR-rogant
LI-mousine
MIS-chievous
AL-gebra
A-djective
IM-potence
IN-dustry
DE-ficit
IN-famous
DE-nigrate
LI-merick
E-chelon
OB-solete
SI-nister
AL-ternate
YES-terday
PHO-tograph
IN-undate
A-libi
DIF-fidence
IM-pudence
IN-tricate
IN-stigate
I-rony
AF-fable
GIB-berish

SY-cophant
E-quable
LU-nacy
LU-natic
BI-gotry
HO-locaust

Words with THREE-SYLLABLES (with the stress on the <u>Second</u> Syllable)
Ex-HI-bit
an-CES-tral
De-CI-sive
Ge-NE-tic
Con-DO-lence
a-DJA-cent
re-SIS-tance
in-CLE-ment
ef-FI-cient
in-I-tial
im-PAR-tial
e-NIG-ma
in-HER-ent
er-RA-ta
e-LIX-ir
in-TRE-pid
aes-THE-tic
in-TER-pret
al-LER-gic
ex-PO-nent
di-LEM-ma
re-SI-lience
ec-CEN-tric
sur-REN-der
in-ER-tia
con-SI-der
fe-RO-cious

Words with THREE-SYLLABLES (with the stress on the <u>Third</u> Syllable)

Among three syllable words, stress on the third syllable is somewhat less common than stress on the first or second syllable. One may notice that most examples are of words in which there is a prefix such as re, dis, or un. In such instances the prefix acquires a secondary stress while the primary stress remains on the final syllable.

Three syllable words derived from French (such as cigarette and refugee) also tend to have the stress on the third syllable.

read-MIT
rea-DJUST
reaf-FIRM
rear-RANGE
disa-PPEAR
disa-GREE
disap-PROVE
under-RATE
under-TAKE
under-NEATH
Unem-PLOYED
Unre-SOLVED
Resur-RECT
Under-STAND
Ciga-RETTE
Person-NEL
Repre-SENT
Exper-TISE
Remin-ISCE
Refu-GEE

POLYSYLLABIC WORDS

We notice a tendency among Indian learners of English to place equal stress on every syllable. This causes problems of understanding for native speakers. And native speakers are accustomed to the sing song sound patterns created by stressing. On the other hand they might think we have a sing-song pattern without stressing.

Indians should remember that in polysyllabic words it is common to have both a primary and secondary stress. Unfortunately, there are no consistent rules as to which of the syllable should receive prominence. All one can say is that if the third syllable receives primary emphasis it is common for the first syllable to get secondary emphasis. Likewise, if the second syllable is fully stressed the fourth syllable may be partially stressed. Look at these words and listen to them as often as is needed while you look at the way spelling is arranged. We have used capital letters to indicate stressed syllables. We also have phonetic spelling alongside each of the words.

MAN-datory
de-RO-gatory
pre-RO-gative
ma-CHI-nery
MIS-sionary
mi-CRO-meter
ther-MO-meter
con-GE-nital
inco-HE-rent
incom-PA-tibte
in-VES-tigate
in-VES-tigative
medi-O-crity
chro-NO-met
vi-CAR-ious
ne-FAR-ious
e-MA-ciate
e-QUI-vocal
IG-nominy
Ignor-A-mus
Repre-SEN-tative
A-miable
I-deograph
de-LI-very
er-RO-neous
eco-NO-mic
am-BI-valent
eso-TE-ric
COW-ardlines

em-PI-ricism
CRI-ticism
ME-lancholy
e-QUI-valent
i-DEN-tify
i-DEN-tity
i-DEN-tical
appa-RA-tus
AR-bitrary
a-NA-chronism
NE-potism
ir-REV-ocable
ca-CO-phony
cal-LI-graphy
im-PLA-cable
inac-CES-sible
hy-PO-thesis
schizo-PHREN-ic
di-A-meter
lexi-CO-graphy
ki-LO-meter
i-NE-vitable
pe-RI-meter
an-NU-ity
he-XA-meter
hy-PER-bole
superin-TEN-dent
E-quitable
a-STIG-matism
e-PI-tome
cinema-TO-graphy

SHIFT IN STRESS

Certain words in English do double or triple duty. They function as nouns, adjectives, verbs and so on. It means, the same word is used as a noun, an adjective or as a verb. In these words the stress often shifts with the part of speech. We have nouns and corresponding verbs. There is a stress difference.

NOUNS and Corresponding VERBS—Stress Difference

CON-flict (n)
con-FLICT (vb)
IN-crease (n)
in-CREASE (vb)
CON-vict (n)
con-VICT (vb)
AD-dress (n)
ad-DRESS (vb)
EX-ploit (n)
ex-PLOIT (vb)
CON-vert (n)
con-VERT (vb)
IN-sult (n)
in-SULT (vb)
DIS-card (n)
dis-CARD (vb)
DIS-charge (n)
dis-CHARGE (vb)
SUR-vey (n)
sur-VEY (vb)
CON-trast (n)
con-TRAST (vb)
ES-cort (n)
es-CORT (vb)
COM-bine (n)
com-BINE (vb)
EX-cise (n)
ex-CISE (vb)
Let us look at some sentences:
The CON-trast is clear.
He con-TRAST-ed the two.
He was a CON-vict.
He was con-VICT-ed.
He is a CON-vert from Islam.
He has been con-VERT-ed.
The IN-crease is very little.
Let's in-CREASE it.

The SUR-vey showed nothing.
They sur-VEYED the scene.
Where's the AD-dress?
Let's ad-DRESS the envelopes.

NOUN / ADJECTIVE versus VERB

AB-sent (adj)
ab-SENT (vb)
PRO-gress (n)
pro-GRESS (vb)
PRO-ject (n)
pro-JECT (vb)
PRO-duce (n)
pro-DUCE (vb)
RE-search (n)
re-SEARCH (vb)
CON-tract (n)
Con-TRACT (vb)
FRE-quent (adj)
fre-Quent (vb)
RE-bel (n)
re-BEL (vb)
TRANS-fer (n)
trans-FER (vb)
PER-mit (n)
per-MIT (vb)
AC-cent (n)
ac-CENT (vb)
SUB-ject (n)
sub-JECT (vb)
RE-cord (n)
re-CORD (vb)
DE-sert (n)
de-SERT (vb)
IM-port (n)
im-PORT (vb)
PRO-ceeds (n)
pro-CEEDS (vb)
COM-press (n)

com-PRESS (vb)
EX-port (n)
ex-PORT (vb)
PRE-sent (n)
pre-SENT (vb)
RE-call (n)
re-CALL (vb)
PUR-port (n)
pur-PORT (vb)
Let us look at some sentences:
He is AB-sent.
He ab-SENT-ed himself.
It is a DE-sert.
Friends de-SERT-ed him.
He was PRE-sent there.
He pre-SENT-ed himself.
He is a RE-bel.
He re-BELLED.
He pro-CEEDS to Bombay.
The PRO-ceeds go to a fund.
It is a SUB-ject.
It is sub-JECT-ed to a condition.
We need a PER-mit.
We per-MIT-ted ourselves to go.
The AC-cent is on the money.
The word is not ac-CENT-ed.
We wanted PRO-gress.
We pro-GRESSED.

"Be able to correctly pronounce the words you would like to speak and have excellent spoken grammar."

– Marilyn vos Savant

CHAPTER 3

VOCABULARY

3.1 How to improve your vocabulary?

Step 1: Read books, magazines, poems, plays, stories and more. The more language you're exposed to, the more new words you'll learn.

Step 2: Make it a habit to find a new word every day. Look in the dictionary, sign up for "A Word a Day" (See dictionary.com) or make swapping new words a game with a workmate or fellow student.

Step 3: Speak to people. You'll be exposed to an amazing range of cultural influences and occupations, all of which will introduce you to new words.

Step 4: Write down words you don't know. Keep a pad in your briefcase or purse just for that purpose.

Step 5: Look up the words in a dictionary so you'll understand what they mean, how they're spelled and their various usages. This will also help you remember the words.

Step 6: Make flashcards of the words and go through them regularly.

Step 7: Create or play word games.

Following are a few methods for expanding your vocabulary with words you will feel comfortable using.

1. Vocabulary Tree

Improving vocabulary skills requires constant attention. How to do that? This 'how to' focuses on a basic strategy for increasing vocabulary in specific subject areas through the use of a Vocabulary Tree. Here is how:

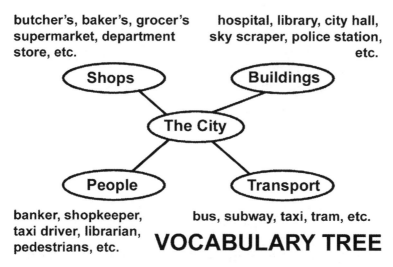

butcher's, baker's, grocer's supermarket, department store, etc.

hospital, library, city hall, sky scraper, police station, etc.

Shops

Buildings

The City

People

Transport

banker, shopkeeper, taxi driver, librarian, pedestrians, etc.

bus, subway, taxi, tram, etc.

VOCABULARY TREE

(Fig. 5—The Vocabulary Tree)

1. Choose a subject area that interests you very much.
2. Write a short introduction to the subject trying to use as many vocabulary words concerning the subject as possible.
3. Using your introduction, arrange the principle ideas concerning the subject into a vocabulary tree.
4. To create a vocabulary tree, put the subject (head word) at the center of a piece of paper.
5. Around the central subject, put some related category of words coming under the central subject. See Figure 5 above.
6. In each of these categories, write the appropriate vocabulary. If you need to, write sub-categories.
7. Create the same vocabulary tree in your native language
8. Your native language tree will be much more detailed. Use this native language tree as a reference point to look up new words and fill in your English tree.
9. Rewrite your introductory essay concerning the subject taking advantage of the new vocabulary learned.
10. To make this vocabulary active, practice reading your essay aloud until you can present it by memory.
11. Ask a friend or fellow classmate to listen to your presentation and ask you questions about the subject.

Tips:

1. Remember that vocabulary goes from passive knowledge to active knowledge—this means that you need to repeat a word often before it becomes active vocabulary.
2. Be patient with yourself, it takes time for this process to work.
3. Try to always learn vocabulary in groups of words instead of random lists. In this manner, words are related to each other and are more likely to be remembered over the long-term.

2. Vocabulary Themes

Create a list of vocabulary themes; include the vocabulary, a definition and an example sentence for each new item. Here is an example of a household appliance vocabulary theme sheet. These are appliances we use every day in our house. Each word includes a definition and example sentence:

✦ broiler—device for broiling meat

That steak was done to perfection. Where did you get that broiler? It's fantastic.

✦ can opener—a device to open cans by cutting around the edges of the rim.

Don't open that by hand. Use the can opener!

✦ compactor—device for pressing together; crusher

You'd be surprised at how much garbage the compactor can put into one bag!

✦ dishwasher—dishwasher - device that washes dishes

I don't know what I'd do without my dishwasher. I can't imagine having to wash all those dishes by hand!

✦ dryer—device or appliance for removing moisture, as by hot air

Honey, where's the dryer? I've just taken a shower and I need to dry my hair.

✦ fan—device for creating a current of air or a breeze

I really don't like using the air-conditioning. I much prefer this fan to keep things cool.

✦ freezer—one that freezes, as a thermally insulated cabinet

He goes shopping and buys enough food to put into his freezer for a month.

✦ furnace—structure or apparatus for generating heat

Could you check if the furnace is working? It seems so cold in here. It's a good idea to put a humidifier in the room for young babies when they have a cold.

+ icebox—insulated chest or box in which ice is put to cool
We have an icebox out in the backyard where we keep the beer. Feel free to help yourself!

+ iron—instrument used for taking the wrinkles out of a piece of clothing through heat
The production of modern materials such as permanent press has almost made the iron a thing of the past.

+ oven—chamber or enclosed compartment usually used to cook in, as in a stove
I like cooking potatoes in the oven instead of frying them.

+ refrigerator—appliance for maintaining foods at a low temperature, or producing ice
We keep the bread in the refrigerator.

+ shaver—one that shaves; a device used in shaving
I prefer using a shaver instead of a razor.

+ stove—device used to provide heat (either electric or gas) to cook food
I really don't know how to cook. About the only thing I can do is boiling an egg on the stove.

+ toaster—device used to toast bread, esp. by exposure to heat
Could you pop this bread into the toaster?

+ vacuum cleaner—appliance using suction to clean surfaces
I used the vacuum cleaner to clean all the rugs—they really needed it.

3. Specific Vocabulary Lists

Rather than studying a long list of unrelated vocabulary, use specific vocabulary lists to help you prepare for the type of vocabulary you need for work, school or hobbies. Here there is a Specific Vocabulary List of words related to Arts.

❖ abstract adj.
❖ academy n.
❖ aesthetic adj. n.
❖ aesthetics n.
❖ album n.
❖ architect n.
❖ canvas n.

4. Word Formation Charts

Word formation is one of the keys to success for advanced level learners. These word formation charts provide the concept of noun, adjective and verb forms of key vocabulary listed in alphabetical order.

work n.

1. application of mental or physical effort to a purpose; use of energy. 2. task to be undertaken. 3. thing done or made by work; result of an action. 4. employment or occupation etc., esp. as a means of earning income. 5. literary or musical composition. 6. actions or experiences of a specified kind (nice work!). 7. (in comb.) things made of a specified material or with specified tools etc. (ironwork; needlework). 8. (in pl.) operative part of a clock or machine. 9. Physics the exertion of force overcoming resistance or producing molecular change. 10. (in full the works) colloq. a all that is available or needed. b full, esp. harsh, treatment. 11. (in pl.) operations of building or repair (road works). 12. (in pl.; often treated as sing.) factory. 13. (usu. in pl.) Theol. meritorious act. 14 (usu. in pl. or in comb.) defensive structure (earthworks).

work v.

1. do work; be engaged in bodily or mental activity. 2. be employed in certain work (works in industry). 3. make efforts (works for peace). 4. (foll. by in) be a craftsman in (a material). 5. operate or function, esp. effectively (how does this machine work?; your idea will not work). 6. operate, manage, control (cannot work the machine). 7. a put or keep in operation or at work; cause to toil (works the staff hard). b cultivate (land). 8. a bring about; produce as a result (worked miracles). b colloq. arrange (matters) (worked it so that we could go; can you work things for us?). 9. knead, hammer; bring to a desired shape or consistency. 10. do, or make by, needlework, etc.

work out n.

1. a solve (a sum) or find (an amount) by calculation. b solve, understand (a problem, person, etc.). 2. (foll. by at) be calculated. 3. give a definite result (this sum will not work out). 4. have a result (the plan worked out well). 5. provide for the details of (has worked out a scheme). 6. engage in physical exercise or training.

work out v

1. examine thoroughly. 2. colloq. treat with violence. work through arrive at an understanding of (a problem) etc. work to rule (as a protest) follow official working rules exactly in order to reduce output.

work up
1. bring gradually to an efficient or (of a painting etc.) advanced state. 2. (foll. by to) advance gradually to a climax etc. 3. elaborate or excite by degrees. 4. mingle (ingredients). 5. learn (a subject) by study

> *workable adj.* that can be worked, will work, or is worth working.
>
> *workaday adj.* ordinary, everyday, practical.
>
> *workaholic n.* colloq. person addicted to working.
>
> *workbook n.* student's book with exercises.
>
> *workbox n.* box for tools, needlework, etc.
>
> *work camp n.* camp at which community work is done, esp. by young volunteers.
>
> *workday n.* day on which work is usually done.
>
> *worker n.* 1. person who works, esp. for an employer. 2. neuter bee or ant. 3. person who works hard.
>
> *work experience n.* scheme intended to give young people temporary experience of employment.
>
> *workforce n.* 1. workers engaged or available. 2. number of these.

5. Visual Dictionaries

A picture is worth a thousand words. It's also very helpful for learning precise vocabulary. There are a number of excellent English learner visual dictionaries for sale. Here is an example of a Visual Dictionary (Figure 6).

Cherry n.   1 [C] a small soft round fruit with a stone in the middle.

2 [C] a tree on which cherries (1) grow

(Fig. 6–Cherry)

6. Learn Collocations

Collocations refer to words that often or always go together. A good example of a collocation is to do your homework. These lists of important verb + noun collocations will help you learn some of the most important collocations.

Choose which one of the following first three verbs (underlined) goes with the expressions listed afterwards.

❖ Collocation Use with: *Take/Have/Break*

a break /a leg /a headache /a window /a haircut /an exam /a seat / breakfast /the law/ a holiday/ a taxi/a world record/ someone's heart/ a bath / someone's temperature/ a relationship / a look / a promise/ a chance/ a drink / the rules/ notes/ time/ a habit / the ice/ a rest / a rest / someone's place / the news to someone / a problem

❖ Collocation Use with: *Catch, Pay, Keep*

a cold/attention/ a pet /a bus /control /the bill /a promise /interest / someone's attention / a ball /calm //the price /someone's place /by check /a thief /someone a visit/ a fright/ an appointment/ by surprise /a salary /quiet / fire /cash /a secret /a diary /someone a /compliment /someone's eye /a mouse /the change /wages

❖ Collocation Use with: *Save, Find and Go*

time /a partner /mad /wild /time /money /the answer /crazy /someone's life /energy /happiness /white /abroad /the money /someone a seat /oneself trouble /a solution /missing /quiet /electricity /space /one's strength /a way / bad /space /dark /a replacement /a cure /a penalty /overseas

❖ Collocation Use with: *Come, Get and Feel*

first /ready /tense /comfortable /married /last /right back /happy / started /free /divorced /early /close /burnt /nervous /prepared /drunk /old / disappointed /angry /late / /lost /second /complete with /sleepy /worried / direct /wet /hurt

❖ Collocation Use with: *Miss, Get, Do and Make*

a goal/home /homework /progress /an effort /the shopping /a chance / frightened /the sack /the point /money /the housework /someone a favor / permission /a flight /a mess /business /a surprise /one's family /a mistake / nothing /furniture /the message /a lesson /one's home /a noise /the washing up /lost /ready /trouble /an opportunity /the cooking /a job /peace /an appointment /a job /nowhere /a change /someone's help /one's best

7. Elaboration

Elaboration is an easy technique that will increase your retention of new words more and more.

e.g.   act →acting→action→actor→active→activity→activism→activate.

You can form so many words in this process. But remember you have to use these words in sentences in order to know the meaning and usage.

8. **Personal Dictionary**
   Why should you write your own Personal Dictionary/Vocabulary Book?
   ❖ You can put in important information that is not in other dictionaries.
   ❖ You can put in information in any language
   ❖ You can put in pictures
   ❖ You can put the sentence where you first found the word, and translate the whole sentence
   ❖ You can put in collocations (words that often go together; e.g. a light meal)
   ❖ You can put in different connotations (words which describe the same thing, but give you a good or bad impression; e.g. 'freedom fighter' and 'terrorist').
   ❖ You can put in different parts of speech for the same headword (headword is an entry in a dictionary, e.g. jump. You could put in jump, jumped, jumping, and jumper.)
   ❖ You can compare how to use the word in English and in your own language, for example, Cantonese has a word for cup, but English divides cups into cups, mugs, beakers and glasses.
   ❖ You can put in whether the word is formal or informal; e.g. 'a meeting' or 'a get-together'
   ❖ You can put in whether the word is derogatory (rude) you can put it any other useful information, for example where you first heard the word. It is faster. See below, how will it save your time?

Using your own dictionary is faster because:

   ❖ It only contains words you need, so it has fewer entries and you don't need to search so much for a word.
   ❖ You can put in words that are not headwords in a normal dictionary, such as 'jumped', rather than 'jump'.
   ❖ You can put the words in any order, for example, you can group together all the technical words about your academic subject. Therefore you should use a book where you can insert pages at any point, like a ring binder.
   ❖ You can put information from different types of dictionary together in one entry, for example, information from technical, picture, mono-lingual and bi-lingual dictionaries. Therefore you only need to look in one dictionary to find all the information.

❖ You can write abbreviations in full, so you don't need to check the meaning in the front or back of the dictionary. For example, you can write 'Uncountable noun' instead of [U]

Example of a Personal Dictionary / Vocabulary Book: a noun, an expression, an adjective, an adverb, an idiom,

1. A Noun
   Word: 'Fluke'
   Pronunciation: /flu:k/
   Meaning: something good that happens by accident and good luck
   (It also means a whale's tail, but this is a rare and technical meaning.)
   Example: 'The goal was a total fluke; the ball went between the goalkeeper's legs.'
   Grammar: countable noun. Plurals are unusual, but grammatically possible; e.g. "Their goals were all flukes, but ours were skillful!"

2. An Expression
   'It's raining cats and dogs.'
   Meaning: It's raining heavily. Note: This expression is a bit old-fashioned; it is not used much nowadays. A modern equivalent is "It's pouring."
   Continue with this process . . .

3. An Adjective
   Word: 'bad'
   Note: In late 1990s British English teenager slang, 'It's bad!' means 'It's very good.'
   Pronunciation: /bæd/

4. An Adverb
   Word: 'badly'
   Meaning: adverb of 'bad'
   Examples:
   ❖ 'He did very badly in his test, so he will have to study the material again.'
   ❖ 'This is a badly-written assignment.'
   Pronunciation: /bædli/

5. An Idiom
   'to swallow the dictionary' / 'to swallow a dictionary'
   Meaning: to use long and unnecessarily complicated words and expressions, especially in normal conversation.

Example: "He talks like he has swallowed a dictionary, I can't understand half of what he says."

9. Collection of Common Words
Common Prefixes:

A prefix is a letter or a group of letters attached to the beginning of a word that partly indicates its meaning. For example, the word prefix itself begins with a prefix—pre-, which generally means "before." Understanding the meanings of the common prefixes can help us deduce the meanings of new words that we encounter. But be careful: some prefixes (such as in-) have more than one meaning (in this example, "not" and "into").

The table below defines and illustrates 35 common prefixes.

Prefix	Meaning	Example
a-, an-	without	amoral
ante-	before	antecedent
anti-	against	anticlimax
auto-	self	autopilot
circum-	around	circumvent
co-	with	copilot
com-, con-	with	companion, contact
contra-	against	contradict
de-	off, away from	devalue
dis-	not	disappear
en-	put into	enclose
ex-	out of, former	extract, ex-president
extra-	beyond, more than	extracurricular
hetero-	different	heterosexual
homo-	same	homonym
hyper-	over, more	hyperactive
il-, im-, in-, ir-	not, without	illegal, immoral, inconsiderate, irresponsible
in-	into	insert
inter-	between	intersect
intra-	between	intravenous

macro-	large	macroeconomics
micro-	small	microscope
mono-	one	monocle
non-	not, without	nonentity
omni-	all, every	omniscient
post-	after	postmortem
pre-, pro-	before, forward	precede, project
sub-	under	submarine
syn-	same time	synchronize
trans-	across	transmit
tri-	three	tricycle
un-	not	unfinished
uni-	one	unicorn

Common Suffixes: A suffix is a letter or a group of letters attached to the end of a word to form a new word or to alter the grammatical function of the original word. For example, the verb read can be made into the noun reader by adding the suffix -er; read can be made into the adjective readable by adding the suffix -able.

Understanding the meanings of the common suffixes can help us deduce the meanings of new words that we encounter. The table below defines and illustrates 26 common suffixes.

Noun Suffixes:

Suffix	Meaning	Example
-acy	state or quality	privacy
-al	act or process of	refusal
-ance, -ence	state or quality of	maintenance, eminence
-dom	place or state of being	freedom, kingdom
-er, -or	one who	trainer, protector
-ism	doctrine, belief	communism

-ist	one who	chemist
-ity, -ty	quality of	veracity
-ment	condition of	argument
-ness	state of being	heaviness
-ship	position held	fellowship
sion, -tion	state of being	concession, transition

Verb Suffixes:

-ate	become	eradicate
-en	become	enlighten
-ify, -fy	make or become	terrify
-ize, -ise	become	civilize

Adjective Suffixes:

-able, -ible	capable of being	edible, presentable
-al	pertaining to	regional
-esque	reminiscent of	picturesque
-ful	notable for	fanciful
-ic, -ical	pertaining to	musical, mythic
-ious, -ous	characterized by	nutritious, portentous
-ish	having the quality of	fiendish
-ive	having the nature of	creative
-less	without	endless
-y	characterized by	sleazy

Word Roots:

A root, as its name suggests, is a word or word part from which other words grow, usually through the addition of prefixes and suffixes. The root of the word vocabulary, for example, is voc, a Latin root meaning "word" or "name." This root also appears in the words advocacy, convocation, evocative, vocal, and vociferous.

Understanding the meanings of the common word-roots can help us deduce the meanings of new words that we encounter. But be careful: root words can have more than one meaning and various shades of meaning. In addition, words that look similar may derive from different roots. So when you meet up with a new word, be sure to rely on a dictionary to check its definition.

The table below defines and illustrates 30 of the most common Greek and Latin roots. The letter in parentheses indicates whether the root word is Greek (G) or Latin (L).

Root	Meaning	Examples
ast(er)-(G)	star	asteroid, astronomy
-audi- (L)	hear	audible, audience
-auto- (G)	self	automatic, autopsy
-bene- (L)	good	benefit, benign
bio- (G)	life	biography, biology
-chrono- (G)	time	chronic, synchronize
-dict- (L)	say	dictate, diction
-duc- (L)	lead, make	deduce, produce
gen- (L)	give birth	gene, generate
geo- (G)	earth	geography, geology
-graph- (G)	write	autograph, graph
-jur-, -jus- (L)	law	jury, justice
log-, -logue- (L)	thought	logic, obloquy
luc- (L)	light	lucid, translucent
-man(u)- (L)	hand	manual, manure
-mand-, -mend- (L)	order	demand, recommend
-mis-, -mit- (L)	send	missile, transmission
-omni- (L)	all	omnivorous
-path- (G)	feel	empathy, pathetic
-phil- (G)	love	philosophy, bibliophile
-phon- (G)	sound	phonics, telephone
-photo- (G)	light	photograph, photon
-port- (L)	carry	export, portable
-qui(t)- (L)	quiet, rest	acquit, tranquil
-scrib-, -script- (L)	write	ascribe, script
-sens-, -sent- (L)	feel	resent, sensitive

-tele- (G)	far off	telecast, telephone
-terr- (L)	earth	terrain, territory
-vac- (L)	empty	evacuate, vacate
-vid-, -vis- (L)	see	visible, video

Common words those sound alike:

Many words sound alike but mean different things when put into writing. This list will help you distinguish between some of the more common words that sound alike.

Forms to remember:

Accept, Except

❖ accept = verb meaning to receive or to agree: He accepted their praise graciously.

❖ except = preposition meaning all but, other than: Everyone went to the game except Alyson.

Affect, Effect

❖ affect = verb meaning to influence: Will lack of sleep

❖ effect = noun meaning result or consequence: Will lack of sleep have an effect on your game?

❖ effect = verb meaning to bring about, to accomplish: Our efforts have effected a major change in university policy.

Remember, Affect is a Verb and Effect is a Noun.

Advise, Advice

❖ advise = verb that means to recommend, suggest, or counsel: I advise you to be cautious.

❖ advice = noun that means an opinion or recommendation about what could or should be done: I'd like to ask for your advice on this matter.

Conscious, Conscience

❖ conscious = adjective meaning awake, perceiving: Despite a head injury, the patient remained conscious.

❖ conscience = noun meaning the sense of obligation to be good: Chris wouldn't cheat because his conscience wouldn't let him.

Idea, Ideal

❖ <u>idea</u> = noun meaning a thought, belief, or conception held in the mind, or a general notion or conception formed by generalization: Jennifer had a brilliant idea—she'd go to the Writing Lab for help with her papers!

❖ <u>ideal</u> = noun meaning something or someone that embodies perfection, or an ultimate object or endeavor: Mickey was the ideal for tutors everywhere.

❖ <u>ideal</u> = adjective meaning embodying an ultimate standard of excellence or perfection, or the best; Jennifer was an ideal student.

Its, It's

❖ <u>its</u> = possessive adjective (possessive form of the pronoun it): The crab had an unusual growth on its shell.

❖ <u>it's</u> = contraction for it is or it has (in a verb phrase): It's still raining; it's been raining for three days. (Pronouns have apostrophes only when two words are being shortened into one.)

Lead, Led

❖ <u>lead</u> = noun referring to a dense metallic element: The X-ray technician wore a vest lined with lead.

❖ <u>led</u> = past-tense and past-participle form of the verb to lead, meaning to guide or direct: The evidence led the jury to reach a unanimous decision.

Than, Then

❖ <u>than</u> = used in comparison statements: He is richer than I.
Used in statements of preference: I would rather dance than eat.
Used to suggest quantities beyond a specified amount: Read more than the first paragraph.

❖ <u>then</u> = a time other than now: He was younger then. She will start her new job then.
Next in time, space, or order: First we must study; then we can play.
Suggesting a logical conclusion: If you've studied hard, then the exam should be no problem.

Their, There, They're

❖ <u>their</u> = possessive pronoun: They got their books.

❖ <u>there</u> = that place: My house is over there. (This is a place word, and so it contains the word here.)

❖ <u>they're</u> = contraction for they are: They're making dinner. (Pronouns have apostrophes only when two words are being shortened into one.)

To, Too, Two
- ❖ <u>to</u> = preposition, or first part of the infinitive form of a verb: They went to the lake to swim.
- ❖ <u>too</u> = very, also: I was too tired to continue. I was hungry, too.
- ❖ <u>two</u> = the number 2: Two students scored below passing on the exam.

Two, twelve, and between are all words related to the number 2, and all contain the letters tw.

Too can mean also or can be an intensifier, and you might say that it contains an extra o ("one too many")

We're, Where, Were
- ❖ <u>we're</u> = contraction for we are: We're glad to help. (Pronouns have apostrophes only when two words are being shortened into one.)
- ❖ <u>where</u> = location: Where are you going? (This is a place word, and so it contains the word here.)
- ❖ <u>were</u> = a past tense form of the verb be: They were walking side by side.

Your, You're
- ❖ <u>your</u> = possessive pronoun: Your shoes are untied.
- ❖ <u>you're</u> = contraction for you are: You're walking around with your shoes untied. (Pronouns have apostrophes only when two words are being shortened into one.)

One Word or Two?
All ready/already
- ❖ <u>all ready</u>: used as an adjective to express complete preparedness
- ❖ <u>already</u>: an adverb expressing time
  At last I was all ready to go, but everyone had already left.

All right/alright
- ❖ <u>all right</u>: used as an adjective or adverb; older and more formal spelling, more common in scientific & academic writing: Will you be all right on your own?
- ❖ <u>alright</u>: Alternate spelling of all right; less frequent but used often in journalistic and business publications, and especially common in fictional dialogue: He does alright in school.

All together/altogether
- ❖ all together: an adverb meaning considered as a whole, summed up: All together, there were thirty-two students at the museum.
- ❖ altogether: an intensifying adverb meaning wholly, completely, entirely: His comment raises an altogether different problem.

Anyone/any one
- ❖ anyone: a pronoun meaning any person at all: Anyone who can solve this problem deserves an award.
- ❖ any one: a paired adjective and noun meaning a specific item in a group; usually used with of: Any one of those papers could serve as an example.

Anyway/any way
- ❖ anyway: an adverb meaning in any case or nonetheless: He objected, but she went anyway.
- ❖ any way: a paired adjective and noun meaning any particular course, direction, or manner: Any way we chose would lead to danger.

Awhile/a while
- ❖ awhile: an adverb meaning for a short time; some readers consider it nonstandard; usually needs no preposition: Won't you stay awhile?
- ❖ a while: a paired article and noun meaning a period of time; usually used with for: We talked for a while, and then we said good night.

Maybe/may be
- ❖ maybe: an adverb meaning perhaps: Maybe we should wait until the rain stops.
- ❖ may be: a form of the verb be: This may be our only chance to win the championship.

PRACTICE
Fill up the blanks.
1. _____is my jacket? I wanted to _____it today, and if I can't find it, _____ going to be late. (where/wear/were)
2. Jane wanted _____go on the school trip, but her mother said that _____hundred dollars was _____much for the family budget. (to/ two/too)

3. As she waited for Rodney to become _____, Selma was seized with an attack of _____was there anything she could have done to prevent the accident? (conscious/conscience)
4. The map _____the intrepid treasure hunters to a _____box of precious stones. (led/lead)
5. Have you seen _____coats? _____going to need them; it's cold outside. I last saw the coats over _____. (their/they're/there)
6. After conducting careful research, Shufang had a brilliant _____; she'd write a paper on Thomas Moore's concept of the _____society in Utopia. (idea/ideal)
7. Even though Bob would rather play video games _____study, he decided to hit the books and _____play some Halo. (than/then)
8. _____easy to admire a business that puts so much effort into creating _____signs and window displays. (it's/its)
9. _____fortunate to have survived the car crash without a scratch; it must have been because you were wearing _____seat belt. (you're/your)
10. I would _____you to seek qualified legal _____about how to handle this situation. (advise/advice)

3.2 British and American Slang Words and Phrases

BRITISH SLANG WORDS AND PHRASES

after—bars open after normal closing time
all over the gaff—unorganized
arse—butt
arse-over-tit—drunk
ballistic—wild
bangers—sausages
barmy—crazy
bob—shilling
blimey!—Oh geez!
bloke—a male
bobby—policeman
brilliant!—great! awesome!

cabbage—a slow person
cack—crap (What a load of cack, mate!)
cakehole—mouth (Shut your cakehole!)
Charlie—crack, cocaine
chips—french fries
chunder—to throw up
ciggy—cigarette
claret—blood (They were copping it up, claret all over the place!)
cop a feel—to feel someone up
to cop it—to get in trouble
copper—policeman
Crikey!—My God!
damage—cost
Dicky—feeling unwell
doddle—something easy (It was a doddle to get the Charlie.)
dodgy—shady
done over—beat up (He was done over by that bloke.)
Doris—a plain woman
dosh—money
duck and dive—to run from the police
earner—a dishonest laborer
eppy—a fit
faced—drunk
five finger discount—shoplifting
flim-flam—crap (Cut out this flim-flam, you wanker!)
folding—paper pound-notes
For crying out loud!—For God's sake!
Frenchy—a french kiss
full monty—the entire take, all that is desired
funny farm—a mental institution
gab—to talk a lot
gander—to look at
geezer—an old man
get the nod—to get permission
git—an unlikeable person
gob—mouth
greaser—a 50's style person, usually a man
grub—food
gutted—choked up (He was gutted at the funeral, mate.)

hacked off—annoyed (He was really hacked off at that copper.)
having it off—a term for intercourse
headcase—a nutcase
hold it down—keep the noise down, control yourself
hooter—nose
ickle—small, tiny (I like that an ickle bit, mate.)
iffy—doubting, doubtful
in stook—in financial trouble (Your uncle is in stook.)
inside—imprisoned (Barry's inside again.)
jammy—lucky
jar—a pint of beer
jock—a Scottish man
jugs—breasts
juiced up—very drunk
kick it off—start something, a fight with another Brit perhaps
kip—sleep (I need some kip.)
knackered—tired
knock-up—to wake someone up
lairy—loud, brash
larging it—to live large
lip—smart talk
loaded—very rich
lock-in—a term for late-hours in a pub
lolly—money
lost the plot—gone mad (That nutter's completely lost the plot!)
malarkey—stuff and nonsense (What a load of malarkey!)
mate—address for a friend
mental—crazy
miffed—fed up
minger—an unattractive girl
mint—great condition (That's mint, mate.)
mitts—hands
monkey—500 pounds
moose—an ugly girl
mullered—drunk
munch—food (Time for munch, mate!)
naff—nasty, in poor taste (That's naff!)
nipper—a small child
nosh—food

nugget—a pound coin
nutter—a crazy person
offie—a place where off-license alcohol is sold
off your face—very drunk
out of the tree—nuts
parky—chilly (Parky weather today.)
plank, a fool
ponce—a slacker
ramped—drunk
rat-arsed—drunk
readies—cash on hand (Have any readies? I'm all out.)
ruck—a fight
rug—wig
salt—a loose woman
scrounge—to begg food, materials
shafted—screwed, betrayed
shag—sexual intercourse
shell-like—ear (Can I have a word in your shell-like?)
skirt—a young woman
snog—a french kiss
squire—a term for a working man
sussed out—figured out
tanked—drunk
toerag—a tramp
tom—a prostitute
tooled—drunk
top!—wonderful
trainspotter—a nerd, geek
trots—an upset stomach
up for it—enthusiastically available
up the duff—pregnant
wank—to masturbate
wedge—money
wind up—to tease

AMERICAN SLANG WORDS AND PHRASES

ace—to succeed or to do well
blow or bomb—to fail or to be unsuccessful
have the blues—to feel sad
buck—one dollar
chill out or chill—relax or calm down
cool—agreeable; okay
cop—police officer
couch Potato—a lazy person; one who sits and watches TV
cram—to study feverishly before an exam
crash—to go to sleep; or to show up without invitation
down to earth—practical, simple
drive up the wall—to irritate;
Dutch or go Dutch—each person pays for his/her meal
freaking out—to be very anxious
hang out—to gather in a casual and social manner
hang over—the physical effects of heavy drinking (headache)
hit the road—to leave
hit the books—study
hold your horses—be calm!
jock—an athlete
the late Mr. Smith—a term used when the person is dead
lemon—bad buy or purchase
once in a blue moon—infrequent
oops!—said after a small mistake
piece of cake—easy or effortless
pig out—to overeat
pop quiz—an exam that is not announced
rip off—overcharge or steal
R.S.V.P—the formal reply to an invitation, by phone or mail (Please reply.)
shoot the breeze, chatting—talk
take a rain check—do at another time; postpone
take for granted—to assume
"what's up?"—How are you?
dude—friend or man

A Good Teacher—One day, a teacher was attempting to teach the names of animals to a class of 5-year-olds. She held up a picture of a deer, and asked one boy, "Billy, what is this animal?" Little Billy looked at the picture with a disheartened look on his face and responded, "I'm sorry Mr.s. Smith, I don't know." The teacher was not one to give up easily, so she then asked Billy, "Well, Billy, what does your Mommy call your Daddy?" Little Billy's face suddenly brightened up, but then a confused look came over his face, as he asked, "Mrs. Smith, is that really a pig?"!

3.3 Word Groups and Expressions

PREPOSITIONAL AND PHRASAL VERBS

act for	:	to be employed to deal with someone else's affairs for them
e.g.	:	In the absence of the Manager, the Assistant Manager will act for him.
act on	:	to take action on the basis of information or advice
e.g.	:	He acted on impulse when he announced his withdrawal from the election.
back out	:	withdraw from something that is agreed; fail to keep a promise
e.g.	:	When you make a promise, you should not back out of it.
back up	:	to support
e.g.	:	Don't worry. I'll back you up with all the money you need for the project.
break into	:	to enter by force
e.g.	:	The thieves broke into the bank.
break (something) off	:	end something suddenly
e.g.	:	Their engagement has been broken off.
break up	:	to cause to scatter

e.g.	:	The police charged with *lathis* and broke up the demonstration.
bring about	:	cause
e.g.	:	They discussed the factors that brought about the recent floods.
bring in	:	earn
e.g.	:	A good film always brings in a lot of money for the producer.
bring off	:	succeed in doing something
e.g.	:	Despite the sound of crackers outside, the show was brought off without interruption.
bring out	:	to make something come out
e.g.	:	We are bringing out a new book on spoken English.
bring up	:	raise a subject
e.g.	:	I told him not to bring up the question of money.
call for	:	require
e.g.	:	He called for help.
call on	:	visit
e.g.	:	The PM called on the President.
call off	:	cancel
e.g.	:	They called off the meeting as the Chief Guest did not turn up.
call up	:	telephone
e.g.	:	I'll call you up tomorrow and give the details of the plan.
carry on	:	to continue
e.g.	:	He carried on reading though the electricity failed.
carry out	:	to do something successfully
e.g.	:	India carried out a nuclear test recently.
catch on	:	become popular
e.g.	:	Pop music has caught on quickly in our country.
come across	:	find unexpectedly
e.g.	:	The other day I came across an old silver coin.
come around	:	become agreeable
e.g.	:	He hasn't come around to our point-of-view yet.
come about	:	happen

e.g.	:	How could such horrible floods come about?
come off	:	be successful
e.g.	:	Although the team worked hard, their film did not come off.
come upto	:	be the equal of
e.g.	:	The new students are not able to come up to the standards of the old.
do without	:	manage without
e.g.	:	I can't do without a cup of tea in the morning.
drop in	:	call on someone without prior notice
e.g.	:	Do drop in if you are ever in this area.
drop out	:	leave an activity
e.g.	:	Many children drop out of school in villages.
fall back on	:	use in an emergency
e.g.	:	We should keep that old scooter because we can fall back on it if anything happens to the new one.
fall through	:	fail
e.g.	:	The deal fell through at the last minute.
figure out	:	discover, determine
e.g.	:	Try to figure out a way to solve this problem.
fill in	:	complete a document
e.g.	:	Would you give me a subscription form to fill in?
fill out	:	complete
e.g.	:	Fill out this application form.
fill up	:	complete
e.g.	:	Fill up the form as soon as you can.
find out	:	discover
e.g.	:	The police are trying to find out who was responsible for match-fixing.
fix up	:	repair
e.g.	:	Would you fix up my tape recorder?
get ahead	:	achieve success
e.g.	:	He was determined to get ahead in life.
get along	:	manage
e.g.	:	My brother and I got along well when we were kids.
get at	:	make clear

e.g.	:	What is he getting at in his speech? I think he is trying to criticize the government.
get away	:	escape
e.g.	:	They got away in a stolen car.
get away with	:	go without punishment
e.g.	:	Everybody knew that he wouldn't get away with killing the minister.
get on	:	progress
e.g.	:	He is new here, but he seems to be getting on fine.
get over	:	overcome
e.g.	:	He got over his illness quickly.
get through	:	succeed
e.g.	:	He got through his driving test.
get together	:	meet
e.g.	:	It's ages since I got together with my classmates from school.
get up	:	awake
e.g.	:	What time did you get up this morning?
give away	:	give as a present
e.g.	:	That man was so rich that he gave some of his fortune away.
give in	:	submit
e.g.	:	They argued back and forth until Shiela gave in.
give up	:	stop doing something
e.g.	:	He is trying to give up smoking.
go against	:	contrary to
e.g.	:	Prem went against his father's wishes.
go ahead	:	continue
e.g.	:	The newspaper decided to go ahead and publish the story.
go for	:	try to get.
e.g.	:	She is going for that job in sales.
go in for	:	take part
e.g.	:	Are you going in for the proficiency exam?
go off	:	turn out
e.g.	:	Did your birthday party go off alright?
go on	:	happen

e.g.	:	What is going on in this office?
go through	:	look at something carefully
e.g.	:	Let's go through the text once again, from the beginning,
go without	:	manage without
e.g.	:	If there is no salt for my meal, I'll go without it.
hand over	:	give something to someone
e.g.	:	Aruna handed over the amounts to her assistant.
hang around	:	move about idly
e.g.	:	The game was over but people were still hanging around in the stadium.
hang on	:	to hold
e.g.	:	Hang on a second while I look Swamy's number up.
hold on	:	wait
e.g.	:	I'll hold on for a few minutes if you like.
hold up	:	delay
e.g.	:	The building work has been held up by bad weather.
hurry up	:	go fast
e.g.	:	Please hurry up, we're going to be late.
keep away from	:	not to be near
e.g.	:	Keep away from that dog.
keep out of	:	stay away
e.g.	:	We have always tried to keep out of local politics.
keep up	:	continue
e.g.	:	Keep up the good show.
let down	:	disappoint
e.g.	:	I won't let you down.
let off	:	excuse
e.g.	:	I'll let you off this time, but don't do it again.
long for	:	wish for
e.g.	:	I'm longing for a cold drink.
look after	:	take care of
e.g.	:	They looked after us well.
look ahead	:	plan for the future
e.g.	:	You should always look ahead and prepare for the worst.

look back on	:	remember
e.g.	:	When I look back on those days, I realize I was unhappy.
look down on	:	ill-treat
e.g.	:	He looks down on anyone who hasn't had a college education.
look for	:	search
e.g.	:	I'm looking for Saritha. Have you seen her?
look forward to	:	anticipate
e.g.	:	I'm looking forward to our vacation.
look into	:	investigate
e.g.	:	The CBI is looking into the match-fixing scandal.
make out	:	understand
e.g.	:	I can scarcely make out his writing
make up	:	decide
e.g.	:	He made up his mind to leave the company.
pass by	:	move
e.g.	:	I was looking at the clouds passing by.
pass off	:	take place
e.g.	:	The meeting passed off without any incident.
put down	:	write
e.g.	:	I put his address down to remember it.
put in	:	spend time
e.g.	:	He has put in 20 years of service.
put off	:	postpone
e.g.	:	Because of his mother's illness, he had to put his trip off for some weeks.
put on	:	add
e.g.	:	He put on weight.
put up with	:	bear
e.g.	:	I can't put up with his laziness anymore.
ring up	:	make a telephone call
e.g.	:	Ring me up tomorrow.
run after	:	chase
e.g.	:	The policeman ran after the thief.
run away with	:	steal
e.g.	:	They found that the treasurer had run away with all the cash.

run down	:	talk rudely
e.g.	:	He always runs his Wife down in front of others.
run into	:	hit or collide with
e.g.	:	His car skidded and ran into a lamp post.
see through	:	to realize the truth so that one is not deceived
e.g.	:	He saw through her lies
see off	:	go to a place to say good bye
e.g.	:	I think they have gone to the airport to see their daughter off.
see to	:	care for
e.g.	:	Will you see to it that this letter is sent by airmail today?
set aside	:	reserve
e.g.	:	He has set some money aside for emergencies.
set off	:	start
e.g.	:	We are setting off on a shopping trip.
set out	:	start
e.g.	:	Nitin set out for the U.S.
set up	:	establish
e.g.	:	We are thinking about setting a business up.
show off	:	display proudly
e.g.	:	Jagan wanted to show off his new Matiz
stand by	:	support
e.g.	:	Don't worry. I'll stand by you.
stand for	:	be a symbol for
e.g.	:	The initials T.S. stand for Tirimala Sampath.
take back	:	return
e.g.	:	The shoes don't fit, so I'll take them back to the shop.
take down	:	write down
e.g.	:	The policeman took down the evidence.
take in	:	listen to
e.g.	:	The students took in every word of their teacher's speech.
take off	:	fly
e.g.	:	The flight to Delhi took off ten minutes late.
take over	:	buy
e.g.	:	Our firm was taken over last year.

take up	:	start to do
e.g.	:	He has taken up painting
think over	:	consider seriously
e.g.	:	Think it over and give me your answer tomorrow.
try on	:	test
e.g.	:	The-saleswoman gave Mr. Raju a deodorant to try on.
try out	:	test the ability
e.g.	:	The coach is trying out some players for the game
turn down	:	refuse
e.g.	:	I was offered the job but I turned it down.
turn in	:	produce
e.g.	:	He turned in a good performance.
turn off	:	stop the flow
e.g.	:	Please turn the water off.
turn on	:	cause to operate
e.g.	:	She turned the light on.
turn up	:	arrive
e.g.	:	Half the guests didn't turn up.
wear out	:	become useless
e.g.	:	He wore out a pair of shoes last year.
work out	:	do well
e.g.	:	His plan did not work out.
write off	:	cancel
e.g.	:	He couldn't pay. So I wrote off his debt.
write up	:	describe fully in writing
e.g.	:	He wrote up the notes he had taken in the class.

COMMON IDIOMS

by accident	:	unexpectedly
e.g.	:	I met her quite by accident.
take into account	:	consider
e.g.	:	You should take his problems into account.
take advantage of	:	to make use of something in an unfair way
e.g.	:	Don't lend them the car. They are taking advantage of you.

in agreement	:	all have the same opinion
e.g.	:	A decision will not be taken until everyone is in agreement.
on the alert	:	ready to deal with a situation
e.g.	:	Be on the alert for pickpockets at the bus stop.
above all	:	especially
e.g.	:	He values his wife's love, above all.
after all	:	considering everything
e.g.	:	Your work is not so bad, after all.
at all	:	used in negatives and questions to emphasize
e.g.	:	They weren't at all happy.
all in all	:	considering every part of a situation
e.g.	:	All in all, it has been a comfortable year for Shankar
by all means	:	certainly
e.g.	:	"Can I bring Vinod to the party? "By all means!"
to begin with	:	first of all
e.g.	:	Well, to begin with, he should not have been driving my scooter.
make the best of	:	accept an unsatisfactory situation and do something to make it less bad
e.g.	:	We are held up here, so we might as well make the best of it.
in brief	:	in as few words as possible
e.g.	:	Don't tell me the whole story. Just say what happened in brief.
by the by	:	used when mentioning something interesting but not important
e.g.	:	By the by, Rekha said she might call round in the evening.
by and large	:	generally
e.g.	:	Donations are, by and large, exempt from income tax.
in case	:	if
e.g.	:	In case someone comes in, I'll be in my room.
by any chance	:	to politely ask if something is true
e.g.	:	Are you Mr. Bharat, by any chance?
for a change	:	as something different
e.g.	:	Let's go to a restaurant for a change.

under the circumstances	:	in a particular situation
e.g.	:	The result was the best that could be expected under the circumstances.
on condition	:	if
e.g.	:	You can have my car on condition that you drive slowly.
in confidence	:	as a secret
e.g.	:	I am giving you this information in confidence.
on the contrary	:	used for disagreeing
e.g.	:	You said he is stupid; on the contrary, he's intelligent.
at all costs in	:	regardless of difficulties
e.g.	:	I must finish my work at all costs,
in due course	:	at some time in the future when it is the right time
e.g.	:	Your application will be considered in due course.
of course	:	certainly
e.g.	:	"Are you coming with me?" "Of course, I am"
give credence to	:	believe or accept something as true
e.g.	:	I don't give any credence to these remarks.
on credit	:	arrangement to buy and pay later
e.g.	:	I bought a coat on credit from that shop.
in danger	:	in a situation in which something unpleasant may happen
e.g.	:	A fast driver is always in danger,
to date	:	up to now
e.g.	:	To date he has borrowed more than 5 lakh rupees.
day after day	:	continuously
e.g.	:	Day after day the boy would ask me for money.
day by day	:	slowly and gradually
e.g.	:	His health was improving day by day.
day in, day out	:	everyday for a long time
e.g.	:	She cooked and cleaned day in, day out for forty years.
in demand	:	wanted by a lot of people
e.g.	:	That style of furniture is in demand. It is selling well.

in detail	:	pay attention to all the details
e.g.	:	The manager will tell you the conditions of employment in detail.
under discussion	:	being discussed
e.g.	:	The prisoner's case is under discussion now.
in disguise	:	in a changed appearance
e.g.	:	Babu went to the party in disguise.
at ease	:	relaxed
e.g.	:	I always feel at ease when I get home after work.
in the end	:	finally
e.g.	:	If you go on like that you will be disappointed in the end.
on end	:	without stopping
e.g.	:	It rained for days on end.
in any event	:	in any case
e.g.	:	In any event, we don't need the documents. You can keep them.
for example	:	to give an example of what one is saying
e.g.	:	There are many sources of air pollution. Exhaust fumes are one of them, for example.
to an extent	:	to a degree
e.g.	:	Although his argument has many flaws, it is correct to an extent.
keep an eye out/ keep an eye out for: watch		
e.g.	:	Could you keep an eye out for my blue pen? I seem to have misplaced it.
face to face	:	very close
e.g.	:	I have never met her face to face. We have only talked on the phone.
in fact	:	really
e.g.	:	They told me it would be cheap but in fact it cost me nearly 1000 rupees.
as a matter of fact	:	really
e.g.	:	Vidisha is very intelligent. As a matter of fact, she is one of the top students in our class.
by far	:	by a great degree
e.g.	:	Mehta is the smartest, by far.
in fashion	:	stylish
e.g.	:	That style of dress is in fashion now.

at fault	:	wrong
e.g.	:	I couldn't determine who was really at fault.
at first	:	in the beginning
e.g.	:	At first we were shocked by the news, but then we got over it.
look forward to	:	anticipate
e.g.	:	We are looking forward to meeting you soon.
make friends with	:	meet people and become friendly.
e.g.	:	Mahesh makes friends with everybody he meets.
in full	:	completely
e.g.	:	We paid in full and left.
for good	:	permanently
e.g.	:	He is going back to Chandigarh, for good.
at hand	:	near in time or space
e.g.	:	There are shops and buses close at hand.
in haste	:	in a hurry
e.g.	:	They left in haste, without even saying goodbye
at heart	:	really
e.g.	:	Our professor is a nice man at heart.
at home	:	at ease
e.g.	:	Sunil makes me feel at home.
in bad humour	:	bad temper
e.g.	:	You'd better not talk to him now. He is in bad humour.
in good humour	:	cheerful
e.g.	:	He reacted to this criticism with his usual good humour.
for instance	:	for example
e.g.	:	There are some mistakes in your letter. For instance, the second word is spelled wrong.
on the job	:	as part of a job
e.g.	:	We'll put our best people on the job.
jump to a conclusion	:	make a deduction too quickly
e.g.	:	If you jump to a conclusion on this sensitive subject, you may regret it.
keep to oneself	:	keep secret
e.g.	:	He kept the facts to himself.
at large	:	free of legal check I absconding
e.g.	:	Two of the prisoners are still at large.

by and large	:	usually
e.g.	:	By and large, his novels bring him a lot of money.
at last	:	finally
e.g.	:	At last I see what you are getting at
at least	:	minimum
e.g.	:	This T.V. set must cost 20 thousand rupees, at least.
at leisure	:	at one's convenience
e.g.	:	Take the brochure home and read it at your leisure.
at length	:	in detail
e.g.	:	We already discussed the subject at length in previous meetings.
little by little	:	gradually
e.g.	:	The ship was sinking, little by little.
by all means	:	of course
e.g.	:	"Can I bring Shyam to the party? "By all means."
in mind	:	thinking about something
e.g.	:	He has a good idea in mind; wait until he tells you what it is.
keep in mind	:	remember
e.g.	:	Keep that in mind. Don't forget it.
by mistake	:	without intention
e.g.	:	Someone must have left the door open by mistake.
at most	:	cannot be larger
e.g.	:	At most I will get twenty thousand rupees for my car.
get on one's nerves	:	make nervous
e.g.	:	His talking and laughing got on my nerves
from now on	:	starting from now
e.g.	:	Promise that you will come to class regularly from now on.
all at once	:	suddenly
e.g.	:	All at once there was a loud banging on the door.
at once	:	immediately
e.g.	:	Get me some paper at once.
once and for all	:	definitely and finally

e.g.	:	Let's settle this matter once and for all.
once in a while	:	sometimes
e.g.	:	It'll be nice if you'd write to me once in a while.
in the open	:	without secrecy
e.g.	:	No one could accuse him of corruption; everything he did was in the open.
in order	:	appropriate
e.g.	:	Is your passport in order?
on order	:	ordered but not received
e.g.	:	It's on order. It should be in next week.
in part	:	partially
e.g.	:	He has only been paid in part for all his work.
in particular	:	specifically
e.g.	:	He has nothing in particular to say to you.
in peril	:	in danger
e.g.	:	The fire put the people living upstairs in peril.
in person	:	do it personally
e.g.	:	He will forward the documents to you in person.
be on the phone	:	to be using the telephone
e.g.	:	He told me the good news on the phone.
in place	:	in the correct position
e.g.	:	After the maid washed the floor, she put everything back in place.
to the point	:	pertinent
e.g.	:	The message was short and to the point.
in principle	:	in general
e.g.	:	The scheme seems OK in principle, but I would like to know more details.
in all probability	:	very probably
e.g.	:	In all probability, you will succeed in your job.
in progress	:	happening at present
e.g.	:	Work is now in progress on the new dam.
on purpose	:	deliberately
e.g.	:	Why did he go there by train when he could go by car?
e.g.	:	I think he did it on purpose.
in question	:	under consideration
e.g.	:	The whole programme is in question now.

out of the question	:	impossible
e.g.	:	I can't go to the wedding in this old dress. It's out of the question.
at any rate	:	at least
e.g.	:	You should eat when you are ill. Or, at any rate, you should have some juice.
within reach	:	close to
e.g.	:	All the main tourist attractions are within reach of the hotel.
off the record	:	not for publication
e.g.	:	He spoke off the record to the journalist.
in the long run	:	later in the future
e.g.	:	The more you do exercise, the better it will be for your health in the long run.
in some respects	:	in some ways
e.g.	:	That is a good plan in some respects
ahead of schedule	:	earlier than expected
e.g.	:	We completed the project ahead of schedule.
behind schedule	:	later than expected
e.g.	:	His article is already two days behind schedule.
on schedule	:	at the specified time
e.g.	:	We finished the work on schedule.
on second thoughts	:	after reconsidering
e.g.	:	I'll have a coffee please. Oh no, no second thoughts make it a tea.
in a sense	:	in a particular way
e.g.	:	In a sense, you are right; but your conclusion is not entirely convincing.
in short	:	in brief
e.g.	:	In short he told me that he wouldn't accept it.
for a song	:	very cheaply
e.g.	:	He sold his car for a song.
stand to reason	:	be logical
e.g.	:	It stands to reason that we should write him a letter of complaint.
in style	:	done to win admiration
e.g.	:	Sampras won the title in style, not losing a single game.
in succession	:	one after another

e.g.	:	She won the championship four times in succession.
as such	:	in itself
e.g.	:	This toy is useless without a battery. As such it is only a piece of plastic.
for sure	:	certainly
e.g.	:	No one knows for sure what really happened.
by surprise	:	unexpectedly
e.g.	:	The recent floods had taken us all by surprise.
in tears	:	crying
e.g.	:	The poor lady was in tears after the discussion.
for the time being	:	temporarily
e.g.	:	For the time being, I'm staying at my friend's house.
from time to time	:	occasionally
e.g.	:	I still see her from time to time.
in time	:	giving enough time for someone to do something
e.g.	:	You will hear about my plan in time.
in time	:	sufficiently early
e.g.	:	We reached the airport in time.
on time	:	punctually
e.g.	:	Mr. Kapoor always comes to the office on time.
by turns	:	alternately
e.g.	:	The two men drove the bus by turns.
as usual	:	in the habitual way
e.g.	:	As usual, Sheela turned up to the party late.
in view	:	for the reason
e.g.	:	In view of his recent conduct, he has been suspended from service.
by the way	:	incidentally
e.g.	:	By the way, what time does your plane leave?
in a way	:	from one point of view
e.g.	:	In a way, Vijay was right in his answer.
on the (your, my, his) way to:		while travelling from one place to another
e.g.	:	Why don't you bring some bread on your way home?
as well	:	also
e.g.	:	We are going to the cinema today. Why don't you come along as well?

all the while	:	all the time
e.g.	:	Yesterday they were playing cards all the while.
on the whole	:	in general
e.g.	:	Sekhar is a good fellow on the whole.
in a word	:	in short
e.g.	:	"Did you enjoy the film?" "In a word—no."

Common Proverbs

1. As you make your bed you must lie in it.
    Everyone must bear the consequences of his or her own acts.
2. Set a beggar on horseback, and he'll ride to the devil.
    There is no one so proud and arrogant as a person who has suddenly grown rich.
3. Well begun is half done.
    Anything which is started well can be easily accomplished.
4. The belly has no ears.
    A hungry man will not listen to advice or arguments.
5. A bird in hand is worth two in the bush.
    It is better to be content with what one has than to risk losing everything by being too greedy.
6. It's the early bird that catches the worm.
    The person who arrives or gets up first will be successful.
7. Birds of a feather flock together.
    People of the same sort are found together.
8. Old birds are not to be caught with chaff.
    Experienced persons cannot be deceived easily.
9. To kill two birds with one stone.
    To achieve two aims with a single action.
10. Keep your breath to cool your porridge.
    Keep your advice to yourself.
11. To make bricks without straw.
    To try to do something without having the necessary material.
12. You cannot have your cake and eat it too.
    You cannot spend money and yet keep it. You cannot enjoy benefits from two alternative courses of action.
13. You cannot burn the candle at both ends.
    You cannot spend your energies on too many things.

14. Care killed the cat.
    Worry and anxiety can destroy anybody.
15. See how the cat jumps.
    Weigh the pros and cons of a matter before taking any decision on it.
16. When the cat is away the mice play.
    Servants will ever take advantage of the absence of their master.
17. All cats love fish but fear to wet their paws.
    Everybody wants to obtain good things, but nobody wants to work for them.
18. Charity begins at home.
    A person's first duty is to care for his/her own family.
19. Don't count your chickens before they are hatched.
    Do not be too confident that something will be successful.
20. The burnt child dreads the fire.
    You are not likely to make the same mistake twice.
21. Every cloud has a silver lining.
    There is some good in the worst of things.
22. To carry coals to Newcastle.
    To take something to a place where it is already plentiful.
23. Every cock crows best on its own dunghill.
    It is easy to boast of your deeds or bravery at your own place.
24. Cut your coat according to your cloth.
    Live within your means.
25. Great cry and little wool.
    Those who boast too much do too little.
26. Curses like chickens come home to roost.
    One must suffer for one's ill deeds.
27. It may be fun to you but it is death to the frogs.
    One man's fun may be another man's tragedy.
28. Do not put all your eggs in one basket.
    Do not risk everything you have on the success of one plan.
29. A soft fire makes sweet malt.
    Nothing should be done in haste. Unhurried effort will give excellent results.
30. A friend in need is a friend indeed.
    A true friend is one who is helpful in difficulty.
31. Out of the frying pan into the fire.
    To change over from a bad situation to one that is worse.
32. Adding fuel to fire.

Saying or doing something which worsens an already bad situation.

33. The game is not worth the candle.
     In certain situations the gains from doing something are not worth the trouble and expenses involved.

34. To take the gilt off the gingerbread.
     To do something which makes a situation or achievement less attractive or worthwhile.

35. Those who live in glass houses should not throw stones on others. We should not criticize others for faults similar to our own.

36. To strain at a gnat and swallow a camel.
     Having scruples about doing or allowing something only slightly wrong, but remaining unconcerned about doing or allowing something really wrong.

37. Whom God would destroy he first makes mad.
     People who lose their common sense come to grief. God robs those of wits who He wants to destroy.

38. God helps those who help themselves. If you need God's help, help yourselves.

39. God tempers the wind to the shorn lamb.
     A blind man can see with his hands. There is compensation, of one kind or other, for every loss.

40. Whom the gods love die young.
     Heaven gives its favourites early death. Good people often die young.

41. A good name is better than a golden girdle. Fame is better than wealth.

42. Good wine needs no bush.
     Anything of good quality will be appreciated on its own merits and does not need to be advertised.

43. To teach one's grandmother to suck eggs.
     To tell somebody how to do something that he can do perfectly well.

44. Hamlet without the Prince.
     It is like a play without a hero.

45. He who hunts two hares leaves one and loses the other. It is unwise to try to achieve two aims at the same time.

46. Better be the head of an ass than the tail of a horse.
     It is better to rule in hell than to serve in heaven. It is better to be the master of a small concern than a servant in a big one.

47. Two heads are better than one.
     Two people working together achieve much more than one person working alone.

48. Honey is not for the ass's mouth.
    Stupid people do not appreciate fine remarks or ideas.
49. Don't look a gift horse in the mouth.
    Do not refuse or criticize something that is given to you for nothing.
50. One may steal a horse, while another may not look over the hedge.
    Some people are specially privileged, and can commit crimes with impunity (without any fear of punishment), while others get punished for trivial offences.
51. It's a good horse that never stumbles.
    Everyone makes mistakes some time or other.
52. Go and tell that to the horse marines!
    Tell such unbelievable stories to somebody else.
53. You can take a horse to water but you cannot make him drink.
    You can give a person the opportunity to do something but he may still refuse to do it.
54. When the horse is stolen, lock the stable door.
    It is no use taking precautions after a loss has occurred.
55. Win the horse or lose the saddle.
    In certain desperate situations, you have a choice between a great success and a total failure.
56. To hunt with the hounds and run with the hare.
    To try to remain friendly with both sides in a dispute.
57. Strike while the iron is hot.
    Do not miss a good opportunity.
58. A good lather is half the shave.
    If you start a thing well, you can accomplish it easily.
59. It's a long lane that has no turning.
    Every calamity (serious misfortune) has an end.
60. Man proposes but God disposes.
    We may make plans, but it is God that decides whether they will be realized or not.
61. Give a man luck and throw him into the sea.
    Those who are lucky survive any calamity.
62. A whistling maid and a crowing hen is fit for neither God nor men.
    A woman who behaves like men is good for nothing.
63. Money makes the mare go.
    You can do anything if only you have the money.
64. Murder will out.
    A crime such as murder cannot be hidden.

65. Looking for a needle in a haystack.
   Looking for a very small article amidst a big mass of other things.
66. A nod is as good as a wink to a blind horse.
   However clear a hint or suggestion may be, it is useless if the other person is unable to see it.
67. He who would eat the nut must first crack the shell.
   Nobody can achieve anything without the required amount of labour.
68. To cast pearls before swine.
   To offer beautiful or valuable things to people who cannot appreciate them.
69. Penny wise pound foolish,
   To be thrifty (economical) in small matters and careless in large ones.
70. A penny saved is a pound earned.
   Saving is as good as earning. Small savings can ultimately add up to great amounts.
71. In for a penny, in for a pound.
   Once a thing has been started, it must be carried through, no matter what difficulties arise.
72. To rob Peter to pay Paul.
   To take away from one person in order to give to another.
73. He who pays the piper calls the tune.
   The person who provides the money for something should control how it is spent.
74. Touch pitch, and you will be defiled.
   Evil company will corrupt anybody.
75. Possession is nine points of the law.
   A person who occupies or controls something is in a better position to keep it than somebody else whose claim to it may be greater.
76. The pot calls the kettle black.
   We should not accuse others of faults similar to those committed by us.
77. A little pot is soon hot.
   A small person is quickly annoyed.
78. A watched pot never boils.
   Watching and anxiety will not hasten matters.
79. You cannot make a silk purse of a sow's ear.
   You cannot make something good of what is by its nature bad in quality.
80. All roads lead to Rome.

Any of the methods, or means, being considered will bring about the same result in the end.

81. Rome was not built in a day.
    Achievements of great importance take a long time to accomplish.
82. When in Rome, do as the Romans do.
    It is wise to adapt oneself to the manners and customs of those among whom one lives.
83. No rose without a thorn.
    Every sweet has its sour. Even the best things have a bad side.
84. The sauce was better than the fish.
    Accessories (extra minor fittings) were better than the main part.
85. There's black sheep in every flock.
    In every group of persons, there is sure to be one or two hady characters.
86. (There is) many a slip 'twixt the cup and the lip.
    Everything is uncertain till you possess it.
87. Speech is silver, silence is golden.
    (Sometimes) silence is better than speech. It is sometimes best not to say anything.
88. Store is no sore.
    Things stored up for future use are a great advantage.
89. One swallow does not make a summer.
    A single fortunate incident, example, etc. does not mean that all the others will be as good.
90. Stolen sweets are always sweeter.
    Things illegally acquired are more palatable (likable) than those honestly earned.
91. What you lose on the swings you get back on the roundabouts.
    If you have bad luck on one day, you have good luck on another.
92. More worship the rising than the setting sun.
    More persons pay respect to rising than to fallen greatness.
93. Time and tide wait for no man.
    We should not put off a favourable opportunity to do something because we cannot delay the passing of time.
94. Two of a trade did never agree.
    Two individuals in the same trade or profession seldom agree.
95. A tree must be bent while it is young.
    You cannot teach an old dog new tricks. If you want to teach something to somebody, start when he/she is young.

96. The tree is known by its fruit.
    One is judged by what one does, not by what one says.
97. You cannot judge of a tree by its bark.
    Do not go by appearances.
98. It's an ill wind that blows nobody good.
    Someone profits by every loss.
99. The wish is father to the thought.
    We are always ready to believe what we most want to believe.
100. No wool is so white that a dyer cannot blacken it.
    No one is so free from faults that he cannot be criticised.
101. A word to the wise.
    A hint is enough for wise people.

COMMON EXPRESSIONS

THANKS
    Thank you. (for lunch / the coffee)
    Many thanks.
    Thanks a lot / very much.
RESPONSES TO THANKS
    Not a bit.
    Not at all.
    Don't mention it.
    My pleasure.
    You're welcome.
    That's all right.
INTRODUCTION
    May I introduce (you to) Dr Das? (formal)
    This is Bimal Mahanty.
    This is my husband, (familiar)
    Have you met Renu?
    Do you know Renu, Mr. Das?
    I'd like you to meet Mr. Das.
    Let me introduce you to Mr. Das (rather formal)
GREETINGS ON INTRODUCTIONS
(Formal introduction is responded to in a formal style, and the familiar one in a similar manner.)
    How do you do? (formal)
    Glad/Pleased/Nice to meet you.

A pleasure to meet you. (familiar)
How are you?
Hello (informal)

SAYING GOODBYE
Well, I must be going now.
I have to go now. Goodbye, Dilip.
(I'm) See you (later).
Bye! (informal)
So long!
Cheerio! (informal)
See you tomorrow.
I'm afraid I really must go.
Well, I've got to go now.

"One forgets words as one forgets names. One's vocabulary needs constant fertilizing or it will die."

– Evelyn Waugh

CHAPTER 4

ON THE SPOT

1. SPEAKING ENGLISH FLUENTLY

Arpita is a student. She gets guidance from her teacher Mr. Mishra for speaking English fluently.

Arpita	:	Good morning sir.
Mr. Mishra	:	Very good morning. How are you Arpita?
Arpita	:	I'm fine sir. I have some urgent discussion with you. I hope you will help me.
Mr. Mishra	:	What happened, you are looking so worried?
Arpita	:	Sir, I'm not so fluent in English. That makes me so worried.
Mr. Mishra	:	Oh! Then why don't you watch English movies and listen to English news?
Arpita	:	OK sir. From today I'll start watching movies.
Mr. Mishra	:	That's fine
Arpita	:	Thank you for your valuable suggestion sir.
Mr. Mishra	:	It's OK.

2. TRYING FOR A JOB

Maya is on the lookout for a suitable job. She meets Ganga and talks.

Maya	:	Hi.
Ganga	:	Hi, How is your job hunting going? Any luck yet?
Maya	:	I haven't really started yet because I'm still working on my career portfolio.
Ganga	:	Is that the same as a resume or CV?
Maya	:	It's similar but it's more detailed. It will give potential employers a complete picture of my qualification, experience and capabilities. I'm planning to upload it to my website.
Ganga	:	Wow! That sounds really impressive.

Maya	:	Why are you sitting here?
Ganga	:	Nothing really. Just sitting.
Maya	:	OK. Bye.
Ganga	:	Bye.

3. IN THE COMPUTER LABORATORY

Mini wants to refer to a few topics on the internet. She asks Anu if she could help.

Mini	:	Excuse me. Do you mind if I use your PC for browsing the Net?
Anu	:	Well, actually, I do. Rather you don't. It had a virus attack the other day, when I was surfing the net.
Mini	:	Oh, hard luck. How about my borrowing your copy of the Guinness Book of World Records?
Anu	:	I'm sorry, Mini. But, that won't be possible, either. My brother is working on a project, and he needs it for the next two weeks.
Mini	:	Oh, I give up.
Anu	:	Why don't you try the central library in the city? It may have multiple copies of this book.
Mini	:	That's a good idea. Thank you, so much.
Anu	:	You're welcome.

4. FITNESS WORKOUT

Gayatri is working on her physical fitness. Mosumi is curious.

Mosumi	:	Well, that's another working day over. Let's go for a cup of coffee.
Gayatri	:	Not today, thanks. I have to go to my health club.
Mosumi	:	Health club? I didn't know you belonged to one.
Gayatri	:	Yes, I joined one, last week. I've been getting a bit worried about my fitness.
Mosumi	:	So what are you planning to do?
Gayatri	:	Well, I've decided to go for a workout three times a week after work.
Mosumi	:	That'll get you really fit if you can keep it up. May be I ought to join too.
Gayatri	:	The bus hasn't come yet.

5. PAINTINGS

Chitra likes paintings. Jenny is surprised at Chitra's talents.

Jeny	:	Wow! These paintings are really good.
Chitra	:	I'm glad you like them. I painted them last year.
Jeny	:	Oh, you painted them yourself? They're so good. I can't believe it.
Chitra	:	They're not that good, but I'm glad you like them.
Jeny	:	You're so talented. I wish I had your skill.
Chitra	:	You should try, I'm sure you could do better. See that one. Oh, Wow!
Jeny	:	Wow!

6. RENTING A VIDEO

Judy just finished her exams. She wants to rent some videos for viewing.

Vimla	:	Hey Judy. What are you up to these days?
Judy	:	I just finished my 4th semester exams. Now I am just relaxing till the next semester begins.
Vimla	:	I am going to rent out a couple of movies. Do you want to come with me to Planet M?
Judy	:	Yea, sure! That place has a good collection.
Vimla	:	What type of movies do you like?
Judy	:	I love watching thrillers and horror movies. What about you?
Vimla	:	I prefer movies with a strong story line
Judy	:	Well, this place caters to varied tastes. So we won't have a problem choosing.

7. START A FAMILY

Choosing between a career and a family is difficult. Jenny broke up with John and is sad.

Mary	:	Hi, Jenny, how have you been?
Jenny	:	Not very well.
Mary	:	Why? Looks like you feel very down. What happened?
Jenny	:	Nothing.
Mary	:	Come on. For a woman who's so down, there're usually two reasons. Either her career is going downhill, or she has a broken heart. Since you're so successful, it must be the other one.
Jenny	:	Well, you're right. I just broke up with John.
Mary	:	Well, I thought you two were made for each other.

Jenny	:	Well, you never know. I'm ready for a commitment and want to settle down, but he says he wants to pursue his career while he's still young.
Mary	:	Well, you can't blame him. It's always difficult to choose between career and family.
Jenny	:	May be you're right.
Mary	:	Jenny, I don't know what to say to comfort you, but cheer up. There's plenty of fish in the sea and you'll find your soul mate, your perfect match.
Mary	:	Yeah, but it's hard to forget him at the moment. You know, we were together for almost five years. It's really hard . . .

8. MAY I HELP YOU?

Rani and Lekha are good friends. They help each other.

Rani	:	I feel very thirsty. Can I have a glass of water?
Lekha	:	Of course. It is very warm, isn't it? Could I open the window, please?
Rani	:	Certainly.
Lekha	:	(Take.) Would you like to eat something?
Rani	:	Can I have one or two biscuits?
Lekha	:	Certainly, eat all you like.
Rani	:	Will you courier these letters for me on your way?
Lekha	:	Surely. Would you mind lending me Rs. 100?
Rani	:	OK.

9. PLAYING CRICKET

Tinu is crazy about cricket. She not only plays but likes to talk about it.

Vineetha	:	Hi Tinu. You look tired. What have you been doing?
Tinu	:	I was playing cricket with my friends. We had an exciting match.
Vineetha	:	Were you batting?
Tinu	:	I prefer to bowl.
Vineetha	:	Did you get any wickets today?
Tinu	:	I got three. I felt so happy.
Vineetha	:	Do you play any other games?
Tinu	:	No. I love playing cricket. What about you?
Vineetha	:	Oh, I like cricket but I play tennis too.

10. HOW TO OR NOT TO SAY?

Jenny likes John, but she's afraid to ask him. Her friend Clara is trying to encourage her.

Jenny : Hey, Clara, is John coming with us?

Clara : Yes. Why?

Jenny : Nothing. I'm just asking.

Clara : Just asking? But why is your face burning like that of a mad? Ah, someone has a crush on John, doesn't he?

Jenny : Who has a crush?

Clara : Come on, Jenny, don't be such a chicken. You've got to let him know. May be he likes you.

Jenny : But I don't have the guts to ask him out.

Clara : What're you so afraid of?

Jenny : I'd totally die if he turned me down.

Clara : But that's better than keeping everything to yourself. You've got to let him know. Come on! You've got to take a chance.

Jenny : I don't know . . . Well, may be, you're right, but how am I going to tell him?

11. BUYING A PC

Sally is bored with her old computer but she is not sure if she should go for a new one or not.

Mary : Hi. "PC World?" What are you reading that for? Thinking of buying a new PC?

Sally : You've got it. This machine is four years old and it's a bit slow for the latest video games.

Mary : That's a museum piece. You've got to get a new one right away.

Sally : I want to, but my brother told me that in about six months they'll sell PCs with even more powerful chips than the latest ones today.

Mary : It's always like that.

Sally : Yea. So, I'm of two minds, whether to buy now or to wait for six months.

Mary : Oh, go for it. If you wait for the next most powerful chip, you could be waiting forever.

Sally : True.

12. DISTANCE EDUCATION

Kusum wants to study further. Deepa shares her experience.

Kusum	:	I would really like to do a course in journalism but I can't afford the time and money for the course.
Deepa	:	I suppose you're talking about a full-time course, but that's not the only option you know.
Kusum	:	Well, what else could I do?
Deepa	:	You could do it by distance learning. My brother just completed a distance learning course in HR management.
Kusum	:	Was he satisfied with it? Was it any good?
Deepa	:	Yes, he was. Although he said it was tough to come home tired after a day's work and then do two or three hours of study before going to bed.

13. DECIDING ON VACATION

Anju, Teena and Bini talk about their vacation.

Anju	:	Why don't we go to Chennai this time?
Teena	:	It's really a nice place to visit. But I am afraid our trip will be very expensive.
Bini	:	Teena is right. Shall we go to some other place? Why not Kodaikanal?
Anju	:	Oh, that's a good idea! But we have been there before.
Bini	:	Then why not Kanyakumari?
All	:	Oh, that's wonderful.

14. HOSPITALITY MANAGEMENT COURSE

Dale is busy with studies. Preeta asks her if she forgot all her friends.

Preeta	:	Hey Dale. We never see you these days. Have you lost interest in your friends?
Dale	:	No, of course, not. But I'm taking a correspondence course in hospitality management.
Preeta	:	What's that all about?
Dale	:	It's about hotel management, catering, organising events, and things like that.
Preeta	:	That sounds like a lot of stuff to cover.
Dale	:	It is and I have to work hard because they keep mailing assignments which I have to complete.
Preeta	:	How do they grade you?

Dale	:	They value my assignments and if I get 70% marks they will allow me to appear for the final exams.
Preeta	:	Oh, you must be working hard.
Dale	:	Um.

15. INTERIOR DECORATION

Chithra bought a new house. Teena visits Chithra and appreciates the interior.

Teena	:	Um. Nice. So this is your new apartment.
Chithra	:	Yes, I moved in a month ago.
Teena	:	Well, I have to say it looks really fantastic. Did you decorate and furnish it yourself?
Chithra	:	Yes, I did. It took me quite a lot of time. My husband too helped me out.
Teena	:	Well, I must say you have such good taste in interior decoration. It could have been done by a professional designer.
Chithra	:	Oh, I don't think so, but I'm glad you think it's nice. Come let's move into the next room.
Teena	:	Yea. OK.

16. TERRIBLE NOISE

Rose is sorry for breaking a stack of plates.

Alka	:	What happened?
Rose	:	I'm sorry. I just dropped a stack of plates.
Alka	:	Were you hurt?
Rose	:	Fortunately, no. But I'm terribly sorry.
Alka	:	I'm glad you're not hurt, but why did you drop the plates?
Rose	:	I couldn't help it. The plates were too greasy and slippery.
Alka	:	You've got to be careful next time, OK.
Rose	:	I will. Trust me.

17. BOARDING SCHOOL

Ritu talks about her boarding school experience to Tintu.

Tintu	:	Is it true that you went to boarding school?
Ritu	:	Yes, I started staying in a hostel when I was 10 years old. I was there till I left school.
Tintu	:	Didn't you get homesick living away from home for such a long period?

Ritu	:	Well, I did at times, especially in the early days. But I gradually made quite a few friends and came to enjoy it.
Tintu	:	My cousin went to boarding school and she hated it.
Ritu	:	Well, it's true that it doesn't suit everyone. But I have to say that staying in a boarding school makes you self-reliant from an early age itself.
Tintu	:	Um. May be.

18. MARKETING MANAGER

Kirti is applying for a job. She talks to Kajol about it.

Kirti	:	I'm thinking of applying for a marketing manager's job.
Kajol	:	Well you've got plenty of experience. So you should have a nice chance.
Kirti	:	I'm going to work on my resume tonight at home.
Kajol	:	I'd wait to get the job description if I were you.
Kirti	:	Why do you say that?
Kajol	:	Well, then you'll be able to tailor your resume to fit the job.

19. A BUILDING PROJECT

A few people are committed to a building project. They are discussing about ways and means to fund it.

Member 1	:	Well, girls there aren't many ways open to us to raise money at the moment except, of course, asking for contributions.
Teacher	:	Teachers are willing to donate Rs. 5000 from their side.
Member 2	:	We will collect some money from the people.
Member 3	:	Why not organise a magic show to raise money?
Member 1	:	Any more suggestions . . .
Member 4	:	How about distributing surprise prize coupons?
Member 1	:	Wonderful, if all of us work together, surely we will complete this project soon. Yea.

20. LIKES AND DISLIKES

Rekha and Anita are watching a movie. But they like different types of movies

Rekha	:	I like animation very much. Haven't you seen Ice Age, The Lion king, Finding Nemo . . . ?
Anita	:	No, I like all types of movies—English, Hindi, Odia.
Rekha	:	I think all animation look alike. I like movies with spices like romance, fights, crimes, etc.

Anita	:	Animation can create anything our mind can visualise or imagine.
Rekha	:	Really!
Anita	:	Animation can produce what is normally impossible in real life. The graphical depiction makes it simply funny and exciting.
Rekha	:	OK.

21. ABOUT ACCIDENT

Renuka describes Nimi about an accident she saw recently.

Renuka	:	I saw a terrible accident last week. I was working in my computer lab. And I wanted to see if the rain had stopped. So I walked over to window and I looked outside.
Nimi	:	And what did you see?
Renuka	:	Nothing at first. But then a car came along. It stopped at the pedestrian crossing opposite my office. A man and a woman started to cross just as another car came along, straight over the crossing without even slowing down.
Nimi	:	Oh no. Was anybody hurt?
Renuka	:	Well the woman jumped out of the way and the car just missed her. But the man was knocked down.
Nimi	:	So what did you do?
Renuka	:	Oh, I immediately called the police.
Nimi	:	Did it take long for them to come?
Renuka	:	No, they arrived in a couple of minutes.

22. A NEW PET

Sapna and Asha have pets. Sapna recently bought a Boxer.

Sapna	:	Ruben, go-go.
Asha	:	Is that your new dog?
Sapna	:	Yes, we've only had him a week.
Asha	:	He's really handsome and lively.
Sapna	:	He should be. He cost a fortune.
Asha	:	Why was he so expensive?
Sapna	:	He's a thoroughbred Boxer with an outstanding pedigree, that's why. We got him from a top breeder.
Asha	:	I have a dog too. He is a mongrel, . . . quite ugly but very intelligent.

23. DRY UP SOON

Usha got wet in the heavy rain. Stela wonders at her ignorance of the weather report.

Stela : Wow! You look like a drowned rat. Didn't you know there's a thunderstorm today?

Usha : I knew there would be a shower, but I didn't realise it would rain cats and dogs today.

Stela : Well, you'd better towel yourself dry right now or you'll catch a cold.

Usha : I know. I don't want to fall ill.

24. BORROWING A MOBILE

Manju borrows Shruti's mobile phone. She wants to have it for a few more days.

Manju : OK. Bye. Shruti, thanks so much for the mobile. Can I keep it until Monday?

Shruti : I'm sorry I can't let you do that because I need it myself on Monday for the college festival.

Manju : I'm sorry I didn't know about it. Is it all right if I returned it to you on Sunday?

Shruti : That's fine.

Manju : Do you want to buy something.

Shruti : Yea, let me see.

25. BUYING A MOBILE PHONE

Remya wants to buy a mobile phone online. Hema warns her of the dangers.

Remya : I have just seen a mobile phone advertised at an amazing price on the Internet.

Hema : I know you've been searching to buy one for some time. Is it a good make?

Remya : Oh yes, it's one of the top brands and it is described as in excellent condition. It has a lot of additional features also. See.

Hema : Are you going to buy it?

Remya : The price is so good. I think I have to go for it.

Hema : I'd be very careful if I were you. Any Tom, Dick or Harry can set up as any kind of dealer on the Internet. You might be dealing with a crook.

26. STAY CONNECTED

Rupali is going on a vacation. Susan advises Rupali to take her cell phone along with her.

Susan   :   Always make sure that you've got an international roaming cell phone with you when you go on vacation.

Rupali   :   Why, I don't always take my cell phone with me on vacation. I hate being disturbed when I want to relax.

Susan   :   Well, I've just been reading how cell phones are useful for rescuing tourists

Rupali   :   How's that?

Susan   :   Well, many were stranded by the tsunami in the remote area of the country where they had been staying. They couldn't get out. The authorities were able to locate them when they made calls on their phones.

Rupali   :   That's really useful to know. I'll definitely take your advice in future.

27. RESCUE OPERATION

All the places are flooded. It is the old and the weak who suffer during such times.

Pallavi   :   The people who are trying to cope with the rescue operations in the flooded areas have an incredibly difficult job.

Chithra   :   Yes, my brother is a doctor and when he phoned home last night he told us that it was a race against time.

Pallavi   :   And there's also the problem of bringing help to the people in that place.

Chithra   :   Yes, some of them are in very remote areas apparently.

Pallavi   :   They are, and it's another race against time to get food to them before they become weak and die of malnutrition or disease.

Chithra   :   I know. It's the very young and the very old who are most at risk.

Pallavi   :   True.

28. AIRPORT CHECK-IN COUNTER

Geeta lets an airport official verify her ticket and clears her doubts.

Geeta   :   Good morning.

Employee   :   Good morning. May I have your ticket please?

Geeta	:	Certainly. Can I take this as hand luggage? Yea. Can I have an aisle seat in the smoking section?
Employee	:	I'm afraid this is a non-smoking flight, But you can have an aisle seat. Here's your boarding pass and have a nice flight.
Geeta	:	Thank you.

29. CUSTOMS DUTY FOR EXTRA

Customs official questions Sonya about her belongings and luggage she is carrying.

Employee	:	Do you have anything to declare, Madam?
Sonya	:	Just some wine and gold.
Employee	:	How much wine do you have?
Sonya	:	Four bottles.
Employee	:	That's fine, and how much gold?
Sonya	:	I have 2 kilogram.
Employee	:	I'm afraid you're allowed only 1 kilogram of gold. You'll have to pay duty on the rest.
Sonya	:	Oh.

30. BEAUTY TREATMENT

Raje and Vineeta argue about beauty treatment.

Vineeta	:	Bye. I'll call you . . .
Raje	:	Hey, look! She's pretty, isn't she? Her skin looks baby smooth.
Vineeta	:	Well, it's just that she puts lots of make-up on her face. Actually, natural beauty should come from within.
Raje	:	Aha, I can smell jealousy in the air.
Vineeta	:	She has nothing that deserves my jealousy. I don't have to put things on my face to look pretty. Don't you think so?
Raje	:	All right! But what was that you put on your face last night? Those little greenish things?
Vineeta	:	That's cucumber. They're natural skin soothers. Haven't you heard them say on television that they soften the skin, wipe out the roughness, counter irritation, and build up strength and resilience? Besides they are natural, absolutely free of chemicals. They remove wrinkles and signs of ageing.
Raje	:	Oh, you do know quite a lot about it. Don't you?
Vineeta	:	What's the song?
Raje	:	"E . . . Goura."

31. ESCAPE FROM DISASTER

Natural calamities are disastrous. Escaping one is nothing short of a miracle.

Maya	:	I've been really depressed by all the sad stories about the earthquake which I've heard on the news this week.
Jane	:	Well, that's understandable—whole families have been killed. On the other hand, there have been some incredible survival stories.
Maya	:	I haven't heard about those.
Jane	:	There was one man who was rescued after being trapped under the debris of a building for more than twenty-four hours.
Maya	:	He was one of the few lucky ones.
Jane	:	Yes, he escaped death by the skin of his teeth.

32. TWO FRIENDS IN A HOSTEL

Falguni is not well. She doesn't want to go to college but wants to attend her favourite concert.

Anjali	:	Get up. It's getting late. Your bus will be here in 15 minutes.
Falguni	:	Well, I don't feel well. I think I've got a cold.
Anjali	:	Well, I don't think you should stay at home just because you've a cold. Just take a bath in hot water and after that I'll give you some lime juice with honey in it. That'll cure your cold.
Falguni	:	But, I don't feel like getting up. I think I've got a splitting headache too.
Anjali	:	Oh, so you will miss your concert tomorrow as you are so ill.
Falguni	:	No, I'll be all right tomorrow.
Anjali	:	OK. Too sick for your college, but OK for your concert, right? Up you get young lady and off to college you go.

33. GARDENING

Fanny's parents have a very good garden. Gita is amazed . . . commend the efforts.

Gita	:	What a beautiful garden your parents have?
Fanny	:	I'm glad you like it. They certainly spend a lot of time on it.
Gita	:	And the indoor plants are also very attractive.
Fanny	:	They're my mother's specialty. She's really got a green thumb—plants seem to respond to her.

| Gita | : | She must be really interested in gardening |
| Fanny | : | They make money out of it too. The nursery they run is very popular. |

34. IN A COLLEGE CAMPUS

Malika is trying to borrow Deepti's Chemistry note book.

Malika	:	Hi. As I was unwell I couldn't attend the class for last two days. Will you be able to give me notes of the Chemistry classes?
Deepti	:	Yes. But I need the notes to study for the exam. Could you please return it tomorrow?
Malika	:	Sure. I'll take photocopies and return it to you.
Deepti	:	Fine.
Malika	:	Thank you.

35. CAR REPAIR

Malavi speaks out her bitter experience at the garage to Renjini.

Renjini	:	Hey, you look angry. What happened?
Malavi	:	Nothing. I'd rather not talk about it.
Renjini	:	Come on. You shouldn't keep your feelings pent-up. Tell me, may be, I could help you.
Malavi	:	All right. Yesterday morning I took my car to the garage to have them check the air-conditioner. They said that they had repaired it and presented me with a hefty bill. But you know what—the a/c just worked for 10 minutes.
Renjini	:	No wonder you look so livid.
Malavi	:	And they were rude. They said that I didn't know anything about cars, which I don't, but they didn't have to be so blunt.
Renjini	:	You should file a complaint with the consumer protection agency.
Malavi	:	Well.
Renjini	:	It's not opening.
Malavi	:	Let's go.

36. HOLIDAY PLANS

Mary was on holiday in Kerala. She tried some Ayurvedic treatment.

| Jyothi | : | Well, did you enjoy your week of relaxing in Kerala? |
| Mary | : | Oh yes, I did. |

Jyothi	:	You've had a lovely ayurvedic treatment in Kerala, haven't you?
Mary	:	Yea, I feel very relaxed.
Jyothi	:	Are you holidaying there soon?
Mary	:	I hope to, but I don't know when I'll be able to. George came with me last year.
Jyothi	:	Did he? Where else did you go?
Mary	:	Well, we made a tour of several countries in Europe.
Jyothi	:	Have you ever been to Australia? You sound like a travel agent. Have you changed your job?
Mary	:	Of course not. But I was reading a brochure about Australia yesterday. It's a very lovely country.
Jyothi	:	Yes, it is!

37. ANXIOUS ABOUT THE FUTURE

Rhea is worried about getting admission to a class.

Liza	:	Rhea, you look so worried. What happened?
Rhea	:	Well, I want to get into that class, but I just found out that there are so many people on the waiting list. I guess chances are pretty slim.
Liza	:	I wouldn't say that. Many people might drop the class and then there will be some openings. You never know.
Rhea	:	I hope so.
Liza	:	Come on, cheer up. Don't worry so much. Everything will be just fine.

38. EATING AT A RESTAURANT

Maya and Neha disagree about food they had from a restaurant.

Maya	:	Do you remember the restaurant we went on Friday?
Neha	:	Sure, I do. It was the 'Silver Castle.'
Maya	:	No, we've never been to the 'Silver Castle.'
Neha	:	May be, it was the Gold Coin.
Maya	:	No! It is on the tip of my tongue.
Neha	:	Never mind. The food was terrible. We won't go there again
Maya	:	Well, I don't think that it was too bad.
Neha	:	The food was too spicy for my taste.

39. MIGRAINE HEADACHE

Judi is suffering from migraine. She does not want to go out with Saira

Saira	:	Hi. Are you coming to the restaurant with us, Judi?
Judi	:	No, I'm sorry. I can't. I've got a splitting headache. I'm having one of my migraines.
Saira	:	Oh, is there anything I can do?
Judi	:	No, it's all right. I've taken all my pills and I'll just stay at home and lie down.
Saira	:	That's a miserable way to spend the day. Anyway, I'll come back after lunch and see if you are better.
Judi	:	That's very kind. It'll give me something to look forward to.

40. CARING FOR AUNT

Minu visits her aunt. Her visit was of some help to her aunt.

Minu	:	Aunty, may I leave you now?
Aunt	:	Just a moment, darling. Get me a tablet, please.
Minu	:	Yes, please.
Aunt	:	Give me a glass of water too.
Minu	:	Certainly. (Here it is. Aunty.)
Aunt	:	Thank you dear. I would also like to have a cup of hot black coffee. Will you make it for me?
Minu	:	Just a minute, Aunty.
Aunt	:	Remember, don't put any sugar.
Minu	:	I know Aunty. Relax please. Coffee will be ready in a minute.

41. AT A MOBILE SHOP

Neena doesn't have enough money with her. She enquires about payment by credit card.

Neena	:	All right, can I pay by card?
Cashier	:	I'm afraid we don't accept credit cards.
Neena	:	Can I pay by cheque then?
Cashier	:	I'm really sorry, madam. We don't accept anything other than cash.
Neena	:	That makes my job difficult because . . . I don't think I have enough money on me.
Cashier	:	Oh, sorry ma'am.

42. TIGHT SCHEDULE

Viola is too busy to find some time to talk to.

| Cynthia | : | Do you think it's possible for us to have a talk sometime today? |

Viola	:	I'd love to, but I've got a pretty tight schedule today.
Cynthia	:	Oh, what have you got going on?
Viola	:	Well, I've got to finish a report by 10 AM. Then I have to go to the airport to pick up a client of mine at 11. After that, I'll have a meeting with him over lunch. I guess I won't have a break until two o'clock. But then, from three until five, I have to attend a senior staff meeting.
Cynthia	:	Wow! That's cutting it close.

43. WAKE-UP CALL

Jaya is a heavy sleeper. She needs several clocks to wake her up.

Rani	:	Hey, you have so many clocks in your bedroom.
Jaya	:	Yes, I want to make sure I can get up early in the morning.
Rani	:	But is there something wrong with them? None of them has the same time.
Jaya	:	I do it on purpose. I set this clock ahead ten minutes, and this one behind ten minutes, but I always set that clock to the right time.
Rani	:	So the alarms ring every ten minutes?
Jaya	:	Yes. I am a heavy sleeper. I need thunder to wake me up.

44. A STUDENT AND A TEACHER

A student is unwell. One of her teachers advises her to submit a leave application.

Teacher	:	Why are you standing here?
Student	:	I don't feel well. I have a fever and sore throat. Could you please grant me permission to leave at lunch break?
Teacher	:	All right. Please fill in the leave application form and leave it at the Principal's office, OK.
Student	:	Thank you. I'll do that right away.

45. LATE AT HOME

Helping somebody is good but at times could be misunderstood by others.

Mother	:	Why did you come back so late from grandma's house?
Deepa	:	Mom, I was about to leave when granny said she wanted to have a tablet. So I gave her a tablet and I gave her a glass of water.
Mother	:	But that couldn't have taken this much time.

| Deepa | : | She also asked me to make a cup of hot black coffee for her. Granny was too weak to get up. So I made her a very nice cup of hot black coffee without sugar and asked her to relax. |
| Mother | : | Hum. |

46. POLICE COMPLAINT

Jessy's house has been burgled. She makes a complaint at the police station.

Police	:	City Police Station. Can I help you?
Jessy	:	Sir, please help me. My house has been burgled.
Police	:	Where do you live?
Jessy	:	My address is 28-B, M.G Road.
Police	:	When did you discover the burglary?
Jessy	:	We were out of station for a week. And we had just arrived half an hour ago.
Police	:	What are the things that were stolen?
Jessy	:	The jewels we had kept in the safe are gone, and my computer too has been stolen.
Police	:	How did they get in?
Jessy	:	They forced the back door open.
Police	:	An officer will be a round in about half an hour. Please don't touch anything.
Jessy	:	Fine.
Police	:	OK.

47. A NEW JOB

Karishma had an interview for a new job. Ruby is asking about the details.

Ruby	:	I heard you're looking for a new job.
Karisma	:	Yeah. I just had an interview yesterday.
Ruby	:	Oh, how did it go?
Karisma	:	I think I did well. They said they would take a decision by this Friday.
Ruby	:	This Friday? I think they want to hire the person as quickly as possible.
Karisma	:	Yeah. I think so, too.
Ruby	:	Well. What are your chances of getting that job?
Karisma	:	I believe I have a very good chance. The director seems to like me.

Ruby   :   Oh, that's cool.

48. LOOKING FOR AN APARTMENT

Sheela wants to move to a new apartment. She talks to a property dealer.

Sheela   :   Hello. I'm calling to know more about the apartments that you had advertised.

Dealer   :   Yes. What kind of apartment are you interested in?

Sheela   :   I'm interested in a one-bedroom apartment. Do you have such a flat available?

Dealer   :   Yes. I have one. When do you need it?

Sheela   :   Well, almost immediately. What can you tell me about this apartment?

Dealer   :   Well, it's a one-bedroom apartment. The monthly rent is 2000 rupees, with 3 months' rent as advance payment. You have to give a monthly maintenance charge, which is 550 a month. You'll be assigned a sheltered parking space at no extra charge.

Sheela   :   Sounds good. May I come over tomorrow to take a look?

Dealer   :   Sure. What time would you like to come?

Sheela   :   How about 10 AM?

Dealer   :   OK. May I have your name, please?

Sheela   :   My name is Sheela.

Dealer   :   I'll see you tomorrow OK. Goodbye.

49. FILM FESTIVAL

Tina explains about one of the foreign films she saw at the film festival.

Emy   :   Hey Tina. How was the film festival?

Tina   :   It was quite interesting. I saw a lot of foreign movies. The last one I saw was really good.

Emy   :   Oh, where was it made?

Tina   :   In Sweden. I didn't even think it had a movie industry.

Emy   :   Neither did I. What was it about?

Tina   :   It was about an old man on his deathbed looking back on his life in flashback.

Emy   :   Oh, sounds a bit depressing.

Tina   :   Not at all. He had led a very exciting life.

Emy   :   Oh, what about the technical side.

Tina   :   It displayed a fantastic choreographic style.

| Emy | : | OK. Let's hope that such brilliant movies will come again in the near future. |
| Tina | : | Yea sure. |

50. JANE'S BOYFRIEND

Jane likes Jack. Jane and Michelle talk about him.

Michelle	:	I heard you're going out with Jack.
Jane	:	Yes. To be frank, I really love him to death.
Michelle	:	You're so lucky.
Jane	:	Why do you say that?
Michelle	:	Why? Are you kidding me? A boy like him is so hard to find, so patient, so caring . . . Did I mention—so handsome.
Jane	:	It's very nice of you to say so.
Michelle	:	Well, it's not a compliment. I'm saying it from the bottom of my heart. It's obvious that he's head over heels in love with you.
Jane	:	I sure hope so.

51. EXERCISE

Rehna is working on her fitness. Alisha finds out that it is good for her too.

Alisha	:	You are looking quite trim these days. Have you been working out?
Rehna	:	Yeah, as a matter of fact, I've been going to the gym for nearly six months.
Alisha	:	I see. You look really good. Even your waist has reduced. Have you been lifting weights?
Rehna	:	Yes and I also do an hour of aerobics every other day. I tell you, it's really good if you want to lose weight! I feel like a new woman.
Alisha	:	May be, I too should give it a try. You certainly could but you shouldn't give it up after a couple of days. You should stick to the schedule.

52 INTRODUCING ONESELF

Prema and Jaya meet at a travel agent's office. They talk about their states.

| Prema | : | Ay God! Excuse me. My name is Prema. What's your name? |
| Jaya | : | Jaya |

Prema	:	Where are you from Jaya?
Jaya	:	I'm from Delhi. Where are you from?
Prema	:	I'm from Mumbai.
Jaya	:	Is this your first visit to Delhi?
Prema	:	Yes, I have read a lot about the national capital.
Jaya	:	So, how do you like our state?
Prema	:	It's really beautiful and the people are quite friendly, I feel life is more relaxed here.

53. INVITATION TO A PARTY

Diana is invited to a party. She confirms her participation over phone.

Diana	:	Hello Kay. It's Diana here. I just received the invitation to your party.
Kay	:	Can you make it?
Diana	:	Well, let's see. It's on Saturday night, 7:00 PM, at 201 Liberty's, Champaign. Right?
Kay	:	It's right. I hope you can come?
Diana	:	It would be my pleasure. Can I bring anything?
Kay	:	No. Just yourself.
Diana	:	OK, I'll be there with bells on. I'm looking forward to it. Take care. Bye-bye.
Kay	:	OK then. Bye.

54. ASKING FOR A DIRECTION

A visitor wants to find out where the nearest SBI ATM is. Reena helps her out.

Visitor	:	Excuse me.
Reena	:	Yes
Visitor	:	Can you tell me how to reach the bank, please?
Reena	:	Which bank? There are two: the State Bank of India and the Bank of Baroda
Visitor	:	I have an SBI ATM card and I want to withdraw money from bank.
Reena	:	You need to go to the SBI which is near the Railway Station.
Visitor	:	How do I get there? I have no knowledge of this area.
Reena	:	It's the road and turn left at the other side. Walk along the footpath until you reach the traffic lights. You will see a shopping centre on the right hand side. And walk across the road to the Railway Station. The bank is to your left.

Visitor	:	It sounds very complicated. How far is it from here?
Reena	:	It's not so complicated. It's about five minutes walk from here. I can draw a map for you if you wish.
Visitor	:	Oh, I would really appreciate that. Will I be going North or South?
Reena	:	You will be going northwards. You are now in the Western part of the city and the SBI is situated in the North East. Here's a rough sketch of the area.

55. ORDERING FOR FOOD

Celina and her friends go to a restaurant. She is finalising the menu.

Waiter	:	Good evening.
Celina	:	A table for two, please.
Waiter	:	Certainly, ma'am.
Celina	:	Could we sit by the window?
Waiter	:	I'm sorry. The window tables are all reserved.
Celina	:	OK.
Waiter	:	Would you like to have a buffet?
Celina	:	Oh, I don't think we'll go for the buffet.
Waiter	:	In that case can I take your order, ma'am? Would you like to have some soup?
Celina	:	No, thanks. We'll order the main course straight away. We'd like to have fried rice and a chicken dish, which is not too spicy. What do you recommend?
Waiter	:	I suggest you try our Chinese dishes—they are quite bland.
Celina	:	Oh, then we'll have a portion of garlic chicken and some smoked fish.
Waiter	:	Is that all ma'am?
Celina	:	Yes. We'll order dessert later. Thanks.
Waiter	:	Thank you, ma'am.

56. PLANNING A PARTY

Rita invites Malati for dinner at her home. They talk about their preferences.

Malati	:	Um, Thank you.
Rita	:	Hey, I've sent out the invitations for the dinner party.
Celina	:	Um. That's good. Now what should we do?
Rita	:	We've got to plan the menu.
Celina	:	Oh, that's right. Do you have anything in mind?

Rita	:	I think I'm going to make the chicken curry you like. Your mother has given me the recipe.
Celina	:	Yeah, but did you forget that Vishnu doesn't eat chicken?
Rita	:	Thanks for reminding me. I will definitely include a vegetarian dish.
Celina	:	Don't make it too spicy.
Rita	:	Um, let's see.

57. EATING OUTSIDE

Sonya is working. She doesn't have time to cook food at house. She always eats food from hotels. Preeti envies her.

Preeti	:	How often do you eat out, Sonya?
Sonya	:	Well, very often. I eat out almost five times a week.
Preeti	:	Wow! I really envy you. I hardly get a chance to eat out. It's home cooked breakfast, lunch and dinner for me. And I have to do the cooking.
Sonya	:	Don't envy me. It's for business. In fact, I'm sick and tired of restaurant food. Sometimes I just want a home-cooked meal. Hotel food is far too spicy for me. But I have no choice as I have to travel a lot as part of my job.

58. AT THE ICE CREAM PARLOUR

Shalu wants Mini's company for buying ice-cream. But Mini is on diet.

Shalu	:	Hey, would you like to have some ice cream? This ice cream parlour has got a variety of flavours for you to choose from. They have strawberry, peach, chocolate, black currant, mango and butterscotch.
Mini	:	Wow! What a temptation! I wish I could, but I just can't. I'm on diet to lose weight.
Shalu	:	Oh, come on, it's just a bit. It doesn't really hurt to have just a bit.
Mini	:	I'd better not. Please don't tempt me. Please.
Shalu	:	Wow! You are really strong-willed.
Mini	:	You're right. I'm not so easily coaxed into doing something that I think is wrong.
Shalu	:	Well, I'd better not tempt you.
Mini	:	OK.

59. EAT OUT DINNER TONIGHT

Terri wants to take Feba for an outing in order to relax.

Feba	:	What's the occasion? You won the lottery?
Terri	:	No, just want to relax a little bit. You don't have to win the lottery to relax, do you?
Feba	:	Well, I'm kind of broke.
Terri	:	Really? It's very nice of you.
Feba	:	Don't be silly. I'll take you anywhere you want to go.
Terri	:	Wonderful! You know what, I wish you wanted to relax every day.
Feba	:	Um. Dream on.

60. DIET WATCH

Terri was hungry. She ate salt biscuits Saira made at home.

Saira	:	Terri, where are the biscuits I made? Don't tell me you ate them all.
Terri	:	Yes, I did. I couldn't help it. They were so good.
Saira	:	I thought you didn't like biscuits.
Terri	:	Well, I don't like biscuits flavoured with chocolate at all. But vanilla is different. They are so delicious. I must say you are a good cook.
Saira	:	Thank you for the compliment but I think that you should watch your weight.
Terri	:	Well, then you should stop tempting me with such good food.

61. BOOKING A FLIGHT TICKET

Priya is flying to Singapore. She goes to the travel agent to book the tickets.

Agent	:	Yes, ma'am.
Priya	:	I'd like to book a flight to Singapore, please.
Agent	:	Which airline would you like to use?
Priya	:	Which airline would you recommend?
Agent	:	When do you want to travel?
Priya	:	Next week, the 15th.
Agent	:	Would you like a return ticket?
Priya	:	Yes, I'm coming back on the 30th.
Agent	:	Let me see . . . Air Alpha costs Rs. 10,000. And Jet Set is the cheapest . . . direct flight at Rs. 8000.
Priya	:	How long does the Air Alpha flight take?

Agent	:	Total time is 6 hours. Air Alpha takes 7 hours as there is a stopover at Mumbai.
Priya	:	I may as well go with Jet Set then.
Agent	:	How many seats would you like?
Priya	:	Three tickets, please.

62. FOREIGN EXCHANGE

Kamla is going abroad on vacation. She wants some cash converted to US dollars.

Cashier	:	Yes, ma'am.
Kamla	:	I'm going on holiday, and I need some foreign currency.
Cashier	:	Cash or traveler's cheque?
Kamla	:	I think cash will be enough.
Cashier	:	Which currency do you want the cash in?
Kamla	:	I need some dollars. What is the rate of exchange?
Cashier	:	Rs. 57 for a US dollar.
Kamla	:	I see. Please exchange Rs. 2000 for me and debit the money from my account.
Cashier	:	OK. Please sign here.
Kamla	:	Thank you.

63. FORGETS PHONE NUMBER

Meena doesn't have Juliet's phone number. She calls her friends to find out.

Meena	:	Do you know what Juliet's phone number is?
Bindu	:	Oh, Juliet's phone number? I don't have my address book on me . . . Hm. I can't think of it right off hand.
Kamla	:	That's too bad. I've got to find her. If I can't find her today, I'll be dead.
Bindu	:	Well, why don't you call Michelie? She has Juliet's phone number.
Kamla	:	I've tried, but no one answered.
Bindu	:	Oh, you are so dead.

64. INTRODUCING A PERSON

Sania and Dolly are friends. Sania introduces her cousin Claire to Dolly.

Sania	:	Hi Dolly. How are you?
Dolly	:	Fine. Thank you. How about you?
Sania	:	Great! Let me introduce you to my cousin, Claire. Claire, meet my friend Dolly and she works with me at the office.

Claire	:	Hi, Dolly.
Dolly	:	Hi, Claire.
Sania	:	Dolly, this is actually my brother, John's, daughter.
Dolly	:	Pleased to meet you. Actually I didn't know John had a daughter? Where's he been hiding you?
Sania	:	She's been actually living out East with his Wife's sister.
Dolly	:	What part of the East, Claire?
Claire	:	Boston, near the harbour.
Dolly	:	OK. It must be a great change coming back here?
Claire	:	Yea, but I'm glad to be back and see all my friends.
Dolly	:	OK.

65. BIRTHDAY PARTY

Sara and Priti plans to throw a birthday party for Rakhi.

Sara	:	Do you know its Rakhi's birthday on Thursday?
Priti	:	Oh, I'd forgotten all about it.
Sara	:	I suppose we should buy a present for her.
Priti	:	I think we ought to have a party for her.
Sara	:	What can we get her?
Priti	:	It depends on how much we want to pay.
Sara	:	I think we should pool in and buy a present for her. And also invite a few friends over for a birthday party on Thursday evening.
Priti	:	We could but she's got an interview on Friday and she might want to get ready for it.
Sara	:	Let's see till the weekend. Anyway, more people will be free on Saturday.
Priti	:	OK. It will be a nice surprise for Rakhi.
Sara	:	Cool!

66. TRAFFIC SPEED LIMIT

Chitra has been fined for over-speeding. Devika reads out the charges.

Chitra	:	Just my luck. Look at this letter.
Devika	:	Ah, Yes. I thought it was something official looking. Oh, you have been fined for exceeding the speed limit, it says. Why weren't you fined on the spot?
Chitra	:	Because I was photographed by a speed camera. I didn't even know it was there.

Devika	:	They're installing more and more of them around here. Two of my friends were caught by them last month. You're going to have to be more careful in future.
Chitra	:	You're not kidding—the fine is Rs. 250. That's a lot of money and it would be double if I got caught again.
Devika	:	I know, speeding is an expensive hobby.

67. CALL BACK MESSAGE

Steffy wants to talk to Amit. As he is in a meeting she leaves a message with Poonam.

Poonam	:	Good afternoon. Infotech. May I help you?
Steffy	:	Extension 237, please.
Poonam	:	I'm sorry, the line is busy, and will you hold the line please?
Steffy	:	Yes, I will.
Poonam	:	I'm putting you through.
Steffy	:	Could I speak to Amit Menon, please?
Poonam	:	Sorry. He's in a meeting at the moment.
Steffy	:	Do you know when he'll be back?
Poonam	:	He should be back around four. Can I take a message?
Steffy	:	Yes. Please ask him to call Steffy on 240983.
Poonam	:	240983, right?
Steffy	:	That's right.
Poonam	:	OK, I'll see that he gets your message. Thank you.

68. BUYING CD's

Ivy is in a music shop to buy a CD. She wants to get a copy soon.

Ivy	:	Do you have the new Jay Johns CDs?
Salesperson	:	I'm afraid that it's sold out. Oh, your pardon. Sorry, It's been selling like hot cakes.
Ivy	:	Are you serious?
Salesperson	:	Yes, it's really popular. As soon as we stock them, they sell out.
Ivy	:	When do you think you'll have more in stock?
Salesperson	:	We should be getting some by this evening.
Ivy	:	Wow! Great! Can you hold one for me? I can't wait to get my hands on one.
Salesperson	:	OK.

69. BUYING A SHIRT

Beena is looking for a shirt at a ready-garment shop.

Assistant	:	Can I help you?
Beena	:	Yes, I'm looking for a shirt.
Assistant	:	What size are you?
Beena	:	I'm medium size.
Assistant	:	How about these?
Beena	:	Yes, that's nice. Can I try it on?
Assistant	:	Certainly, the changing rooms are over there.
Beena	:	Thank you, your are welcome.
Assistant	:	How does it fit?
Beena	:	It's too tight. Do you have a larger size?
Assistant	:	Yes. Here you are.
Beena	:	Thank you. I'll have it, please.
Assistant	:	How would you like to pay?
Beena	:	Do you take credit cards?
Assistant	:	Yes, we do.
Beena	:	OK.

70. BUYING A TV

Cema wants to buy a new TV. She is at an electronics shop talking to the salesperson.

Assistant	:	Good morning. Can I help you?
Cema	:	Yea, I hope so. I'm looking for a television.
Assistant	:	We have a special offer on Hi Tech television this month.
Cema	:	How much is it?
Assistant	:	You need to pay just Rs. 5000 as down payment for a 27 inch television. And the rest can be paid in easy installments.
Cema	:	What is the total price?
Assistant	:	It will come up to Rs. 25,000.
Cema	:	Oh, it's a little expensive! Do you have a cheaper one?
Assistant	:	Yes, this one's only 15,000.
Cema	:	What make is it?
Assistant	:	It's a Dano.
Cema	:	I'll take it. Do you accept credit cards?
Assistant	:	Yes, we do.

71. BUYING A PAIR OF SHOES

Kiran goes to a shoe market. She prefers a tan coloured shoe.

Shopkeeper : May I help you?
Kiran   : Do you have these shoes in size seven?
Shopkeeper : I'm not sure. If you can't find them on the rack, they may be out of stock. But let me look in the stockroom.
Kiran   : Thanks. I'd like to try on a pair if you have them.
Shopkeeper : I'll be right back. Which colour do you prefer suede or tan?
Kiran   : I think . . . tan.
Shopkeeper : OK.

72. SHOPPING FOR TROUSERS

Kumari wants to buy a pair of trousers for her husband. She is at a readymade garment shop.

Aruna   : May I help you?
Kumari : Yes, I'm looking for a pair of trousers for my husband.
Aruna   : What colour would you like?
Kumari : Black.
Aruna   : And what's the size?
Kumari : His waistline is 34 inch.
Aruna   : OK, then how about this?
Kumari : That's good.

73. A VISIT TO THE DENTIST

Riya got her dental cavity filled. She describes how painful the whole process was.

Aleena : Hey, Riya, what happened to your face? It looks swollen.
Riya   : I had to go get a cavity filled today.
Aleena : Did it hurt?
Riya   : I don't even want to talk about it. It nearly killed me.
Aleena : How long were you in the chair?
Riya   : It took quite a while. But the worst part was getting numbed. They had to give me three shots.
Aleena : Well, I guess you've learned a good lesson. You have to take good care of your teeth.
Riya   : I suppose so. I am really scared of dentists. The sight of all those instruments makes me break out into a cold sweat. And the bill is really huge.
Aleena : Oh, you did have a tough time today.

Riya   :   That's putting it mildly.

74. PLANNING FOR A MOVIE

Arati and Beena decide to go for a movie but yet to decide when and which one.

Arati   :   Let's go for a movie together.
Beena   :   I'd love to. When shall we go?
Arati   :   How about next Friday evening?
Beena   :   Let me see . . . Oh, I am sorry, I'm having dinner with a friend.
Arati   :   How about the following Tuesday?
Beena   :   That'd be great. What shall we see?
Arati   :   'Guru'?
Beena   :   Oh, I've seen it. Why don't we watch 'the da Vinci Code'?
Arati   :   When shall we meet?
Beena   :   At 5 PM. In front of the theatre?
Arati   :   Great! See you later.
Beena   :   Bye.

75. CHECKING INTO A HOTEL

Monica wants a hotel accommodation for one day. She is booking a room.

Receptionist :   Good evening, madam. May I help you?
Monica   :   Yes, what kind of rooms do you have?
Receptionist :   How large is your party?
Monica   :   Three. Two adults and one child.
Receptionist :   Let's see. We have a room with two double beds. How many nights?
Monica   :   Just one. We're only staying overnight.
Receptionist :   OK.

76. CHECK-IN AT A HOTEL

Geeta is talking to the hotel receptionist for an accommodation for couple of nights.

Receptionist :   Good evening, ma'am. May I help you?
Geeta   :   Have you got any rooms?
Receptionist :   Yes. Single or double, ma'am?
Geeta   :   Single, please.
Receptionist :   Ma'am would you like an air-conditioned room?

Geeta	:	No, an ordinary room will be enough.
Receptionist	:	OK, ma'am. You may please occupy room 319. That'll be Rs. 500 a night, including breakfast. How long will you be staying, ma'am?
Geeta	:	Just a couple of nights. What time would the breakfast be?
Receptionist	:	Breakfast is from 7 to 9 AM.
Geeta	:	And what time is dinner?
Receptionist	:	The dinner is from 7 to 10:30 PM. Ma'am you'd better hurry because the restaurant closes in 15 minutes.
Geeta	:	Thank you, ma'am. Have a nice day.

77. CALL WAITING

Laxmi tried calling Bharat but in vain. Shanti thinks that it was due to Internet browsing.

Shanti	:	Did you call Bharat last night?
Laxmi	:	Yes. I tried to get hold of him last night, but it was so difficult to get through.
Shanti	:	That's strange. Maybe he was on the Net.
Laxmi	:	That's probably it. No wonder the line was so busy all the time! May be he ought to take another line.
Shanti	:	He certainly should do that. Did you try his mobile?
Laxmi	:	Yes, I did. But I kept getting a message saying that the call was on wait. It was really frustrating because I wanted to speak to him very urgently.

78. WAVERING ON COMMITMENT

Olive is disappointed at the way her boss dropped the business project.

Delia	:	I've seen you looking a lot more cheerful than you are at the moment.
Olive	:	Well this isn't the best day I've had this year.
Delia	:	Is it something to do with the new business strategy?
Olive	:	How did you guess? You know, the boss said he would commit 300,000 dollars to my latest business development project?
Delia	:	Yes, you fought very hard for that, I remember.
Olive	:	Well, he's wavering on that commitment. Says the company may not be able to afford it.
Delia	:	Oh, that's a bit of a blow.
Olive	:	Let us go.

79. STRAINED FRIENDSHIP

Elizabeth and Lauri could iron-out some issues through talk.

Laurie	:	This was a very good meeting, Elizabeth.
Elizabeth	:	I'm happy that we've finally cleared up some problems.
Laurie	:	I think we have. Is there anything else to discuss?
Elizabeth	:	No, that's all, I guess.
Laurie	:	Oh, then, let's call it a day, shall we?
Elizabeth	:	All right. See you later, Alligator.
Laurie	:	Okay, Bye, Crocodile. Bye.

80. REVIEWING A PROPOSAL

Mema submits a proposal. Rakhi, her manager, approves of it.

Rakhi	:	Do come in and sit down. How are you?
Mema	:	I'm fine, thanks. Have you had a chance to look at my proposal?
Rakhi	:	Yes, I have. That's what I mainly want to talk about.
Rakhi	:	I wasn't sure whether it was exactly the kind of thing you wanted.
Rakhi	:	Oh, don't worry. It's precisely what we need and your work is absolutely first-class.
Mema	:	Well, I must say that's a great relief.

81. SUMMER TALK

Alice has an air-conditioner but is afraid of electricity bills. She prefers using a fan.

Tina	:	Don't you have air-conditioning in your apartment? It's sweltering here.
Alice	:	Well, there's air-conditioning. But the electricity bills are so high that I dare not switch it on.
Tina	:	So how can you stand the heat?
Alice	:	Well, I open my windows and . . . And I've got an electrical fan. It helps a little.

82. KINDS OF FEAR

Payal and Maya talks about different kinds of fear.

Payal	:	Hey, You know something.
Maya	:	I'm frightened of a lot of things.
Payal	:	Yes, we all are.
Maya	:	Do you know what such unreasonable fears are called?

Payal	:	Is it phobia?
Maya	:	Yes, you are absolutely right. And now tell me, what are you afraid of?
Payal	:	I'm very scared of heights.
Maya	:	Oh, then you have acrophobia—the people who are afraid of closed spaces have claustrophobia. And, of course, we do know there are people afraid of foreigners? Isn't it?
Payal	:	Is that so?
Maya	:	Yes! This fear is called xenophobia. People are afraid of so many unlikely things.
Payal	:	Oh, really?
Maya	:	Some people are ever afraid of open spaces. Such people are called agoraphobic.

83. FEELING FEVERISH

Sonali is feeling feverish. Zara advises Sonali what to do and what not.

Sonali	:	I think I'm running a temperature. My head is spinning, and I have a bad throat.
Zara	:	Let me see. You'd better stay at home today. And don't work on the computer! Staying up late with that thing has obviously played havoc with your health.
Sonali	:	I couldn't help it. I had so many assignments to complete.
Zara	:	Well, I think that you should rest today. And don't watch the TV. You will strain your eyes.

84. NEW NEIGHBOURHOOD

Kusum and Malika talk about one of their neighbours.

Malika	:	Has Prakash moved out yet?
Kusum	:	Yes, He moved out last weekend. He's now living in a very nice and quiet neighbourhood.
Malika	:	I wonder if he's paying more rent now.
Kusum	:	I don't know. Even so, it's still worth it, isn't it?
Malika	:	You're right. I think he's probably very happy to leave that noisy apartment.
Kusum	:	Yes, he is.

85. RECYCLING WASTE

Nitya and Rani are concerned about dumping waste paper.

Nitya	:	Look at all the waste paper in the trash-can next to the photocopier.
Rani	:	What do they do with all that waste paper?
Nitya	:	As far as I know, they just simply dump it outside.
Rani	:	That's really wasteful. There's a better way of dealing with it than that.
Nitya	:	Well, we should try to recycle all our waste paper. That would help the environment . . . save few trees.
Rani	:	We need more awareness about the benefits of recycling . . . Very much.

86. FAILED TO WAKE UP

Radha overslept. She blames the clocks. Franzy teases her.

Radha	:	Hey, I am sorry. I overslept. My clock didn't go off this morning.
Franzy	:	Again?
Radha	:	Yea, that's right. Even though I did set the alarm last night.
Franzy	:	Your clock never works. Perhaps you should buy a new one
Radha	:	Well, if it breaks down again tomorrow, I'll definitely buy a new one.
Franzy	:	May be by then it'll be too late.
Radha	:	But what do you mean "too late"?
Franzy	:	By that time you'll be fired.

87. TRAFFIC ADVICE

During holidays traffic becomes very heavy. Reshma asks Rinku to leave office little early.

Reshma	:	I heard you're going out tonight.
Rinku	:	Yes. I'm having a dinner party with my friends.
Reshma	:	Well, because it's Diwali tomorrow everybody gets off work early today so that they can go back home early. Starting at 3, traffic usually becomes bumper to bumper.
Rinku	:	Oh, I didn't think about that. Well, I'll leave earlier today, say by 2 PM.
Reshma	:	That would be my advice. If you don't have any important things to deal with, leave as early as possible.
Rinku	:	OK, done.

88. EXAMS

Nisha tells Sony that her luck isn't favourable and that she would fail in the exam.

Nisha	:	The history exam was really awful.
Sony	:	Was it really that bad?
Nisha	:	Yes it was. Only a couple of the topics that I had revised for the exam came up.
Sony	:	That was really bad luck. Do you think you managed to do enough to pass?
Nisha	:	No, I think I'll definitely fail that exam.
Sony	:	Oh, come on. Don't be so pessimistic.

89. TV CHANNEL SURFING

Sapna tells Hema what happened the previous day at home while watching TV.

Sapna	:	My mother really got annoyed with my father yesterday evening.
Hema	:	Why? Did he complain about her cooking?
Sapna	:	Oh, no. It was when they were watching television.
Hema	:	Don't tell me he fell asleep in front of the television and started snoring.
Sapna	:	No, he does that sometimes, but this was because he kept changing channels on the remote.
Hema	:	My brother does it all the time. I think that channel surfing is his hobby!

90. TAKING A BREAK

Dhanya is worked up. Kavita suggests taking a short break.

Kavita	:	Dhanya, don't you think you should take a vacation? Even one or two days would be fine.
Kavita	:	There's no way. There's too much work.
Kavita	:	But you look so exhausted. You need it.
Dhanya	:	I know my chances would be better if they would hire more people.
Kavita	:	They won't hire more people?
Dhanya	:	No. They always want to keep the cost down. I am really overwhelmed by heavy of work.
Kavita	:	May be, you should talk to the manager.
Dhanya	:	Yes, I'm going to bring this up in tomorrow's meeting

Kavita	:	Yea.

91. FAIL TO RECOLLECT

Bunty tells Chiku how forgetful she has become in recent weeks.

Bunty	:	Do you know what Rajesh's phone number is?
Chiku	:	Oh, Rajesh's phone number? I don't have my address book with me. I cannot think of it right off hand.
Bunty	:	That's too bad, I've got to find him. It's urgent.
Chiku	:	Oh, why don't you call Michelle? She has his phone number.
Bunty	:	I've tried, but no one answered.
Chiku	:	Um.
Bunty	:	Oh, your memory is going from bad to worse. Yesterday you lost your car keys and you were late for the meeting.
Chiku	:	Yes, I left the keys in the car and it automatically got locked. Luckily I had a spare key inside the house.

92. HEARING FROM OLD FRIENDS

Rakhi tells Sarah about her long lost friends.

Rakhi	:	I just received a letter from one of my old high school buddies.
Sarah	:	That's nice.
Rakhi	:	Well, actually I haven't heard from her in ages. It's really hard to maintain contact when people move around so much.
Sarah	:	That's right. People just drift apart! But you're lucky to be back in touch with your friend again.
Rakhi	:	Great!

93. TROUBLE WITH CAR

Manisha's car broke down. Sonali suggests buying a new one.

Sonali	:	Hey, why didn't you come to class this morning?
Manisha	:	I don't even want to talk about it. My car broke down.
Sonali	:	What happened? Did you check the battery?
Manisha	:	But I just bought this one three months ago. It's still new I think there is something wrong with the engine.
Sonali	:	Oh, no. Have you thought about getting a new car?
Manisha	:	Yeah, I've thought about that, but I can't afford a new car.
Sonali	:	Well, these days financial companies offer loans for second hand cars. Why don't you think about it?
Manisha	:	Let me think.

94. DO YOU REMEMBER?

Shirley tells Lata about Prakash whom she met after a while.

Shirley   :   Hey, guess who I met at the grocery store?
Lata   :   I can't imagine.
Shirley   :   Do you remember Mr. Prakash who used to live in our old
                neighbourhood?
Lata   :   That name rings a bell, but I can't place him.
Shirley   :   He used to live in the building next to ours.
Lata   :   Oh yes. Now I remember. He had dark hair and wore glasses
Shirley   :   You got it.

95. COULDN'T HELP IT!

Darlyn is upset. Smitha has to confess that she is the reason.

Smitha   :   What happened?
Darlyn   :   Ah, I am upset. Somebody told my boss I have a part-time
               job.
Smitha   :   And he doesn't like that?
Darlyn   :   No, he doesn't. He thinks that I am too tired to work.
Smitha   :   I am sorry. I have to admit . . . I told him.
Darlyn   :   You told him? Why?
Smitha   :   I couldn't help it. He asked me point-blank.

96. GOODBYE, TILL WE MEET

Rita got a new job in Mumbai. Rita and Anu agree to keep in touch in
future.

Anu   :   I heard you're moving to Mumbai.
Rita   :   Yes. I've got an offer in 'Jet Set Travels'.
Anu   :   Oh, that's great. But I'm going to miss you.
Rita   :   Me too. Let's keep in touch.
Anu   :   Don't forget to drop me a line when you settle down.
Rita   :   Trust me, I won't. I'll keep in touch.
Anu   :   You have my address?
Rita   :   Well, I have your E-mail Id.
Anu   :   All right. I look forward to hearing from you soon. Thank
               you. Bye.
Rita   :   Bye!

97. PRICING DEBATE

Betty and Litty discuss the government policy on SUVs.

Betty	:	I've been expecting the government to increase taxes on SUVs.
Lity	:	That's what they promised before the election. Those vehicles put out a lot more carbon monoxide than other cars.
Betty	:	But did you see the news last night? The transport minister was being questioned about this.
Lity	:	What did she say? Did she give a clear answer?
Betty	:	No. Of course, not. She said that the government was still studying the practicalities.
Lity	:	Well, they're obviously faltering, aren't they?
Betty	:	I'm sure it's because the motoring organisations have been continuously opposing SUV taxes and some of the newspapers are also very anti.
Lity	:	Well, I hope the government has the guts to resist their demands.

98. NOT ENOUGH SLEEP.

Meeta has not slept well. She looks pale.

Sue	:	Meeta, you look pale. What happened?
Meeta	:	I didn't sleep a wink last night.
Sue	:	Did you have something on your mind? You look so concerned. May be, I can help you.
Meeta	:	Well, I'm under a lot of pressure. My boss is very pushy. He assigned me three projects. Now the deadlines are near and I still haven't finished all of my projects.
Sue	:	Is there anything I can do to help you?
Meeta	:	Well, I guess no one can help me but myself. For the moment, I just need someone one to talk to so that I can relieve my stress.

99. I AM IN A QUANDARY.

Serena wants to know about Kenyon's job plans in Japan. Kenyan is undecided.

Serena	:	Good news in your letter?
Kenyon	:	Hi, please sit down. Have a coffee with me. It's very good news in away.
Serena	:	Hey, don't keep me in suspense.

Kenyon	:	It's from my brother in Japan. He tells me that there are very good jobs available in Tokyo for someone like me.
Serena	:	Wow! Cool! Are you willing to go?
Kenyon	:	Sure, I want to. The problem is that I'm in deep debt and I can't afford to make the move. But I'm desperate to go, because I'm in a crummy job which pays very badly. So I'm in a quandary.
Serena	:	Are you sure?
Kenyon	:	Yea.

100.   TEACHER JOINING A NEW SCHOOL

Gouri is an English teacher. She is interested in joining Global Public School.

Interviewer	:	(Over phone) OK. OK. OK. That's right.
Interviewer	:	Good morning. I'm Mr. Sudhir Rout. What is your name?
Gouri	:	My name is Gouri. And I come from Cuttack.
Interviewer	:	Tell me something more about yourself.
Gouri	:	I am a graduate in English Literature. I have also done my B.Ed.
Interviewer	:	Do you have any experience in teaching?
Gouri	:	I have been working as a teacher in Cambridge Public School for the past five years.
Interviewer	:	So, why do you want to leave your job?
Gouri	:	I have heard a lot about your school and the innovative methods the teachers use here while teaching. I thought I would be able to broaden the horizon of my knowledge if I could get an opportunity to work here.
Interviewer	:	Thank you. We will get in touch with you in a week's time.

"The happiest conversation is that of which nothing is distinctly remembered, but a general effect of pleasing impression."

– Samuel Johnson

CHAPTER 5

SHORT PREPARED SPEECH

A prepared speech is easy to deliver as one knows the main points and issues in it. It has already been shaped and compiled to be presented.

A prepared speech must be memorized according to requirement. It will make the task of deliverance easy and efficient. Otherwise the deliverer must be confused and embarrassed before people. But remember the following points:

1. Don't deliver your speech in a half hazard way which will give an impression to the listeners that you are trying to recall every word.
2. Make your speech short enough (one minute) or as per requirement.
3. Keep your eye contact with audience. A break in the eye contact will spoil the charm and hold of one's speech. Eye contact holds the audience's interest and allows you to note their response to your presentation.
4. Try to stabilize your voice and pace of delivery. Some students have the habit of delivering the speech at a fast speed at the beginning and slowing down at the end. Your voice must not be that loud or slow. It must be normal and stable for all the time of speech.
5. Don't copy your speech from anywhere which will be difficult to memorise. Prepare the speech according to your own capacity and use the words that you know. As you prepare, note important ideas, phrases, quotations and statistics. To increase spontaneity, try to choose some words at the time of presentation.
6. Overhead transparencies and Palm Cards are the most useful aids to people making a prepared speech for the first time in public overhead transparencies with the outline emphasizes the key point in your talk and acts as a prompt to keep your delivery to the prepared points.

Two advantages in using overhead transparencies are that they increase audience understanding and offer the speaker hidden notes.

Palm Cards' use is hidden from the audience. Prepare palm cards with the main points and supporting information written on them and hold these in the palm of the hand as you deliver the speech.

SOME SAMPLE SHORT PREPARED SPEECHES

MY HOME

My home is in Shyampur. We have a small thatched house with mud walls. We have three bedrooms and a kitchen in it. There is a cattle-shed at the back of our house and a garden in front of it. We grow vegetables and flowers in our garden. My father is a schoolmaster. My mother cooks our food and keeps the house neat and clean. We are two brothers and one sister. We love our parents and love each other. Home, home, sweet home, there's no place like home.

MY MOTHER

No one is dearer to me than my mother. She feeds me, clothes me and sends me to school every day. She cooks our food, washes our clothes and takes care of the domestic animals. She is always busy. In my illness she nurses me day and night. Father sometimes gets angry, but mother never. She has always a loving smile on her lips. She is fond of reading holy books and singing prayer songs. She tells me stories of great men of old. A home without a mother is a very dull place.

MY FATHER

My father is the head of our family. He is tall and healthy. Once he was in the Army. Now he is working in our village post office. My father is kind to all. He wakes us up early in the morning. We like to work in the garden with him. He helps us with our lessons and tells us stories of brave deeds. We often go with him to see new places. He always teaches us to be good and honest.

MY PET DOG

Have you seen my pet dog Tipu? He is a large black dog with a white bushy tail. You will always find him at the front door of our house. If you are a stranger, he will look at you with angry eyes and bark loudly to make you afraid. One night a man was trying to get into my father's bedroom through the back door. Tipu heard his footsteps. He ran to the back door in a moment and attacked him. The man ran away with a loud cry. Tipu has driven away many thieves in this way. He is a clever and faithful dog.

OUR GARDEN

We have a small garden in front of our house. There is a green fence around it. So cows and goats cannot get into it. A narrow road divides the garden into two parts. In one part we have many kinds of beautiful flowers. In the other we grow vegetables for our kitchen. I work in the garden every morning with my father and brothers. We dig the plots, weed the garden and water the plants. In the evening I play outside our garden with my brothers and sisters. Our garden is pretty.

MY DAILY LIFE

My father is an early riser. He wakes up the whole house with him before 5 a.m. We work in our little garden for half an hour every day. I finish my breakfast by seven and read newspapers for fifteen minutes. Then I begin my lessons. At about half-past nine I take my lunch and go to school. When I return from school, mother gives me something nice to eat. Then I go out to play. In the evening after prayer I do my lessons again. At ten I eat my last meal and go to bed.

A VILLAGE POST OFFICE

Our village post office has a red letter-box on its wall. It is a small building with only one room. The head of the office is the post master. He has two postmen to help him. One of the postmen brings mail bags from the railway station. The post master opens the mail bags and stamps postmarks on the letters. The other postman distributes the letters. The post master opens the letterbox and sends the letters to the railway station in a sealed bag. He receives money-orders and parcels and sends them to the right persons. I am very fond of collecting stamps at the post office.

A VILLAGE FESTIVAL

Dussehra is the biggest festival in our village. People worship the goddess Durga during the festival. An image of the goddess is placed on a pandal. The pandal is decorated with flowers, festoons of green leaves and coloured paper. On the festival day there is beating of drums and feasting and merry-making. We go about in our best clothes, eat sweets and play games. Our schools are closed. Friends and relatives are invited to take part in the festival. After the festival the image of the goddess is taken out in a procession and put into a pond or river. We are sad when the festival closes and our school opens again.

THE CAR FESTIVAL

The Car Festival at Puri is world-famous. It is held in the month of Ashadha. Thousands of pilgrims visit Puri to see the festival. On the day of the festival the images of Jagannath, Balabhadra and Subhadra are taken out of the temple and placed in three large wooden cars. The cars are decorated with coloured cloth and drawn by pilgrims along the main road. The images are taken to the Gundicha Mandap. They are carried back to the Jagannath Temple on the Bahuda Day. As the cars move along the road, people sing prayer songs and shout for joy. There is a heavy rush on the buses and trains for the Car Festival at Puri. Car festivals are held at many other places in our country.

MY FOOD

I take two important meals every day—lunch at 10 a.m. and supper at 9 p.m. I have a light breakfast before I begin my homework at about seven in the morning. Rice, dal and curries make our daily lunch. We add fish or meat once or twice a week, but I am not very fond of it. For supper we usually have bread and vegetable curry. Between the two important meals I have tiffin in the afternoon when I come back from school. I often forget my glass of milk at bedtime, but my mother always remembers it. She makes cakes, sweets and many other nice things, but I always fall ill when I eat too much of them. Every time I promise to be careful but fail to keep my promise.

MY VILLAGE

Have you ever visited Lake Chilka? Nearly six kilometres west of the lake there is a village named Banpur. It is my village and the birth-place of the late Pandit Godavaris Misra, a well-known poet and leader of Orissa. It is famous for the Bhagabati Temple. The Salia flows south of Banpur. It is a big village with a few big buildings and a large number of thatched houses. We have a police-station, a post-office, three high schools and a college here. At the centre of the village there is a busy marketplace. It is slowly growing into a town. I shall always try to keep up the good name of my village.

MY VILLAGE SHOP

We have a small shop in the middle of our village. The shop opens early in the morning and closes late in the evening. I run to it for biscuits and chocolates when I have a little money. It is a noisy place. Men, women and children gather at the shop to buy rice, pulses, sugar, tea, kerosene, matchboxes and many other useful things. The articles are collected from the village market or nearby towns. They are kept in tins, 'bags and earthen pots. The shopkeeper sits at the door and sells his goods. He uses scales, weights and measures. The villagers trust him.

OUR VILLAGE LIBRARY

We have a small library in our village. There are about one thousand books in it. Except a few English books, all the books in the library are in Odia. Most of them are sets of the Ramayana, the Mahabharata and other holy books. The villagers are very fond of reading these books. We get some newspapers and magazines for our library reading room. After their hard work the villagers gather there in the evening to read books and newspapers. Each villager pays one rupee a month for the library. The government also pay five hundred rupees every year for new books. I work as the librarian to lend books to the villagers and to collect them.

MY HOME TOWN

I live in Cuttack. This town lies between the rivers Mahanadi and Kathjori. There are over four lakhs of people in the town. It is one of the oldest towns and for a long time it was the capital of Odisha. King Markat Kesari built the Kathjori stone embankment and King Anangabhima Dev built the famous Barabati Fort here. Only part of its gateway is left now. The beautiful stadium near the fort is known as the Barabati Stadium. Cuttack is a centre of business. You can see the Odisha High Court, many schools, colleges and hospitals in this town. When I grow up, I shall study in the Ravenshaw College.

OUR SCHOOL

I am a student of Manjupur M.E. School. It stands at the foot of a small hill. We have made a beautiful garden in front of our school. Our playground is behind the school. We play different games there. The school has four classes with nearly two hundred students. There are five teachers and one peon in the school. All our teachers are kind and good. We all love and respect them. We shall always try to keep up the good name of our school.

OUR CLASSROOM

I am in class seven. There are thirty-five boys and ten girls in my class. We sit in front of our teacher. The teacher writes on the blackboard. We begin our work every day after roll-call. Our teachers teach us different subjects in different periods. On the walls of our classroom we have pictures of Mahatma Gandhi, Pandit Nehru, Pandit Gopabandhu and some other great men of our country. The class time-table hangs on the wall on one side. We choose our monitor at the beginning of the year. I am the class monitor this year.

OUR HEADMASTER

Shri K.C. Das is the Headmaster of our school. He is strict with his pupils but very kind. He loves them all as his own children. He is never late and is always busy with school work. He teaches us English. We enjoy his lessons. Sometimes he visits the classes and guides the teachers. We have the highest respect for our Headmaster. Our Headmaster loves to watch our games. We are really proud of him.

OUR CLASS TEACHER

Shrimati S. Mohanty is our class teacher. She is never late for school and never allows us to come late. In the first period, she calls over our rolls and teaches us Arithmetic. Our class teacher receives fees on the days of collection. She forwards our applications for leave to the Headmaster. She looks after our class discipline. She is one of the best teachers of mathematics in our school. In picnics and excursions we always have our class teacher with us. She often visits our homes and tells our parents all about our conduct and progress. She is a good friend and guide to us.

OUR SCHOOL PEON

Everyone in our school knows Narahari very well. He is our school peon. He is always in his khaki uniform. Narahari is the first man to come to the school every day. He sweeps the office room and classrooms clean and keeps the attendance registers ready for the roll-call. He rings the bell and locks the rooms when school is over. He carries chalk, dusters, maps and registers to different classes. Narahari has been working in the school for thirty years. His salary is small, but he has always a smile on his lips. We all love him dearly for his honesty and good behaviour.

A PICNIC

Last Sunday the students of our class had a picnic at Naraj. It is about twenty kilometres from Cuttack. Here the Kathjori flows away from the Mahanadi. We went there by boat and reached the place at about 10 a.m. We had taken rice and vegetables with us and got plenty of fish there. Our cook selected a nice spot near the water to do the cookings. We collected firewood from the hillside and helped him to make the fire. Some of us went up the hill to see the caves and the others played cards or sang songs. When food was ready, we sat in a circle and ate it from banana leaves. We came back to Cuttack late in the evening in a cheerful mood.

THE SPORTS DAY IN OUR SCHOOL

Our Annual Sports Day was held on the 20th of January this year. The sports began at 10 a.m. Many students of the school joined the sports. There were a large number of visitors in the school grounds to see the sports. The high jump, the long jump and the bicycle race were very interesting. It was great fun to watch the arithmetic race and the music chair competition. At the end there was a tug-of-war between the teachers and the visitors. In the evening the Inspector of Schools, Mr. Misra, gave away the prizes to the winners. One of the boys of our class got the championship shield. We clapped our hands and danced for joy.

PRIZE-GIVING CEREMONY

The Annual Prize-giving Ceremony is a great day in our school life. It was held on the 7th of January this year. Many men and women were invited to the ceremony. When the chief guest took his seat, one of the students garlanded him. After the opening song our Headmaster read out the Annual Report of the school. Then the chief guest made a fine speech. After the speech the Headmaster called out the names of the prizewinners. Each of them bowed before the chief guest and received a prize from his hands. At the end of the ceremony the students presented a variety show of dance, music and recitation. The ceremony closed with the singing of the national anthem.

CHILDREN'S DAY

The 14th of November is the birthday of our late Prime Minister Jawaharlal Nehru. He loved children very dearly. So we observe this day as Children's Day all over India. On this day we have no lessons at all. We have a busy programme of speeches, music, dance and games till the evening.

Nehru's photo is placed on a platform in the school hall and decorated with flowers and green leaves. In this hall we hold a meeting of students and teachers and make speeches on the life and work of our great leader. We also hold an exhibition showing Nehru's life in pictures. Parents and other important people are invited to spend the day with us. At the end sweets are distributed to the school children.

TEACHERS' DAY

Dr S. Radhakrishnan, the late President of India, was born on the 5th of September, 1888. He was a learned man and a great teacher. He had high respect for all teachers. So his birthday is observed as "Teachers' Day" all over India. On this day we invite all our teachers to a meeting at the school and honour them. Our parents join us in showing respect to them. They speak highly of the great service of teachers to the nation. We collect some money for Teachers' Welfare Fund and send it to the government. It is a day when we remember our duties to teachers. We should always be grateful to them because they build our lives.

INDEPENDENCE DAY

The 15th of August, 1947, is a great day in our history. On this day India got her freedom. So the day is observed as Independence Day all over the country. On this day schools, colleges and offices are closed. The national flag waves everywhere. Streets and buildings are decorated with chains of green leaves and flowers. Early in the morning children come out in a procession carrying national flags and shouting slogans. In our school our Headmaster hoists the national flag and we sing the national anthem. In a meeting teachers and students pay their respect to the Father of the Nation and other great fighters for freedom. We shall follow the noble examples of these great men.

SARASWATI PUJA IN SCHOOL

Saraswati is the goddess of learning. So she is worshipped in schools. On the day of the Puja, children come to their schools in their best clothes. They decorate the school building with green leaves and coloured paper. The image of Saraswati is placed on a platform covered with flowers. The children place their books, pens and slates at the feet of the image. The priest performs the puja. At the end of the puja the children offer flowers to the goddess and pray for their success in examinations. They finish the day with feasting and merrymaking. Next day the image is taken out in a procession and put into the water in a river or canal.

THE PEASANT

The peasant lives with his family in his small thatched cottage. He keeps his cows and bullocks in a shed. His plough, cart and tools are his wealth. All the men, women and children of his family work hard. When the rains come, he ploughs his fields and sows seeds. He waters his fields, weeds them out and takes care of the plots. In winter the corn becomes ripe and is ready for harvest. He cuts the grain and carries it home on his cart. His family live on plain food and wear plain clothes but they feed us all. He is our best friend.

THE POSTMAN

We know the postman by his khaki dress and bag. He goes from door to door to deliver letters, parcels, money orders and telegrams. He has very difficult work to do. He is not afraid of bad weather when he is out on duty. Sometimes he brings us bad news, but he has always a gentle smile on his lips. Some people in villages do not know how to read and write. The postman reads out their letters or writes a few lines for them. To the children the postman is an interesting fellow. He gives them used stamps. His service is great, but his salary is small.

THE POLICEMAN

The policeman has khaki dress on his body and a turban on his head. He wears a thick leather belt and carries a heavy stick. He looks very smart in his uniform. Thieves and robbers run away at the sight of a policeman. Motor cars and bicycles stop at once when he holds up his hand. He can quiet a whole crowd by raising his stick. He keeps us and our houses safe. He never allows anyone to break the law. Sometimes he puts his own life in danger to save our lives. Every policeman should be honest and dutiful. We should help him with his work.

THE SUN

The sun shines in the sky. It rises in the east and sets in the west. It gives us light and heat. Imagine what would happen without sunlight. Nothing could live on our earth. There would be night all the time and it would be very cold. The rays of the sun are hotter in summer than in winter. On winter mornings we like to sit in the sun and warm ourselves. Sunlight kills germs and makes us safe from diseases. So many people worship the sun as a god. The famous Konark Temple was built for the Sun god.

THE TIGER

The tiger is a wild animal. It is very cruel. It is really a big cat. Its fur is yellow marked with black stripes. Like cats tigers hunt at night. They kill deer, cows, sheep and goats and men too. Hunters kill them with guns. Tiger cubs are caught and put into cages. They are kept in the zoo and in circus parties. The tiger is our national animal.

THE MONKEY

The monkey looks like a man. But it has a tail and it uses its fore legs as we use our hands. Monkeys are tree-animals. They live most of the time in trees and jump from tree to tree. We see two kinds of monkeys in our country, the black-faced langur and the red faced ape. They eat nuts, berries and fruit. They often steal fruit from our gardens. They make a mouth at children when the children throw stones at them. They are fond of copying what they see. So tamed monkeys are taught a few tricks. They can earn money for their masters by showing their tricks.

THE BANANA

It is a large plant without branches. It has very large leaves at the top and long roots in the ground. The trunk of the plant is soft. Each plant bears only one bunch of fruit called bananas. Ripe bananas are very sweet. They are sold in plenty. Plantains are like bananas, but green plantains are cooked as a vegetable. Sometimes we eat from banana leaves. People in Odisha make toy boats with the bark of the plant and float them on the full moon day of Kartik.

RICE

Rice is a kind of tall grass. It needs rich soil and plenty of water. It is planted in the mud under the water. When the plants grow up they rise above the water and the field looks green and beautiful. The corn of the plant becomes ripe in about five months from the time of sowing the seed. The farmer harvests the corn in winter. He binds it in bundles and carries them home in his cart. When the husk is taken off the grain, we get rice.—It is boiled and eaten with dal and curry. Rice is the chief food in Odisha, West Bengal, Andhra Pradesh and Tamil Nadu.

THE BICYCLE

Every schoolboy now wants to have a bicycle. It is cheap and easy to drive. It can carry one or two persons. The bicycle has two wheels with rims, spokes and rubber tyres. The front wheel is fixed to the fork. When the rider turns the pedals, the back wheel moves and pushes the front wheel. He sits on a saddle made of leather. There is a bell fixed to the handle bars and the rider rings it to warn off the people on the road. It is a pleasure to go down a slope on the bicycle. If you are a careless rider, you will meet with accidents and break your head.

A PEN

A pen is a small but very useful thing. Fountain pens and ball points are very common now. In earlier days quill-pens made from birds' feathers were dipped in ink and used for writing. When there was no paper, people in our country used steel pens on palm leaves. People who know how to read and write always carry a pen with them. We need it at home, in the classroom, at the post office, at the bank—everywhere. Without pens we cannot write our letters, writers and poets cannot write their stories and poems for us. Great books have come from the pens of great men and women and changed people's ideas. So we say "The pen is mightier than the sword."

"I often quote myself. It adds spice to my conversation."

– George Bernard Shaw

CHAPTER 6

INTERACTIVE STORIES

Interactive story is a story with full of questions. Two students take part in the story-telling and listening process. One student reads the story aloud with all the questions and the other student answers the questions. The answers can be any imaginary ones which do not change the plot of the story.

The interesting point is that each interactive story is based on one grammar item. The students taking part in the interactive story sessions learn the uses of that particular grammar item.

WORKING WITH INTERACTIVE STORIES

⇨ Get the students to read it to each other like this:

Student A	:	There was a man. He went into a cafe.
Student B	:	Uh-huh.
Student A	:	Was it crowded?
Student B	:	Yes, it was.

⇨ The class can read the text silently to themselves, underlining the target grammar items and their uses.

⇨ The class can (in pairs or groups) try to re-tell the story to each other from memory.

⇨ The class can re-write the story from memory by modifying it and elaborating on it.

⇨ The class can discuss aspects of the story and issues that come up; what they would do in that situation, whether they like a particular character.

⇨ It is very important to develop stories using one grammar item or a particular sentence structure.

Some Sample Interactive Stories

1. THE GRAVEYARD ("be" verbs)

It is a Sunday afternoon in the countryside. Is it hot? A small boy is in a rice field. He is ten years old. When is his birthday? He walks up a hill. Is it a big hill? He goes into a graveyard. Is it an old graveyard? He sees his father's gravestone. What colour is it? He sits down in front of the gravestone. Is he sad?

Suddenly the small boy hears a sound. Is it loud? The boy turns around. He sees a man. Is he tall? The man has very short hair. He has handcuffs on his wrists. The man grabs the boy. Is the boy afraid? The man turns the boy upside down. He shakes him.

There is a rice ball in the boy's pocket. Is it round or triangular? Is it very big? The rice ball falls out. The man picks up the rice ball. He eats it. Is it tasty? He eats very quickly because he is very, very hungry. The boy feels sorry for the hungry man. The man asks for food. He asks for some tools too. He wants to take the handcuffs off.

The boy goes to get food. The man sleeps on the hill behind a tree near the graveyard. Is he very tired? Is he afraid of ghosts?

Two hours later the boy comes back. He has some bread. Is it fresh? He also has some cooked rice. Is it hot? Is it in a bag? He has some fruit too. What kind of fruit is it? He has a bottle of sake too. Is it expensive sake? He has some tools too. What tools are they?

The man is very grateful. He eats the food. He takes the handcuffs off. He runs away.

Two days later the boy is in the rice fields again. Is it a warm day? The boy hears a sound. It is a police siren. A police car comes. What colour is it? Four policemen get out. Are they young or old? They run up the hill. They catch the man. They put handcuffs on him. They put him in the car. The car drives away. Is it fast? The small boy watches the car. He thinks about the man. He feels sorry for the man.

The man is an escaped prisoner. The police take him back to prison. Are the police nice to him? The man is from a poor family. He lives in prison now. Where is the prison? Is it a big prison?

The boy lives with his aunt and his uncle. His father is dead and his mother is dead too. Is he lonely? He lives in an old house in a village. Is it a big house? Is it a traditional Japanese farmhouse?

The boy likes school. Is his school far from his house? What is the name of his favourite teacher? The boy wants to go to university. Is university expensive? The boy wants to go to university but he cannot go to university because his family is poor. Is his uncle a farmer?

At night the boy thinks about his father and his mother and he thinks about his school and he thinks about the escaped prisoner and he thinks about his dream. He wants to go to university. Is he happy?

2.   THE STRANGE OLD WOMAN (there is / there are)

A little boy lives in a small village with his aunt and his uncle. His parents are dead. How many houses are there in the village? The little boy's family is poor. He helps his uncle in the fields.

There is a beautiful little girl in the village. She is about ten years old. Is her hair long? One day the little boy sees the girl. The little boy watches her. He likes her but she does not look at him.

The little boy grows up. He goes to high school and he sees the little girl every day but she does not look at him. How many students are there at the boy's high school? They take the same bus each morning. How many people are there on the bus each morning? What colour is the bus?

There is a strange old woman in the village. She is very, very rich. How old is she? Is her hair white? She owns a lot of rice fields and houses too.

The young high school girl lives with the strange old woman. Her parents are dead. The boy's parents are dead and the girl's parents are dead too. Every day after school, the girl goes home. She talks to the old woman. The old woman talks to the girl but she does not talk to other people. She stays inside the house.

One day a letter comes to the boy's house. It is from the rich old woman. It is an invitation. It is an invitation to the house. The boy wants to meet the girl. The next day he puts on clean clothes. He goes to the house. He walks. It is a big house on a hill outside the village. Is it a beautiful house? There is a big wall around the house. The boy goes to the gate. He rings a bell. The girl comes to the gate. She opens it. He goes inside. The girl says, "Kiss me". The boy kisses her on the cheek. Is her cheek soft? The girl says, "Follow me". The boy follows her. They go inside. The house is huge. How many rooms are there in the house? Is it a three-storey house?

The boy and the girl go upstairs. They meet a man on the stairs. He is a strange man. He has a big red nose. He says "Aaah, very good, very good!" and he nods his head. Is there any hair on his head?

The boy goes into a room. He meets the strange old woman. The old woman lives in a big bedroom. The room is a bedroom. It is very dirty. There is a cake on the table. It is very old. The woman is very thin and she has a strange high voice. She says, "Play cards". The boy and the girl sit on the floor and they play cards. Are there pictures on the cards? The old woman watches. After thirty minutes the old woman says "Enough!" She puts some money in the boy's pocket. She says, "Come back next week." The girl takes the boy to the gate. She does not say "goodbye". The boy goes home. How much money is there in his pocket?

3. THE LETTER FROM A STRANGER (present simple)

A high school boy lives in a village. Every week he goes to a big house on a hill outside the village. A strange old rich woman lives in the village. A beautiful young girl lives with her. The boy plays with the girl. What games do they play? The old woman pays the boy each week. How much does she pay him?

The boy wants to go to university. What does he want to study? Does the girl want to go to university?

One day the boy goes to the old woman's house and the girl opens the gate. Does she say, "Hello"?

The boy goes inside and plays with the girl. After they play, the old woman says, "Today is the last day."

The girl takes the boy to the gate. She says "Am I beautiful?" The boy says, "Yes, you are!" The girl says, "You are ugly!" She slaps him.

The boy goes home. How much money is there in his pocket? Does he love the girl? Does she love him? Is he sad?

The girl goes away to another school in the city. What is the name of the school? Does it have a gym? Is there a swimming pool?

The boy does not see the girl anymore. Does he miss her? He thinks about university. He studies hard at school. What is his favourite subject at school? Does he have many friends? What sport does he play? Does he get good marks at school? How many people are there in his class? The boy wants to go to university but he cannot go because he does not have enough money. How much does it cost per year? He worries about the future.

One day a letter comes to the house. It is a letter from a stranger. The letter says the boy can go to university. It will cost nothing. A rich man will help him. The boy is surprised. Is he happy?

One year later the boy moves to the city. He moves into a small apartment. How many rooms are there in his apartment? Is there a unit bath? Does it have a kitchen?

The man with the big red nose comes to the boy's apartment. He is a lawyer. He tells the boy to come to his office each month. Each month the boy comes and the man with the red nose gives him money. How much does he give him per month? How much is the rent for the apartment? The boy goes to university every weekday. How many classes does he have per week? What course does he do? Does he join a circle? Does he have a part-time job?

One day the boy takes the bus to university. He sees a girl on the bus. It is the beautiful girl from his village. He remembers her and he still thinks about her a lot. Does she remember him? He says "Hello" to her but she does not answer him. She ignores him.

4.   THE ATTACK IN THE PARK (present perfect)

A young guy is a university student. What faculty is he in? Is he a first year student? His parents are dead and he comes from a poor family but he can go to university because a stranger pays his tuition and his living expenses. How much is his tuition per year? How much are his living expenses? Is there a soccer team at his university?

The young guy does not know the stranger. He has never met him. It is exam time. How many tests does the guy have? Is he nervous? He goes to see a lawyer with a big red nose. The lawyer gives him money every month. The money is from a stranger. The young student has never met the stranger. Has he had a letter from him?

There is a girl at the same university. She is from the same village. The young guy is in love with her but she always ignores him. The young guy has a friend. It is another student. The friend is a guy in the same faculty. The young guy tells his friend about the girl. How long has he known his friend? How long has he known the girl? Has his friend ever seen the girl? Has he ever talked to her? Does he like her?

One night the guy is walking home. He walks through a park. Has he ever walked through that park before? He sees a man and a woman. The man attacks the woman. The woman screams. It is the same woman. It is the beautiful girl from the young guy's village. He wants to help her. He wants to save her. He shouts at the man. He hits him. The man stops. He runs away. The girl cries. The young student takes her to a coffee shop. Has he ever been to that coffee shop before? Has the girl ever been there before? What do they order? The two students sit in the coffee shop for a long time. They talk about their village. They talk about the strange old woman. They talk about the lawyer with the big red nose. The young woman gives the young guy her phone number. She has beautiful long hair. The guy holds her hand. Has he ever held a woman's hand before? After several hours they both go home.

The next day the guy calls the girl but there is no answer. He calls her ten times but nobody answers the phone. He goes to his friend's house. He talks to his friend. His friend has a girlfriend. How long has he known his girlfriend? How many girlfriends has he had?

The two friends study for their exams. They both want to work in another country. They both want to get good jobs and travel and see the world. The young guy from the village has never been overseas. Which country does he want to go to? His friend has been to three countries in Asia. Which countries has he been to? Has he been to America?

The final exam period comes. The two friends sit their final exams. They both pass. They both get really high marks. The young guy from the village gets a job at a computer company.

5. THE TRANSFER (present continuous tense)

A young Japanese computer engineer is in his apartment. It is late at night. He is lying in his bed. He is thinking about his life. He is thinking about his parents. Is he thinking about his aunt and his uncle too? Does he miss his aunt and his uncle? Does he visit his village often?

The young engineer comes from a poor family but he has been to university because a rich stranger helped him. He has never met the stranger. The next day he goes to see a lawyer. The lawyer works for the rich stranger. The lawyer is sitting at his desk. He is reading something. What is he reading? Is he wearing a suit? What is on his desk?

The young guy comes in and he sits down. He has known the lawyer for five years. He has asked him about the rich stranger many times but the lawyer has never answered his questions. He asks him again. The lawyer will not answer.

That weekend the young guy goes back to his village. He visits his aunt and his uncle. Are they still living in the same house? What is the uncle doing when he arrives? What is the aunt doing? There is a strange old lady in the village. The young man thinks the old lady is giving him money. He goes to her house. He knocks on the door. A beautiful girl answers. What is she wearing? Is she wearing a hat? The guy has not seen the girl for two years. He still remembers her. He still loves her. He does not want to love her but he does. He cannot stop his feelings.

The young woman takes the young man to see the old lady. She is sitting in the same room. She is sitting in the same chair. She is wearing the same dirty old white dress. She is reading something. What is she reading? Has she read it before? Are there many books in the room?

The young engineer says, "You are giving me money. I know. Thank you, but I don't need money now. I have a good job. I want to pay you back." The old lady laughs. She says, "I have never given you any money."

The young guy is confused. He wants to know who is giving him money. He goes to work on Monday. The boss telephones him. He goes to his boss's office. The boss is sitting in a big leather chair. Is he wearing a suit? Is he wearing a tie? Is he smiling?

The company has a branch in New York City. There are some problems in New York. The young guy has to go to New York. He has to live there and work there for two years. Is he happy about this?

That night he telephones his uncle. What is his uncle doing when the phone rings? What is his aunt doing? He tells them about his transfer to New York. After that he goes to bed. One hour later the telephone rings. It is the beautiful girl from his village. Is he sleeping when she calls? She wants to meet him in New York.

6. THE OLD MAN (should)

An old man is in a big house in New York. He is from Japan originally. He is a criminal. He is sitting in front of the TV. He is thinking about the past. He has broken many laws. He has committed many crimes. Has he ever killed anybody? Has he ever robbed a bank? He has been in prison many times. In Japan the police are looking for him. He is not happy because he wants to go back to Japan. Should he go back to Japan? Should he turn himself in to the police? Would you turn yourself in, if you were him?

In another part of New York City, there is a young engineer. He is working for a Japanese computer company in New York. He knows the old man. The old man has helped him with his education. Should he turn the old man in? Would you turn him in?

The engineer goes to work. His boss is angry. His boss shouts at him. Should he shout back? His boss hits him. Should he hit back? Should he go to the police? He argues with his boss. His boss fires him. He leaves the office. He goes to a bar. He thinks about his life. He thinks about his boss and his job. Should he go back to the office? Would you? He thinks about the waitress from his village. Should he go to the restaurant and see her? Would you? He thinks about the bad man from the restaurant. Should he go to see him? Would you?

Suddenly the engineer's mobile phone rings. It is the old man. He wants to see the engineer. He says, "You are like my son." Should the engineer go to see him? Would you?

The engineer goes to see the old man. He meets him at his house. It is a very big old house in New Jersey. The two men talk about life. The old man tells the young man the story of his life. His mother is Korean. Can he speak Korean? His father is half Korean and half Japanese. Is discrimination a problem in Japan? Should all people be equal?

The young man talks about the beautiful waitress. He talks about the bad man at the restaurant. The old man knows about the bad man and he knows about the beautiful waitress. He says, "The waitress is married to the bad man!" The young engineer is shocked. Should he believe the old man? Would you believe him? The old man says the waitress is selfish. He says she is a bad woman. He says she wants to trick the young engineer. Should the engineer believe the old man? Would you believe him?

The young engineer leaves the old man's house. He goes back to Manhattan. He has no job and he has no girlfriend. He has no parents and a criminal has paid for his education. Should he feel bad? He has to move out of his apartment in one week. What should he do? He has to get a new job. How should he find a new job? Should he go back to Japan?

7. THE NEW JOB (comparatives)

A young engineer is in his apartment in New York. Is it big? Is it bigger than his apartment in Osaka? He looks out the window. Is the view better than the view from his apartment in Osaka? Is Osaka bigger than New York? Is Osaka more interesting than New York? How does Osaka compare to your hometown?

The young guy goes out to a shop. He buys a newspaper. He looks for a job. There are two computer jobs in the paper. One is for a big company and one is for a small company. Which one has a higher salary? Which one has better working conditions? One job is in Chicago and one job is in Boston. Which is closer, Chicago or Boston? Which is closer from Japan?

The guy calls about the two jobs. Which one does he call about first? He arranges two interviews. The interview for the job in Boston is the next day. The guy gets up early. He takes a shower and he puts on a suit. He goes to the interview. There are two interviewers. One is a young man. One is an old man. Which one is taller? Which one is nicer? Which one is handsomer? The young engineer knows one of the interviewers. He knows him from a bar. He likes the interviewer and the interviewer likes him too. He is from Boston. The guy from Boston offers the Japanese guy the job.

He has to move to Boston. Is Boston bigger than New York? Is his salary at his new job higher than his salary at his old job? Does he get more holidays? Does he get a company car? Does he get a free apartment? Does he get a moving allowance?

In his new job the Japanese guy has to travel to Japan five or six times a year. How does Japan compare to the United States?

After two months at the company in Boston, the young engineer makes a trip to Japan. He flies to Tokyo. How does Tokyo compare to Osaka? He stays in Tokyo for two weeks. One weekend he takes the Shinkansen to Osaka than he goes to his village. How does the Shinkansen compare to the local train? Has the village changed much?

The guy visits his aunt and his uncle. Has his aunt changed much? Has his uncle changed much? The guy talks about living in Japan and living in America. How does living in America compare to living in Japan? How does living in the city compare to living in the countryside?

The guy drinks beer with his uncle and then he takes a bath and he goes to bed. The next day he reads the paper. A famous Japanese criminal has turned himself in New York. The engineer looks at the photo of the man. He knows the man. It is the rich stranger from his past. The old man wants to die in Japan. The next day the young engineer goes back to Tokyo then he flies to Boston a week later.

8. AUSTRALIA (superlative)

It's midday in Australia and it is extremely hot. A young Japanese student is working on a mango farm. He is picking mangoes. How much does he earn per hour? How many mangoes can he pick in one hour? Is it a hard job? What is the hardest job he has ever had?

A plane lands in Darwin. Is Darwin the hottest city in Australia? Is it the most humid city in Australia? What is the largest city in Australia? Three Japanese students and a Swiss woman are on the plane. They're travelling south. Who is the oldest? Who is the youngest? Who is the most fun? Who is the most easy-going?

The four friends check into a backpacker hostel in Darwin. Is it the dirtiest hostel in Darwin? Is it the cheapest? Is it the most interesting? How much is a bed for the night?

The four friends meet the fifth member of their group. His name is Yuichi. He has run out of money and he is working at a mango farm. They all have a big drinking party. Who can drink the most? Who can drink the least? Who talks the most? Who talks the least? Does the Swiss woman feel left out? Has she been to Australia before? Is she trying to learn Japanese?

The next morning the five friends have hangovers. Who has the worst hangover? Who has the biggest head-ache? Who has the worst stomach-ache?

The five friends buy a used car. It is an old camper van. The friends travel south. They have had many adventures. Who has had the most dangerous experience? Who has had the most exciting experience? Who has spent the most money? Who has learned the most? Who has met the most people? Who has met the most girls?

In Australia not many people speak Japanese. Everybody has to speak English. Of the five friends, who can speak the most English? Who speaks the least English?

The travellers stop in Katherine. They visit a crocodile farm. How big are the crocodiles? They swim in the river. They see kangaroos and wallabies and birds. Have they ever seen kangaroos before? They meet an aborigine. Is aboriginal culture the oldest culture in the world? The aborigine plays the didgeridoo. Have the friends ever heard a didgeridoo before?

That night the travellers go to a party in the campground. There are lots of other tourists there. They see aborigines dance and play didgeridoos. There are four of them. Their names are Wally, Ernie, Ben and Mick. Which one is the best didge player? Which one is the tallest? Which one is the oldest? Which one is the youngest? Which one is the best-looking?

The next day the five travellers get up early. They drive to the Three Ways then they turn east. They travel for two days. They see a herd of wild horses on the road. There are about two hundred of them.

Finally they reach the east coast. Is Australia the largest country in the world? Is it the oldest? Is it the most peaceful? Is it the safest? Is it one of the most dangerous? Is it the most racist? Is it the most stable? Is it the coldest? Is it the wettest? Is it the hottest? Is it the driest?

9. RETURN TO ANDES CITY (relative clauses; who, which, that)

The year is 2018. A young Japanese Andean couple is sitting on the front veranda of their house on a hill above Andes city. They are looking at the harbour below. There are three ships in the harbour. One of them has come from China, one of them has come from Bolivia and one of them has come from Colorado. Is the one that has come from Colorado American? Is the one, which has come from China American? Where is the one that has come from Bolivia from? What kind of ships are they?

The young couple grow their own rice and vegetables. They also catch fish. Do they sell the fish that they catch in the market? They have a flock of sheep too. Do they sell the wool that the sheep grow? Do they kill the sheep and sell the meat too? Do they sell the rice that they grow?

The young couple has two children. They are both boys. One of them is the son of a pirate king. The other one is the son of the young man. The two boys are playing in front of the house. One of them is standing up and one of them is sitting down. Is the one who is standing up the son of the pirate king? Is the one who is sitting down the son of the pirate king?

That afternoon some of the couple's friends come to their house for a barbecue. They cook roast mutton. Is the meat that they cook from one of their own sheep? They eat the meat with rice. Is the rice that they eat from their own fields? Some of the friends who come to the house are ex-marines. The young man talks to one of his friends. Is the friend who he talks to an ex-marine?

The woman is pregnant with her third child. Does she think about the pirate king sometimes? Is the child that she is carrying the child of the pirate king?

One of the couple's sons comes up to the young man. He listens to the man talk to his friend. He wants to go to another country. He wants to meet people who speak other languages and think different thoughts.

The young man and his friend laugh. Andes City is small and quiet and peaceful. It is a good place to live. They do not want to leave.

The boy who wants to travel is the son of the pirate king. He lives with the Japanese Andean couple but his real father is a Chinese Malay pirate king, who is friends with the president of the US. Does he want to meet his biological father? The boy goes into the house. He sees his mother. He talks to her. What language do they speak? He says that he wants to go overseas. He says that he wants to go to Japan. The woman looks at him. She remembers her life. She remembers the trip to China and her kidnapping. She remembers the pirate king and life at the Bangkok Water Tower. Does she still want to go to Japan? Is she satisfied with her life? Would you be?

10. YAMASHITA'S GOLD (past simple tense)

When did World War two start? When did it finish? Who fought alongside the Japanese? Who fought against the Japanese? Which countries did Japan invade?

The Imperial Japanese army took treasure from Korea, China, French Indo-China, Thailand, British Burma and Malaya and also Singapore. They put all the treasure in ships and sent it back to Japan but the ships never reached Japan. The treasure went missing. It has been missing since the end of World War Two. How long has it been missing? The man in charge of the treasure ships was General YamaShita. He is dead now and his treasure is lost.

Some people say the treasure is in caves in the mountains. Some people say it is hidden in tunnels. Some say Ferdinand Marcos found it and now it is in a bank account in Switzerland. Who was Marcos? Would you live in Switzerland? Some say it is in sunken ships at the bottom of the sea. Is finding treasure at the bottom of the sea difficult?

The castaway from the Imperial Japanese Army says he saw the ships sink. How many ships were there? How many tons of gold were there on the ships? Were there any Ming Dynasty vases on the ships? When did the castaway first come to this island? What branch of the military was he in? What was his rank? Did he serve in China? Did he serve in any other Asian countries? When did America invade Japan? Where are the American bases in Japan now? Should YamaShita's gold belong to the finder or the original owner? Should Hitler's treasure belong to the original owners?

"If you think that grammar is an exact science, get ready for a shock. Grammar is a science, all right, but it is the most inexact. There are no inflexible laws, no absolutely hard and fast rules, and no unchanging principles. Correctness varies with the times.

Grammar follows the speech habits of the majority of educated people— not the other way around."

- Norman Lewis

CHAPTER 7

Micro-Presentation

Micro-Presentation is a group presentation (usually by three members) and it is a micro or short presentation. Normally it has three parts:
1. Introduction,
2. Body and
3. Conclusion.

Presentation Process

1. Introduction:
The introductory part should also include the thesis statement, a kind of mini-outline for the presentation. This is where the speaker grabs the listeners' attention. It tells the listener what the topic or motion is about. The last sentence of the introduction must also include a transitional "hook" which moves the listener to the second speaker and also to the body of the presentation.

2. Body:
This part should include the strongest argument, most significant example, cleverest illustration, or an obvious beginning point. The subject for this part should be in the first or second sentence. This subject should relate to the thesis statement in the introduction. The last sentence in this part should include a transition that signals the listener that this is the final major point being made in the presentation.

3. Conclusion:
This part is the summary part. It is important to restate the thesis and the supporting idea in an original and powerful way as this is the last chance

the speaker has to convince the listener of the validity of the information presented.

A sample Micro-Presentation

Discrimination in Indian Society

Good morning everybody. I'm Lisa with my friends Ashok and Shree. Our topic is "Discrimination in Indian Society". Let me start the topic on behalf of my group.

Introduction: I saw an old peasant who was discriminated against by a salesman when he went to buy a watch at a supermarket in Cuttack two years ago. At first, the old peasant told the salesman that he wanted to buy a watch for his son's birthday. Then the peasant chose one and wanted the salesman to bring it to him, but the salesman refused him roughly. The salesman said, "Don't touch that watch. It's for the other people, not for you. You are a poor peasant and can never afford it! Move away from here!" The peasant was very angry. His face turned red, and his teeth were trembling. He wanted to say something to the salesman, but finally, he walked out from there. Now it is over to my friend Ashok

Body: Thank you Lisa. This situation is caused by several things. One reason why this happened was the different situation between the poor person and the rich person. The rich person always feels condescending and elitist. The rich think that they are cleverer than the poor; therefore, they can earn lots of money and the peasant always is poor. Another cause of this event was that the salesman knew that the peasant's social status was lower. He did not act tolerant because of this. The third cause of this situation was the salesman knew that no one would stand up and help the poor peasant; therefore, the salesman dared to discriminate against the poor peasant. Now let's listen to my friend Shree.

Conclusion: Thank you Ashok. This event teaches us that financial and social elitism lead to discrimination against the poor and lower classes. It also shows that when our fellow humans do not defend each other in this kind of situation, we are allowing discrimination to exist. We must learn to treat each other fairly, and to defend each other against injustice. That's all about our presentation. Many thanks for listening us with so much patience.

MICRO-PRESENTATION TOPICS

⇨ Corruption in India
⇨ AIDS test should be made compulsory.
⇨ Beauty Contests
⇨ T.V. Addiction
⇨ Be Indian and buy Indian.
⇨ Effect of Cinema on Youth
⇨ Dreams can happen.
⇨ Life after Death
⇨ Marriage is a social trap.
⇨ The Decaying Indian Culture
⇨ One Man, One Tree
⇨ Should we celebrate Valentine's Day?
⇨ Students and Politics
⇨ Retirement Age for Politicians
⇨ Adding C to 3R's
⇨ Joint Family System
⇨ Sex Education
⇨ FDI
⇨ Globalisation
⇨ Gay Marriage
⇨ Social Networking - Boon or Bane
⇨ Teasing in College
⇨ Smoking in Public Places
⇨ The Future of Sports in India
⇨ The 2G Scam
⇨ The Mahtma
⇨ The Definition of Success

"Recording at home enables one to eliminate the demo stage, and the presentation stage in the studio, too."

– Warren Zevon

CHAPTER 8

ROLE PLAY

Role Play means an activity in which participants act out characters in a predefined "situation". In the context of Spoken English, role-play is any speaking activity when you either put yourself into somebody else's shoes, or when you stay in your own shoes but put yourself into an imaginary situation!

TIPS ON CLASSROOM ROLE PLAY

The Role of the Teacher:
1. Facilitator—students may need new language to be 'fed' in by the teacher. If rehearsal time is appropriate the feeding in of new language should take place at this stage.
2. Spectator—The teacher watches the role-play and offers comments and advice at the end.
3. Participant—It is sometimes appropriate to get involved and take part in the role-play yourself.
4. Trainer—The teacher can train the students on varieties of skills and concepts through role-play. English grammar can be taught as well.

Error Correction:
1. Self-correction—If you have the equipment to record the role-plays students can be given the opportunity to listen to the dialogue again and may find it easy to spot their own mistakes.
2. Peer-correction—Fellow students may be able to correct some mistakes made by their peers.

3. The teacher should make a note of common mistakes and deal with them in future classes. It ensures that the students don't lose motivation by being corrected on the spot or straight after the role play.

SOME SAMPLE ROLE-PLAYING SITUATIONS

- A doctor and the Mr. Know-All-Patient
- Two friends meeting after a long gap in a railway journey
- Two friend discussing about their future plans
- Brother and sister quarreling over using a computer
- An arrogant son asking for a bike to his poor father
- A disobedient student seeking guidance from his/her teacher just before the exams.
- The buyer and the seller and the hard bargaining
- The traffic police and the stranger asking for help
- The poor husband and the wife demanding a costly jewelry
- The husband and the wife arranging their 10th Marriage Anniversary
- The corrupt police and the thief trying to bribe
- The mother-in-law interviewing the prospective daughter-in-law.
- Two neighbours quarreling over a dog
- The interviewer and the candidate
- The advocate and the false witness
- The receptionist and the student seeking admission into a new course
- The politician and the journalist taking the former's interview
- Friends planning an excursion
- Two strangers sharing about their past
- Two riders blaming each other after the accident
- Two students discussing about the performance of their teacher (positive and negative)
- Two pets discussing about their masters
- Teaching your favourite concept (solo)
- Two friends opposing each other's view about a particular cinema.

TELEPHONIC ROLE PLAY:

- Place two chairs back to back at the front of the classroom.
- Let the students come up to these chairs to perform unprepared Role Plays.

- While each pair is performing, the other pairs should prepare for their Role Play.
- Now, ask the first pair to select the next pair.
- Have these next two students come to the front of the room and repeat the process.

Here there are some telephonic role-playing situations for the students.

- A: You are calling your friend Ravi. You want to invite him to a party this Friday.
  B: You answer the phone. The person on the other end of the line wants to speak to Ravi. You don't know anyone named Ravi.
- A: You want to reserve a table for five at a restaurant called the Hunger. Call the restaurant and make a reservation for 8:00 this Saturday.
  B: You work at a restaurant called the Hunger. Answer the phone. (The restaurant is completely booked for Friday and Saturday nights this week.)
- A: You need to make a doctor's appointment because you hurt your back while you were cleaning the house. Call the doctor's office and make the appointment.
  B: You work in a pediatrician's office answering the phones.
- A: Your friend just borrowed your car to go get some more beer. Call him (on his cell phone) to remind him to get some chips and salad.
  B: You borrowed your friend's car to buy more beer. You have just driven into a lamppost. You're not hurt, but the car is badly damaged. Your cell phone rings.
- A: You're on vacation with your friend in Goa. You have just spent all your money. Your friend is upstairs in the hotel room. Call your friend and ask to borrow Rs. 60/-.
  B: You're asleep in your Goa hotel room. Your friend is still downstairs in the casino. It's four o'clock in the morning. The phone rings.
- A: Call your girlfriend/boyfriend to let them know that you'll be home very late because you have to work.
  B: Your girlfriend/ boyfriend always stays out late. You suspect that she/ he is having an affair outside. The phone rings.
- A: You promised your mother that you would water her plants while she was away on vacation. You forgot. The plants are dead. The phone rings.
  B: You are away on vacation in San Francisco. You have a lot of beautiful plants. Call your son/ daughter to find out how your plants are doing.

- A: You have not finished writing your English essay. Call your teacher and ask if you can turn it in late.
  B: You are an English teacher. The phone rings. It's one of your students.
- A: You live in an old flat. Things break all the time. This time, your toilet is flooding the bathroom. Call your landlady and demand that she fix it.
  B: You own a beautiful old apartment building. You have one tenant who is always calling you to complain. The phone rings.

MORE ROLE PLAYING SITUATIONS

- You lend a friend one of your books. She returns it with pages missing.
- Your friend always asks to borrow a few dollars when you go out, but he never repays you. You begin to resent that he does this all the time.
- A relative calls you late at night just to talk. You are tired and have to get up early in the morning.
- Your friend comes to you with a problem you don't know how to handle. You know your friend has a counselor that she likes and you recommend that she talk to them, but your friend keeps asking you what she should do.
- Your doctor prescribes a medicine but doesn't tell you what it is for or if there are any side effects.
- You are eating lunch and the person next to you smokes throughout the meal; this really bothers you.
- You went to a party with some people but the person who was driving had too much to drink and refuses to let anyone else drive.
- You are walking home with a friend and realize it is getting late. A car pulls up and asks if you want a ride. Your friend is tired and wants to take the ride but you think it's too risky.
- Someone in the van you are riding in decides to sing and does so for 15 minutes. It begins to get on your nerves and you politely ask her to stop, but she doesn't.
- The new shoes you bought three weeks ago are already starting to fall apart. You take them back to the store where you bought them.
- You bring your car to a garage for service. You ask the mechanic to call and let you know how much it will cost before doing the work. He doesn't call and when you call him he tells you he has already done the work and your bill is Rs. 250/-.

- A counselor at the school you want to attend is interviewing you. The counselor notices that you haven't worked or taken any special courses for the last two summers and asks why.
- Someone in your class asks you to work with him on his homework after the teacher has specifically told the class that the assignment should
- You are being interviewed for a job in a new field and the director asks, "Why should I hire you when you have no experience?"

"Sixty years ago I knew everything; now I know nothing; education is a progressive discovery of our own ignorance."

—Will Durant

CHAPTER 9

STORY BUILDING AND RETELLING

STORY BUILDING

Story building means to write a story from any given idea. The idea may come from:

❖ an overhead conversation;
❖ a 'what if' question;
❖ a newspaper article;
❖ something strange you see or hear about;
❖ a family tale;
❖ a desire to try out a style or
❖ a day dream.

Sometimes, finishing an unfinished story is also called story building. Here are some situations:

❖ a picnic party with rain and thunder-storm
❖ a day with a beggar
❖ a teacher who lost his spec
❖ a dream where you are a king
❖ a wife involved with adultery
❖ your sudden rise to the position of a film star
❖ a unique man who can talk of the future
❖ a marriage party sans celebration
❖ a child saving the life of many people
❖ your editorial letter giving you a job
❖ a strange safe from a horrible accident
❖ winning a lottery and getting richer overnight

❖ your unexpected meeting with an alien
❖ a friend winning Nobel Prize by writing a book
❖ forgetting to get down in the proper station in a railway journey

Examples of 'Finishing an Unfinished Story':

1. The clock struck eleven. Puspa looked up from the book of horror stories she was reading. It was still raining hard, flashes of lightening glowing on the windows. Suddenly there was a dark profile of a man on the window pane . . . (Continue.)
2. As Smita was going to school one morning she happened to see two well-dressed men standing under a tree on the roadside, about a hundred meters away from the school gate and they beckoned to her . . . (Continue.)
3. It has been a tiring day and I was looking forward to a quiet evening. My husband would not be back until late. I put my children to bed early and prepared a cold supper and some coffee. Soon I was sitting comfortably with a tray full of food before me. I was about to eat when the phone rang . . . (Continue.)
4. It was a day of hectic activities for me. Running from one office to another and from one person to the other exhausted all my strength. I boarded the evening train to go back home. It was to be a journey for 5 hours. I took my seat by the side of a window and in no time my eyes were shut . . . (Continue.)
5. The news went round that the old man was dead. His sons and daughters living at distant places gathered. They sat in an assembly to divide the dead man's property among themselves . . . (Continue.)

Answer to Story No. 1

1. The night advanced and the silence of the house deepened. Puspa's heart beat faster. The shadow of the man still lingered. She remembered all the stories of devils and ghosts she had heard in her life. She was faint with fear. A ray of light from the street lamp strayed in and cast shadows on the wall. Through the stillness all kinds of noises reached her ears—the ticking off the clock, rustle of trees, snoring sounds, and some vague night insects humming. Every moment she expected the man to break into her room. She did not know what to do. No, she must confront the situation.

Puspa tip-toed to her door-step. As soon as the man entered her room, she caught of him tightly and shouted at the top of her voice. All her family members woke up and moved towards Puspa's room and fell on the man who was a notorious house-breaker of the city.

2. Initially she turned a deaf ear to their words, but later she went to them hesitantly. All on a sudden they threw her into their car. She could not understand anything; she struggled to get rid of them, but in vain.

The two men threatened to kill her, if she shouted. But she screamed at the top of her voice. It caught the attention of the people who were passing by. They blocked the road to prevent them from going forward. The people snatched the miscreants from their vehicle and showered blows on them and rescued the girl.

STORY RETELLING

A number of popular stories can be told and retold in the class. It helps the students to shape their English and build new sentence structures. The example of a popular story is given below.

An Unusual Gift: The Telling Part

George Washington became the first President of the United States of America. On his sixth birthday his father gifted him a little axe with a wooden handle. George liked it very much. He was eager to use it.

In his excited mood, George rushed into the garden. His father had grown beautiful apple trees. George went about cutting everything that came his way, everything that seemed to have grown outsized.

At one corner of the garden, he saw a small apple tree. Somehow George wanted to cut it. He soon cut off all its branches and leaves. The tree's trunk tilted downwards as if dead.

In the evening when his father went into the garden for a stroll, he was surprised to see the small apple tree lying on the ground. He was very annoyed and shouted aloud: "George! Who has done this?" George remained silent for a while. Then an inner voice began troubling him; George couldn't fight it any longer. With tears in his eyes he said: "Father, I was sorely tempted to use the axe you gifted me, so I went about chopping almost everything that I thought worth cutting. This is what I did to the small apple tree. I am sorry."

With much love, his father took him into his arms, kissed him and said, "I am glad you told me the truth. You didn't give in to the temptation to lie. I'd rather lose all the trees in my garden than hear my son tell a lie and so become a prey to temptation."

Moral: Honesty is the best policy.

An Unusual Gift: The Retelling Part

A story which is already told by a student can be retold by another student using his own language and style. It helps the students to be instant communicators.

The previous story can be retold in the following way:

The first President of the United States of America was George Washington. He was a great man. Here we go with a story of George's childhood. He was gifted a little axe by his father on his sixth birthday. George was happy to find such a gift and became ready to use it. So he cut off the branches of a particular apple tree in the garden which his father had grown.

In the evening George's father saw the tree on the ground and asked him about the incident. George was nervous to tell the truth at first. But finally he told the truth. His father was not angry after listening the piece of truth from George. Rather he was happy and hugged George for his honesty.

"My life is storytelling. I believe in stories, in their incredible power to keep people alive, to keep the living alive, and the dead."

– Tim O'Brien

CHAPTER 10

DEBATING

THE DEBATING PROCESS

a. The moderator(s) and the debaters are seated at the front of the audience usually with the team in favour of the resolution to the right of the chairman and the team in opposition to the resolution to the left of the chairman.

b. The moderator briefly introduces the subject and the resolution that is to be debated. It is generally declared before one hour before the debate.

c. The debater for the topic from a particular group speaks on the Topic supporting his/her stand followed by another debater against the Topic and the process continues.

d. The Rebuttal Arguments follow each of the debater's Constructive Arguments. At this time, each debater is given the opportunity to weaken the position of his opponents by further attacking their position and by answering attacks that have been made upon his position. (No new issues may be introduced during rebuttal arguments.)

e. At the end of the debate, the chairman or the moderator makes a few concluding remarks and the debate is over.

f. Evaluation of different aspects of the debaters' performance like the content of their speech, standard of argument, appropriateness of the language, style of delivery, rebuttal, etc. is made at the end.

TIPS FOR THE DEBATERS

Debaters challenge ideas, they do not attack each other. Like other sports, fair play is critical. Regular debaters will be transferred to play on the other side later in their careers, so it does not pay to be too emotionally tied. A debater is a spokesperson for the moment for or against a motion and is not a fanatic for a cause.

During the Debate:

- ❖ Avoid the use of 'never'.
- ❖ Avoid the use of 'always'.
- ❖ Refrain from saying you are wrong.
- ❖ You can say your idea is mistaken.
- ❖ Don't disagree with obvious truths.
- ❖ Attack the idea not the person.
- ❖ Use many rather than most.
- ❖ Avoid exaggeration.
- ❖ Use 'some' rather than 'many'.
- ❖ The use of often allows for exceptions.
- ❖ The use of generally allows for exceptions.
- ❖ Quote sources and numbers.
- ❖ If it is just an opinion, admit it.
- ❖ Do not present opinion as facts.
- ❖ Smile when disagreeing.
- ❖ Stress the positive.
- ❖ You do not need to win every battle to win the war.
- ❖ Concede minor or trivial points.
- ❖ Avoid bickering, quarreling, and wrangling.
- ❖ Watch your tone of voice.
- ❖ Don't win a debate and lose a friend.
- ❖ Keep your perspective—You're just debating.

Before the Round:

- ❖ Find out the topic.
- ❖ Decide your stand whether it is better to speak for the topic or against it.
- ❖ Try to collect literature on the topic and prepare thoroughly making necessary notes.
- ❖ Find out about judges.
- ❖ Find out about the opponents.
- ❖ Find out what they ran the last time (always save pairings).
- ❖ Think of a strategy.
- ❖ Talk to a coach.

❖ Capture the table.

THREE IMPORTANT THINGS TO REMEMBER

1. **Delivery**
   a. A debater's delivery should be slower than usual. Pace your delivery based on the required flow depending on the available time and nature of the content.
   b. Speak in more complete sentences, fewer fragmentary tag lines.
   c. Give summaries about major arguments (contentions, disadvantages, etc.) as you finish with them.
   d. Better sign posting for pages of the flow, pause before moving to another major point.
   e. Watch carefully for non-verbals of agreement/disagreement or understanding/ misunderstanding.

2. **Content**
   a. Debaters are expected to cover, or respond to the major points covered by the other team in their previous speech. When a debater does not cover such points his/her speech fails to gain any mark.
   b. Give a thesis statement before presenting a major argument in order to create a context.
   c. Avoid debate jargon. Explain debate concepts in words everyone would understand
   d. Focus on major points only, not on flow specific arguments, although you must not be perceived as ignoring issues.
   e. Try and create a personal relationship with the judge—which you and the judge understand what is going on and the other team may not.

3. **Argument**
   A. How to Agree Strongly with an Opinion?
   I couldn't agree more!
   That's absolutely true!
   Absolutely!
   I agree with your point.
   I'd go along with you there.
   I'm with you on that.
   That's just what I was thinking.

That's exactly what I think.
That's a good point.
That's just how I see it.
That's exactly my opinion.

B. How to Half Agree with an Opinion?

Yes, perhaps, however . . .
Well, yes, but . . .
Yes, in a way, however . . .
Hmm, possibly, but . . .
Yes, I agree up to a point, however . . .
Well, you have a point there, but . . .
There's something there, I suppose, however . . .
I guess you could be right, but . . .
Yes, I suppose so, however . . .
That's worth thinking about, but . . .

C. How to Disagree Politely with an Opinion?

I am not so sure.
Do you think so?
Well, it depends.
I'm not so certain.
Well, I don't know.
Well, I'm not so sure about that.
Hmm, I'm not sure you're right.
I'm inclined to disagree with that.
No, I don't think so.

D. How to Disagree Strongly with an Opinion?

I disagree.
I disagree with your idea.
I'm afraid I don't agree.
I'm afraid your idea is wrong.
I can't agree with you.
I couldn't accept that for a minute.
You can't actually mean that.
I wouldn't go along with you there.
You can't be serious about that.
You must be joking.

It's possible you are mistaken about that.

A Topic with Hints

MULTINATIONALS—HELP OR HINDRANCE?
You are going to debate the pros and cons of international multi-nation corporations. It is important to remember that you have been placed in your group based on what seems to be the opposite of what you really think. Use the clues and ideas below to help you create an argument for your appointed point of view with your team members. Below you will find phrases and language helpful in expressing opinions, offering explanations and disagreeing.

For Multinationals

❖ Offers employment to local workers.
❖ Promotes peace internationally.
❖ Creates sense of community crossing international borders.
❖ Allows entire world to improve standard of living.
❖ Gives access to quality products regardless of location.
❖ Promotes economic stability.
❖ Raises standard of living for regions involved in production.
❖ Gives local economies new economic opportunities.
❖ Fact of life which needs to be accepted.
❖ Reflects global economy.

Against Multinationals

❖ Ruins local economies.
❖ Depletes local work forces by drawing to metro centres.
❖ Stifles cultural growth and expansion on local level.
❖ Provides little help with problems which are local in nature.
❖ Creates cultural Homogenization.
❖ Too big, little interest in the individual.
❖ Gives political power to outside interests.
❖ Creates economic instability by being subject to the whims of the global economy.
❖ Replaces traditional values with materialistic values.
❖ Makes local economies subject to mass layoffs.

TOPICS FOR DEBATING

1. Should corporal punishment in the school be banned?
2. Is city life better than village life?
3. Are friends the most important things in life?
4. Should we say 'No" to examinations?
5. Should cricket be our national game?
6. Is science a blessing?
7. Should all the politicians be educated?
8. Is money the most important thing in life?
9. Should parents be blamed for children's mistakes?
10. Are Gandhian principles valid today?
11. Do parents and teachers understand teenagers?
12. Is television an idiot box?
13. Are we following western culture?
14. Is reservation in jobs necessary?
15. Is reservation necessary for women?
16. Should education be completely privatised?
17. Should uniform be optional?
18. Are computers harming our creativity?
19. Should English be the compulsory medium of instruction in all the schools?
20. Should we legalise dowry?
21. Are arranged-marriages better than love-marriages?
22. Is development the other name of destruction?
23. Should we ban celebrating certain festivals to save money?
24. What is more important—money or love?
25. Should India attack Pakistan?

EVALUATING A DEBATE

1. Content: The subject matter of the topic including facts and figures.
2. Argument: Logical arrangement of facts, conviction of the speaker and how this conviction for or against the subject is put forward.
3. Language: Appropriate wordings, complete and grammatically correctness of the sentences.
4. Delivery: Correctness and clarity of enunciation, audibility, naturalness, poise, gestures, eye-contact with audience and facial expressions.

5. Rebuttal: (not compulsory) smart and honest reply of the questions asked by the opponents.

(10 POINTS CAN BE AWARDED FOR EACH POINT.)

"If I am asked to speak for an hour, I hardly need any preparation. But if I am asked to speak for 5 minutes, I might prepare for hours."

—Winston Churchill

CHAPTER 11

CROSSFIRE

The Crossfire is an argumentative discussion between two groups of students on different areas of any topic.

CONDUCTING A CROSSFIRE

1. Make the students sit in two rows facing each other.
2. Let the moderator give them a topic which can be divided into different areas. e.g." City Life versus Village Life"
3. Let the moderator start the event by telling some introductory sentences.
4. Let a student of one group speak on one particular area.
5. Let one of the students of the other group also speak on that area with some good arguments and at the same time oppose the opinions of the student of the other group who has already spoken before him.
6. Then let both sides support their views with some good arguments and at the same time oppose the opinions of the members of the other groups.
6. The moderator can interfere if the discussion becomes hostile.
7. Let the moderator give points to the groups according to their performance (2, 1, ½ or 0) at the end of the discussion on a particular area every time.
8. Let the moderator give some remarks to justify his/her evaluation.
9. Proceed to the second area with an observation of the moderator e.g. "Now the City People have one (two or three) point(s) and the next area of discussion is ". . .". Follow the same method.
10. At the end let the moderator sum up the total points of each group and announce the result.

A Sample Crossfire

This is the script of a sample Crossfire where there are 11 students: 5 students in each group and a moderator. The Topic is "City Life versus Village Life" and the areas are:
1. Environment
2. Health
3. Education
4. Peace and Security
5. Culture and Tradition
6. Standard of Living

The Script

Moderator: "Good evening everybody. Welcome all of you to this Crossfire. We have two groups for this Crossfire. They are the Villagers and the City People. Our topic is "City Life versus Village Life" The first area for discussion is Environment. Let us listen to the opinion of one of the Villagers first. Then I shall also allow one of the City People to give his opinions. Then the real cross Fire will start. So one of the Villagers can start. But remember you have to only speak on the environment.

Speaker 1 (from the Villagers): "Well, good evening everybody. As you know, the village environment is full of greenery with a lot of trees, open grass lands and fresh air. All these elements are absent in a city. Therefore, the village life is better than the city life. It's a . . ."

Speaker 2 (from the City People): "It is ok my dear friend. I admit that the village environment is quite fresh and green, but . . ."

Speaker 1 (from the Villagers): Excuse me respected moderator sir, point to be noted that my dear friend is admitting that the village environment is quite fresh and green. Therefore, we should get full one point.

Moderator: Cool down please, let him complete his speech.

Speaker 2 (from the City People): But the city environment is equally good now with so many plantation programmes. We have also beautiful parks and playgrounds in the city. We have . . .

Speaker 3 (from the Villagers): That's not the case, please stop this. Moderator Sir/Madam, how can you compare the man-made park with vast acres of open grass lands of the village?

Speaker 4 (from the Villagers): And also the trees of the plantation programmes of the city people can't be compared with the huge leafy trees of the village.

Moderator: Speaker 4 please. I have not reached in any conclusion. Why are you worried? Speaker 2, do you have any more to say.

Speaker 2 (from the City People): Yes sir, now it is up to my friend Speaker 5.

Moderator: Speaker 5 please.

Speaker 5 (from the City People): By the way the villagers are talking a lot regarding trees and open fields. But in almost all the villages there is no drainage system. As a result, the water logging is a permanent problem there. The water-borne diseases are common in those areas. But . . .

Speaker 6 (from the Villagers): I'm sorry moderator sir. The concept of 'disease' comes under the 'Health' area, not under 'environment' area. Then . . .

Moderator: Speaker 6 please do not disturb the speaker. Environment and health are related to each other.

Speaker 7 (from the Villagers): OK sir, then in the cities also they have dirty and open drains, mounting garbage, more air pollution because of the emission from the vehicles everywhere. They also suffer from more deadly diseases because of these problems.

Speaker 8 (from the City People): No, no, let the moderator, decide whether 'disease' comes under the 'Health' area, or under the 'environment' area.

Moderator: Listen everybody, I have been sincerely listening both the sides for the last ten minutes. In my opinion, the villagers have more points so far as the 'environment' area is concerned. So they are awarded with 2 points.

Now the Villagers have 2 point and the City People have 0. The next area is 'Health' and the City People will start the argument.

Speaker 9 (from the City People): Well, So far as the area of 'health' is concerned the city is definitely ahead of the village. In the city we have got all the facilities of health in terms of the presence of so many hospitals, nursing homes, etc. But in villages they don't have such facilities.

Speaker 10 (from the City People): Not only that, city people are more conscious of their health. They are . . .

Speaker 6 (from the Villagers): Just a minute moderator sir, no doubt there are more hospitals and other facilities in a city. But the city people suffer more from deadly diseases like diabetes, high or low blood-pressure and heart attacks.

Speaker 10 (from the City People): The village people are also suffering from these diseases. But because of their ignorance, they fail to detect and cure these diseases. Therefore, I think our side should get the full 1 point for the area of health.

Moderator: Do the villagers have any other points?

Speaker 4 (from the Villagers): Moderator sir, the village people are very hard-working and eat fresh food every day. Therefore, they suffer from fewer diseases. But the city people are not that much hard-working and fail to eat fresh food like us. Thus, the . . .

Speaker 2 (from the City People): Sir, our nature of work is quite different. But we have modern gymnasium and we go for regular exercises. But the village people don't do that. So far as food is concerned, we are also getting fresh food and the villagers are supplying that to us.

Speaker 5 (from the City People): Moderator sir, I just want to raise another point. The village people are superstitious. They believe on chants and magicians for curing their diseases. Many of them avoid hospitals also.

Moderator: It's all clear now. In my view, the City People have more points so far as the 'health' area is concerned. They did good enough to bag 2 points. Now the Villagers have 2 points and the City People have also 2 points. The next area is 'Education' and the Villagers will start the argument.

Speaker 3 (from the Villagers): Good evening friends. No doubt the city has got more educational institutions and they have more literacy. But ultimately the villagers are coming to the city for better education and becoming city people in the long run . . .

Speaker 8 (from the City People): Point to be noted sir, the villagers is admitting that we have more literacy and more facilities for education. That is enough. Again the point should go to us.

Speaker 7 (from the Villagers): No, no. We have not completely presented our views. Now-a-days, the villagers are also having a lot of facilities. Different educational programmes of the government like Education for All are very effectively working in the villages.

Speaker 9 (from the City People): But don't you think the city still stands ahead of the village? I think we are better in every field of education than the city people. We are . . .

Moderator: That's fine. The City People have more points on 'Education'. So they are awarded 2 more points. Now the Villagers have 2 points and the City People have 4. The next area is 'Peace and Security' and the City People are supposed to start.

Speaker 10 (from the City People): Friends, in my opinion the city is more secured than the village.

All the Villagers: No, no . . . It's absolutely wrong.

Speaker 1 (from the Villagers): How far the city is secured that is clear from the Mumbai Terrorist Attack, from the Kandhamal Communal riots. We all know what is happening in a city.

Speaker 2 (from the City People): Listen my dear friends, we have more police stations here and the security system is far better than the villages.

Speaker 6 (from the Villagers): Moderator sir, the point is not only on 'security'. It is also on 'peace'. The villagers are peace loving people. They are not migrants like the city people. They have been living in the same village for so many years with peace and unity. Therefore, all the points should go to us.

Speaker 4 (from the Villagers): Another point sir. They are telling that they have more security and police stations. In my opinion, they have also more cases of violence and riots. Therefore, they need more police stations. More security is not their qualification rather disqualification.

Moderator: Well it is clear now. I'm sorry my dear city people. No doubt, the villagers have more points on this area. So two more points go to them. Now the Villagers have 4 points and the City People have also 4 points. The next area is 'Culture and Tradition' and the Villagers will start.

Speaker 3 (from the Villagers): What should we say sir? You can see the degradation of Indian culture in every walk of city life. Celebrating festivals is their fashion and merry making only. They also wear such dresses that are beyond our imagination.

Speaker 8 (from the City People): Listen my dear friend, this type of rubbish comments are not at all fair. We are also celebrating festivals with lots of devotion. We are also . . .

Speaker 7 (from the Villagers): And what happens during emersion? Don't you dance drinking wine? Don't you create noise pollution during fares and festivals? Are all these things our culture?

Speaker 5 (from the City People): These things are symbols of a modern society. You are old and outdated. Therefore, you are commenting on our dress.

Speaker 1 (from the Villagers): Oh! It means we can't be modern by wearing Indian dress, observing festivals without much noise. Moderator sir, I think my dear friend does not know what is the meaning of 'modernity'?

Moderator: No more argument please. After listening the arguments of the villagers, I personally feel that the Indian villages are the symbols of their culture and tradition. The villagers have more points on this area. So they are getting1½ points. Now the Villagers have 5½ points and the City People have 4½. The last area for discussion is 'Standard of Living' and we will start with the City People.

Speaker 9 (from the City People): Dear moderator sir, I personally feel that there is nothing to be discussed on this area. Everybody knows that the city people are always better than the villagers in terms of standard of living. We have more earnings, better houses, excellent means of transport and communications, the list is unending.

Speaker 6 (from the Villagers): But I don't agree with you. You have more needs and therefore, more earnings. You have more vehicles and therefore, better means of transport. But these are not indicators of a good 'standard of living'?

Speaker 10 (from the City People): Then what are the indicators of a good 'standard of living'—thatched houses? Muddy roads? People below Poverty Line? All these are the symbols of village life.

Speaker 4 (from the Villagers): You are talking about standard of living or scolding the villagers?

Speaker 8 (from the City People): No, no we are telling the reality. The village people are not financially sound and therefore, their Standard of Living is not good enough. So it can . . .

Moderator: That's fine. I accept that the City People have a better Standard of Living and that is clear from their arguments. So they are getting 1½ and the villagers ½. Now it's all 6. Thus the Crossfire ended in a draw. Both the sides are equally good. Thank you all for taking part in this Crossfire.

More Crossfire Topics:
1. Development is the other name of destruction.
2. Agriculture vs. Industry
3. Science—a boon or a bane?
4. Money vs. Love.
5. Self-employment vs. Wage-employment.
6. Higher Education vs. Vocational Education.

7. Love Marriage vs. Arrange Marriage
8. Joint Family vs. Nuclear Family
9. Awarding Marks vs. Awarding Grade
10. English Language vs. Vernacular Language

TIPS FOR THE TEACHERS

Crossfire as a group activity is subject to generate a lot of argument and noise inside the class. In that case, it may not attain its objective. Therefore, the teachers should be absolutely alert and attentive while conducting the Crossfire. The following tips will be helpful.

1. **Preference**—Let the students select their group with absolute liberty. That will help them to form a group with good cohesion among all the members. They will also be interested to discuss among themselves without any shyness.
2. **Impartiality**—Make it sure that both the sides of a Crossfire topic have enough points to be discussed. Otherwise one side of the group will be in a better position than the other and that will lead to chaos.
3. **Language Function**—The ultimate objective of a Crossfire is to make the students communicative and therefore, absolute importance should be given on the uses of simple and argumentative sentences. Students should not use a lot of chunks in a Crossfire. They should be encouraged to speak in complete sentences.
4. **Equal Opportunity**—Many students have the tendency to dominate the Crossfire without allowing other students to deliver. Moderator should not allow this to happen. Sometimes a moderator can be appointed from the students' side. But he must be unanimously accepted by all the students.
5. **Scoring**—Crossfire scores are like the scores in a football match. The scores are declared at successive stages. The moderator can award it fully (2 points) to a group considering its performance. A group can get ½, 1, 1½ or 2 points.

> "Arguments are to be avoided: they are always vulgar and often convincing."
>
> – Oscar Wilde

CHAPTER 12

DUMB CHARADE

Dumb Charade is a game in which one person explains the name given to him only with actions to his team. Traditionally it is only about Hindi films but now with public demand characters, advertisement, Hollywood films and much more are also included. It is a fun to watch as well as to participate in charade games. In the context of Spoken English, the verbal communication part should be in English and only in English.

RULES FOR CONDUCTING DUMB CHARADE

The rules of the acted charades used vary widely and informally, but these rules, in some forms, are common to most players:

1. The players are divided into two teams.
2. Each player writes a phrase on a slip of paper to create the phrases to be guessed by the other team. Many such slips are collected and put inside two containers (for two teams). A member of a particular team randomly collects a slip from the opposite team's container and then has a limited period of time to convey the message of the slip to his teammates only by signals, not by speech.
3. No sounds or lip movements are allowed. In some circles, even clapping is prohibited, while in others, the player may make any sound other than speaking or whistling a recognizable tune.
4. The actor cannot point out at any of the objects present in the scene, if by doing so he is helping his teammates.
5. Usually, any gesture is allowed other than blatantly spelling out the word, but some play that indicating anything about the form of the

phrase is prohibited, even the number of words, so that only the meaning may be acted out.

6. The teams alternate until each team member has had an opportunity to pantomime.

7. Since so many rules can vary, clarifying all the rules before the game begins can avoid problems later.

STANDARD SIGNALS

A number of standard signals have come into common usage in charades, though they are not required. To indicate the general category of a word or phrase:

Person—Stand with hands on hips.

Book title—Unfold your hands as if they were a book.

Movie title—Pretend to crank an old-fashioned movie camera.

Play title—Pretend to pull the rope that opens a theater curtain, or place both hands out, palms facing the audience and touching at the thumbs, and draw them apart like a theater curtain.

Song title—Pretend to sing.

TV show—Draw a rectangle to outline the TV screen.

Quote or phrase—Make quotation marks in the air with your fingers.

Location—Make a circle with one hand, then point to it, as if pointing to a dot on a map.

Event—Point to your wrist as if you were wearing a watch. Alternatively, hold hands up beside your head and make "spirit fingers" (wave fingers back and forth frantically) simulating confetti or a crowd in the background.

Computer Game—Using both hands out stretched move thumbs like using a game pad.

Website—Hold your hand out, palm down, horizontal to the ground (as if holding a computer mouse). Make a sweeping motion side to side, as if moving a coconut half on table ("navigating"), then stop and tap index finger (as if "clicking").

"Think!" or "intangible" (anything else)—Make the "crazy" signal, i.e. point to your head and wave your finger in a circle.

To indicate other features of the word or phrase:

Number of words in the phrase—Hold up the number of fingers.

Which word you are working on—Hold up the number of fingers again.

Number of syllables in the word—Lay the number of fingers on your arm.

Which syllable you are working on—Lay the number of fingers on your arm again.

Length of word—Make a "little" or "big" sign as if you were measuring a fish.

The entire concept—Sweep your arms through the air.

On the nose (i.e., someone has made a correct guess)—Point at your nose with one hand, while pointing at the person with your other hand.

Sounds like or rhymes with—Cup one hand behind an ear, or pull on your earlobe.

Longer version of—Pretend to stretch a piece of elastic.

Shorter version of—Do a "karate chop" with your hand.

Plural—Link your little fingers.

Proper Name—Tap the top of your head with an open palm.

Past tense—Wave your hand over your shoulder toward your back.

A letter of the alphabet—Move your hand in a chopping motion toward your arm (near the top of your forearm if the letter is near the beginning of the alphabet, and near the bottom of your arm if the letter is near the end of the alphabet).

A colour—Point to your tongue, then point to an object of the color you're trying to convey. If no objects are available, then pantomime an object that typically possesses the color in question.

Close, keep guessing!—Frantically wave your hands about to keep the guesses coming, or pretend to fan yourself, as if to say "getting hotter".

Not even close, I'll start over—Wave hand in a wide sweep, as if to say "go away!" Alternatively, pretend to shiver, as if to say "getting colder". The hand is moved as if flushing a toilet, meaning forget whatever has been done till now and to start afresh.

A synonym—Clasp your hands together and then, rotating your clasped hands from the wrists, simulate multiple figure 8's.

The opposite or the antonym of what you are saying—Form each hand into a hitchhiker's thumb signal, then with the backs of the hands facing away from you, cross your forearms and make the thumbs travel in opposing directions, thus "opposite".

Stop, work on something else—Hold both arms out in front of you, palms of your hands waving, facing your teammates, while simultaneously shaking your head, eyes closed.

Signals for Common Words

Some conventions have also evolved about very common words:
1. "A" is signed by steeping index fingers together.
2. "I" is signed by pointing at one's eye, or one's chest.
3. "The" is signed by making a "T" sign with the index fingers.
4. "That" is signed by the same aforementioned "T".
5. Pretending to paddle a canoe can be used to sign the word "or."

6. For "on," make your index finger leap on to the palm of your other hand. Reverse this gesture to indicate "off." The off motion plus a scissor-snipping action makes "of".

7. Other common small words are signed by holding the index finger and thumb close together, but not touching.

Note that these signals are standardized by general consensus only, and may vary somewhat from place to place.

Dumb Charade as a Speaking Activity

This can be an important speaking activity for learning English if the teachers create some situations to make every participant speak. Every rule of the game will be followed, only the speakers have to speak in English. While deciphering the signals, the speakers should generate a lot of questions and go on speaking in English.

"Most people are other people. Their thoughts are someone else's opinions, their lives a mimicry, their passions a quotation."

– Oscar Wilde

CHAPTER 13

PRESS CONFERENCE

Press Conference is a Role Play. The students play the roles of the reporters and have to take the interview of famous people in a press conference. They need to prepare some general questions they can ask any famous person—actors, singers, sports stars, politicians, etc. Give some examples, like, 'Good morning sir. I am from Zee News. My question is: 'Do you enjoy your job?' or 'Are you happy being so famous?' Also ask the students for playing the role of different famous people. They can get the questions in advance and prepare.

QUESTIONS FOR SOME FAMOUS PEOPLE

FILM ACTOR
1. What prompted you to be an actor?
2. Well, you are the inspiration of so many youths. Who is your inspiration?
3. What was your first film? Please share some of your memory from that film?
4. How did you feel when you faced the camera for the first time?
5. What is your next film sir?
6. What is the secret of your physical fitness sir?
7. Who are your favourite co-actress and director?
8. How do you react when films become flop like your last film?
9. Most of the Indian youths are film-crazy. What is your message for them?
10. Why don't Indian films get Oscar awards?

FILM ACTRESS

1. Indian society is a conservative society. Still then why did you become an actress?
2. Had you not been actress, what would have been your profession?
3. Which is your best film till today and why?
4. Don't you feel shy to dance with so many boys in front of the camera?
5. What is the secret of your beauty madam?
6. Which particular role do you love to play madam?
7. What advice do you want to give to those who want to make acting their career?
8. How do you react when actresses play in nude roles?
9. Do you want to join politics madam like Jayalaitha and Jayaprada?
10. Finally something personal madam. When do you want the family of your own?

POLITICIAN

1. Women are still fighting to get justice in Indian politics. They are yet to get 33% reservation in the parliament? How do you feel as a lady politician and the education minister?
2. You are the role model for millions of Indian women. Who is your role model?
3. Madam, what is your opinion on compulsory education and for all the politicians?
4. You are the Minister of Education now. What is your explanation on so many vacant posts in schools and colleges?
5. Most of the people think that the politicians are corrupt and root of all evils. What is your comment?
6. As an Education Minister do you think that there should be special Spoken English classes for Odia medium students?
7. What is your solution to unemployment Madam?
8. Corporal punishment is still going on in many schools. Many teachers are beating the students mercilessly even after the Supreme Court's ban. What is your opinion?
9. Why is Odisha one of the poor states of India?
10. What is your comment on the plan of not conducting the matriculation examination?

TEACHER

1. Why did you choose the teaching profession?
2. What is your comment on the changing teacher-tot relationship?
3. Now-a-days more and more technology is used in teaching. Even the new concept of online teaching is gaining popularity. What is your comment?
4. What is the best way to control student agitation?
5. Most of the students like to be doctors and engineers, not teachers. Why?
6. What changes will you recommend in the present-day educational system?
7. How can our students be self-employed without running after wage-employment?
8. Some of the subjects like History are losing their importance in schools and colleges. How do you accept it?
9. What is your comment on privatization of education?
10. There is severe malpractice in examinations particularly in rural areas. How to check it?

CRICKETER

1. You are a very popular cricketer in India. Have you made it large?
2. What is your comment on the match-fixing scandal?
3. Now-a-days more and more cricketers are involved with different kinds of advertisements. Don't you think it hampers their performance?
4. Do you think that cricket should be our national game?
5. Most of the youths are cricket crazy. What is the solution?
6. What changes have been taken place after the emergence of Twenty20?
7. How can our players remain fit and free from injury?
8. Do you accept cricketers joining politics?
9. Should India hire foreign coaches?
10. Who is your ideal and why?

POLICE COMMISSIONER

1. Sir, even today a police man is not a symbol of peace; it is a symbol of fear. Why?
2. What is your comment on the changing security situation in our country?
3. Why do you fail to curb the Naxalite problem?

4. Sir, I have a personal question. Can you arrest your relatives if they are found guilty?
5. Most of the terrorists are better trained than the police. Why is it so?
6. Who is your role-model?
7. It is a general conception that police officers are taking a lot of bribe. Should we accept it?
8. Share one of your successful operations against any culprit?
9. The popular Hindi films show the relation between the police and politician in a critical way. Any comment?
10. What is your message to the society?

DOCTOR
1. Sir, you are a famous surgeon of this area. How do you feel after becoming so much successful in life?
2. Doctors are very busy in their private practice. How do you accept that?
3. Doctors are called the Second Gods. But these Gods are going on strike in most of the time neglecting their patients. Is it justified?
4. What is the most successful operation in your life?
5. People say that once you had left a pair of scissors inside a patient's belly during the operation. Is it true?
6. Which branch of medicine is more effective—Allopathic, Homeopathic or Ayurvedic?
7. It is a general conception that some doctors are associated with the rackets of exporting human organs to foreign countries. How true is it?
8. Do you donate blood?
9. The private nursing homes are looting the patients. How can this problem be checked?
10. AIDS is prevalent all over the world now. What is the solution?

TERRORIST
1. Don't you think that you are an anti- social and harmful against the whole humanity?
2. Which organization do you belong to?
3. Can you change yourself if government listens to your demand?
4. What are your demands?
5. How do you raise money for your organization?
6. What is the biggest achievement of your life?
7. Ajmal Kasab was hanged to death. The same thing may happen with you. Don't you fear?

8. What is your next target?
9. Do you think violence is the only way to solve any matter?
10. Is there any solution that you can provide to end terrorism?

SCIENTIST
1. Sir, you are a famous scientist. What prompted you to be a scientist?
2. What was your first invention?
3. What is your latest invention?
4. I have heard that the scientists have their own world. They pass most of their time with their experiments. They are crazy. Any comment?
5. What is your dream project?
6. Don't you want to go abroad like other scientists?
7. Besides being a scientist, what are your other interests?
8. Sir what is your solution to global warming?
9. Is cloning essential?
10. What is your dream for India?

A MODEL HOUSEWIFE
1. Good evening madam, tell something about your family.
2. You are a housewife, but today you are in the press conference. Why?
3. There is news that you have brought a lot of changes in your locality with other housewives. How was it possible?
4. Why did not you want to be a working lady?
5. Do you think that the housewives in India have proved themselves?
6. If your husband interferes in your work, what will be your reaction?
7. Should the housewives join politics?
8. Who is your role model?
9. What is your comment on the dowry system?
10. Why are most of the joint-families disintegrating now?

Note: Don't give importance on the contents of the questions and answers. Rather give importance on the language.

Model Answers to the Film Actor's Questions

1. From my childhood I was fond of watching films. My father is a lover of film too. So, he prompted me to be an actor.
2. I am a great fan of Amitav Bachhan. I like his acting a lot. Therefore, he is my inspiration.

3. My first film was 'Fool'. I was playing the role of a young guy. I was of course very frightened in that film. But my director helped me to gain confidence and supported a lot to remove my fear.

4. For the first time when I faced the camera, I was very nervous. Even I forgot my dialogues most of the time.

5. My next film is "The Lake". It is a horror film and I think will be very popular.

6. Physical fitness, well, that's a good question. There is no such secret. I only attend the gym and in my leisure I play some outdoor games like cricket and football with my friends.

7. My favourite co-actress is Katrina Kaif. It is because, her acting is really natural and she is also very disciplined. My favourite director is Nil Nitin Mukesh. He gives a lot of freedom in playing any particular role.

8. Listen when my films become flop, I don't become sorry. Rather without realizing a lot, I concentrate on my next film and try to do it better.

9. Well, films are for entertainment. But we should not be mad after films. We should do our duty first and during leisure we should think of watching films. Again, the youths should not try to imitate the actors and the actress.

10. Oscar Awards are basically for movies with English language. There is only one category for foreign language movies where a country can compete with one film only. So there is a cut-throat competition in that category as there are so many non-English movies. That's the main problem. Anyway, I have a shooting programme. I have to leave now. Thanks a lot for inviting me here.

"The informed, unmanaged question. That's the most dangerous thing at a press conference anywhere."

– Ron Suskind

CHAPTER 14

Public Speaking / Extempore

Anyone can improve the art of Public Speaking. You need to get rid of the initial stage-fright that you may experience. You have to ignore it. Remember the common saying: "You cannot learn swimming from a book while sitting on the edge of the pool; you need to get your feet wet first."

How to Structure Your Speech?

A good talk should have four parts:
1. Introduction-
   You might start with a story or an incident that engages the attention and interest of the audience.
2. An indication of the structure of your talk-
   This might be something like the following: "We should oppose this amendment for three reasons: first of all, it will be extremely expensive; secondly, it will be ineffective; and thirdly, it is completely unnecessary."
3. The body of your talk-
   Don't be artificial in presenting your speech. Present the facts and figures honestly.
4. Conclusion-
   You summarize your arguments and perhaps return to the story or incident you began with to do so.

How to Begin Your Speech?

Hundreds of people, tons of baggage and fuel, limited runway: an Air-India 747 needs the full thrust of four powerful jet engines to get off the ground and air-borne. So also it takes a strong start to pick up an audience and carry it with you. Here are some hints for a good start.

1. Grab the attention of the audience with an incident, a 'slice of life', from your own experience.

Example: "Late last night by the Institute gate, a man suddenly caught my arm."

2. Arouse curiosity.

Example: "Next week a visitor is coming to this centre that has the power to change the course of your life."

3. Present arresting facts or startling statistics.

Example: "Twenty-four human beings, eighteen of them children under five years of age, die as a consequence of hunger every minute of every hour of every day", or, "At the end of 1993, for the fourth consecutive year, the average per capita income decreased worldwide."

4. Ask a question.

Example: "Do you know what enabled Jyotirmoyee Sikdar to win the Asian 800 metres crown ?"

5. Show the audience something connected with the main point of your remarks.

Example: Hold up a contract, a key, a book or pen.

6. Look friendly, sound friendly, be friendly.

Example : 'Friends', 'Romans', 'countrymen', etc.

7. If you are speaking on the anniversary of an organization, look up the newspapers of the day it started and contrast those circumstances with the present.

Example : "Last year was not a good year; it was a great year."

8. If you are speaking on the anniversary of an organization, look up the newspapers of the day it started and contrast those circumstances with the present.

How to End Your Speech?

1. When you have said what you wanted to say, stop. Speaking is like drilling for water: when you've struck water, stop boring. Remember the advice: "Be clear, be brief and be seated."

2. Go back to the story or incident with which you started. Connect the main point of your talk with it and finish. For example, if you started

your talk with a story about the tennis player, Vijay Amritraj, then at the end go back to that story.

3. Often a little summary is helpful. As someone has remarked: "Tell them what you're going to tell them, tell them and then tell them what you told them."

4. Have a strong finish. 'Free at last, free at last, thank God almighty. We're free at last as Osama is no more.'

5. Don't leave the speaker's stand while saying the last few words. After you have spoken the last word, pause for just a moment. Then sit down or leave the platform with purpose and decision.

6. What do you think of the following as conclusions to a talk?
   a. "Well, ladies and gentlemen, I think that is about all I have to say. I am sorry for taking so much of your time, and I hope you will pardon any mistakes I have made."
   b. "Victory at all costs, victory in spite of terror, victory however long and hard the road may be, for without victory, there is no survival."

Speak with Your Whole Body

Think how much Odissi, Bharata Natyam, Kathakali, Kathak and Manipuri dancers convey just by means of swaying their eyes, hands, fingers, feet, etc. Many feel that body language conveys far more than words. In fact, some think that most of our message, most of the meaning we convey is in our posture, facial expression and gestures. To appreciate the part our body plays in our exchanges, do the following exercises in groups of two or three:

1. Tell an amusing story or joke with a straight face.
2. Tell an exciting story without gestures.
3. Now tell the same story with gestures.
4. Convey bad news with a smiling face; e.g., "Hello, Ravi, you failed in the examination." "Hello, Sangeeta, you have not been selected for the post of computer software engineer."
5. Convey good news with a sad face.
6. Let one person tell a long story or give a long explanation of some subject. While the person is talking, let another use facial expressions and other gestures, but no words, to communicate to him/her:
   ❖ To continue talking.
   ❖ To speak louder.
   ❖ To speed up and get to the point.

- ❖ To slow down.
- ❖ That you are not following him/her.
- ❖ That you wish him/her to expand on the point.
- ❖ That you think he/she is talking rubbish.
- ❖ That you are bored.
- ❖ That you feel offended by what he just said.
- ❖ To stop and let you talk.
- ❖ To end the conversation.

One Minute Speech Practice

Choose one of the following subjects and speak for one minute. Let someone else keep time and indicate when only ten seconds are left.

1. Who am I?
2. If animals could talk.
3. When I am dead, think this of me.
4. The actor/actress that I have always admired.
5. If you want peace, work for justice.
6. You (one person) can make a difference.
7. The most unforgettable character I ever met.
8. You are what you read.
9. Young people today do (do not) have heroes.
10. "Give me a fish and I live for a day. Teach me to fish and I live for a lifetime."

6 P's of Public Speaking

1) Prepare: Put your ideas in a logical order and use appropriate connectives.
2) Pronunciation: Follow the commonly accepted standard pronunciation.
3) Practice: Practise alone or in front of a full length or half length mirror.
4) Posture: No one pays attention to a sloppy speaker. So learn to stand erect, with your shoulders square with your hands either at the side or at the back. Of course, you have to use your hands for emphasising your ideas and for gestures.
5) Presentation: Presentation includes:
   a) Voice modulation which is necessary to reduce boredom and monotony.
   b) Expressions of your eyes and face.
   c) Eye contact.

6) Personalise: Put yourself in the shoes of the writer and try to relive his
    feelings sentiments and emotions while he wrote the piece.

EXTEMPORE

In the case of extemporaneous speech you have to think on your feet, and
this is more difficult, though not impossible. The difference here is that the
topic is given to you and you have very limited time or no time to prepare.
The techniques are, however, the same as described before in the 'Public
Speaking'. The participants will be allowed to pick up chits with the topics.
They may speak either for or against the proposition. Time factor is decided
before. The topic for 'extempore' is therefore, relatively easier and something
within our reach that we use in our daily life.

SOME EXTEMPORE TOPICS

- ❖ AIDS
- ❖ Be Indian, buy Indian.
- ❖ Cinema
- ❖ Democracy
- ❖ Exercise
- ❖ Facebook
- ❖ Grapes are sour.
- ❖ Health is wealth.
- ❖ Illiteracy
- ❖ Jagannatha
- ❖ KISS
- ❖ Love
- ❖ M.K. Gandhi
- ❖ Naxalism
- ❖ One man—one tree
- ❖ Person I like the most
- ❖ Quest for Happiness
- ❖ Riots
- ❖ Science
- ❖ Time
- ❖ Unity is strength
- ❖ Valentine's Day

- ❖ War is outdated.
- ❖ Xmas
- ❖ Yesterday
- ❖ Zeal
- ❖ All is well.
- ❖ Bike I like the most.
- ❖ Cell Phone/ Computer
- ❖ Dating
- ❖ English Language
- ❖ Friendship
- ❖ Hinduism
- ❖ India, my motherland
- ❖ Jai Jawan, Jai Kissan
- ❖ Kindness
- ❖ Luck
- ❖ My Name
- ❖ Nature
- ❖ Odisha
- ❖ Pets
- ❖ Quack Cures
- ❖ Retirement Life
- ❖ Social Service
- ❖ Tit for Tat
- ❖ UNO
- ❖ Vegetarianism
- ❖ Water
- ❖ X-chromosome
- ❖ Yoga
- ❖ Zero

"Public speaking? I speak to myself on the street!"

– Eliot Spitzer

CHAPTER 15

INSTANT TRANSLATION

Translation—the best way to develop vocabulary of a foreign language.

Translating the vernacular (Odia) language into a foreign language (English) is one of the best ways to increase vocabulary. Students find it difficult at the beginning, but ultimately it helps the learners to struggle for new words and learn them by heart. But this is the case of written language. Translation also helps in developing sentence structures. Here we are introducing a novel way of oral translation. It is a great helper of increasing fluency. The instructions to have such an activity are as follows.

PROCEDURE

* Place two chairs facing each other at the front of the classroom.
* Let the students in pair come up to these chairs to perform Oral Translation.
* One partner should either read or speak an Oriya paragraph giving space to her/his partner after each sentence so that the latter can translate it into English.
* The text for translation should be paragraphs, not independent sentences.
* While each pair is performing, the other pairs should prepare for their Oral Translation.
* Now, ask the first pair to select the next pair.
* Have these next two students come in front of others and repeat the process.

Example of an Odia Passage:

ଆମେ ରୋଗରେ ପଡ଼ିଲେ ଡାକ୍ତରଖାନା ଯାଉ ।
ସହର ଓ ନଗରମାନଙ୍କରେ ଡାକ୍ତରଖାନା ଥାଏ ।
ଡାକ୍ତରଖାନାରେ ଡାକ୍ତର, ନର୍ସ ଓ କମ୍ପାଉଣ୍ଡରମାନେ
ଥାଆନ୍ତି । ଡାକ୍ତର ରୋଗୀମାନଙ୍କୁ ଚିକିତ୍ସା କରନ୍ତି । ନର୍ସ ଓ
କମ୍ପାଉଣ୍ଡରମାନେ ଡାକ୍ତରଙ୍କୁ ସାହାଯ୍ୟ କରନ୍ତି । ଗୁରୁତର
ରୋଗୀଙ୍କ ପାଇଁ ଡାକ୍ତରଖାନାରେ ଶଯ୍ୟାମାନ ଥାଏ ।
ସେମାନେ ସେଠାରେ ରହନ୍ତି ଓ ଉପଯୁକ୍ତ ଚିକିତ୍ସା ପାଆନ୍ତି ।
ରୋଗୀମାନଙ୍କୁ ଔଷଧ ଓ ଇଞ୍ଜେକ୍ସନ୍ ଦିଆଯାଏ ।
ବେଳେବେଳେ ଶଲ୍ୟ ଚିକିତ୍ସା ଦରକାର ପଡ଼େ । ଏହିପରି
ଡାକ୍ତରଖାନାଗୁଡ଼ିକ ଆଧୁନିକ ସମାଜର ଆବଶ୍ୟକୀୟ ଅଙ୍ଗ
ଅଟେ ।

Instant Translation of the above Odia Passage into English:

When we become ill we go to hospital. There are hospitals in towns and cities. There are doctors, nurses and compounders in the hospital. The doctor treats the patients. The nurses and compounders assist the doctors. There are beds for serious patients in hospitals. They stay there and get proper treatment. The patients are given medicines and injections. Sometimes surgery becomes necessary. Thus, hospitals are necessary parts of modern society.

"Translation is like a woman. If it is beautiful, it is not faithful. If it is faithful, it is most certainly not beautiful."

– Yevgeny Yevtushenko

CHAPTER 16

TEACHING FOR BETTER FLUENCY

Sometimes an average student becomes a better teacher. Ultimately teaching helps him to be a good communicator. Here are some tips for teaching as an activity for developing Communicative Skill.

- ❖ Select a topic which you can explain.
- ❖ Collect more information on the topic for more explanation.
- ❖ Now, organise every fact and figure—from the beginning to the end.
- ❖ Go for rehearsals, may be many times, alone or among the friends.
- ❖ Finally give a shape to your teaching. Look at the time and the content.
- ❖ Start the class comfortably. Be very simple in your language.
- ❖ The topic can be introduced by a story or any such devices.
- ❖ Use black board and other teaching aids if possible and necessary.
- ❖ Make your students participate in the discussion.
- ❖ Be prepared to be repeatedly questioned. Avoid irrelevant questions.
- ❖ Conclude the topic and ask the students whether they have doubts.
- ❖ Declare the closing of the class and wish the students.

"Participation makes the class more useful; both for the teacher and the students."

CHAPTER 17

FORUM

The forum is a public gathering where everyone has an opportunity for expressing his views on a controversial topic or issue. In the sense described here, it is a public discussion in which brief expositions of conflicting views are presented by two/three/four/ persons teams under a moderator.

Uses

1. To provide for and provoke public discussion of a current event or controversial subjects.
2. To ensure presentation of key points of opposing views.
3. The charm and effectiveness of the forum lies in the condensed presentation, which usually provokes significant audience participation, while the audience is still fresh.

Setting

1. A table for each team, and the moderator.
2. For large audiences, microphone arrangement on the stage and among audience.

Procedure

1. Two teams are formed, each consisting of two/ three/ four persons representing the two sides or viewpoints on the issue in question. After a brief introduction of the topic or the issue by the moderator each speaker presents a summary of his position. No interruptions or questions are allowed.

2. For a brief period the team speakers question one another (through the moderator)
3. Then the issue is thrown open to the floor. Teams alternatively reply to questions.
4. Finally, the non-evaluative summary is presented by the moderator.

"You have to test your ideas in a public forum."

– Hillary Clinton

CHAPTER 18

DESCRIPTION

It is a very interesting speaking activity in which the participant has to describe a person, an animal, a place, an object, a process, etc.

Description of a Person

Loose, wavy brown hair hung down to her waist at the back she had a fringe over her forehead that almost hid her pale blue eyes. The nose-not her best feature-was long but no ugly. She had a regular set of white teeth and was full lipped. Her round face looked rather pale; she wasn't very tall or slim, and she walked with drooping shoulders.

When I knew her she must have been in her early thirties may be thirty-fivish even and she had one or two tell-tale wrinkles round the mouth.

Description of an Animal

The leopard is one of the largest members of the cat family, reaching a height of 75 cm and a length of 2.1 m including the tail. Only the lion and tiger are bigger. It is a powerful animal and an expert tree-climber. It hunts and eats almost any wild domestic animal which it can find. Leopards are found throughout Africa and in Asia from Turkey to China.

Description of an Object

A telephone comes with a bell which can ring a microphone which converts human speech into electrical signals, an earphone which converts incoming electrical signals back into speech, and a dial which is used to send electrical pulses along the line to an automatic exchange.

When we pick up the handset a selector in the exchange searches for and connects our phone to the automatic selector equipment. We then hear the dial tone. When we dial the number the equipment connects us to an outgoing junction cable linked to the exchange we want, or to a junction cable going in the direction of the wanted exchange, if it is a distant one that has to be reached via intermediate exchanges.

When the wanted exchange is reached, the equipment there connects the wires from our phone through to the phone we want. Then a low frequency current known as 'the ringing current' is sent along the wires to the phone we wish to contact. A similar current is sent back over the wires to us and we hear the ringing tone.

The ringing current operates the bell in the handset of the person to whom we wish to speak. When he/she lifts his/her handset to answer, both the ringing current and ringing tone are disconnected and we can begin speaking. If his/her phone is already in use, the wires from our phone are not connected through to it.

Instead an interrupted current known as the engaged tone is sent back over the wires to us.

Description of a Place

Ootacamund, or Ooty (as it is popularly known), which nestles in the Nilgiri Hills, lies on the borders of Kerala, Tamil Nadu and Karnataka. Tourists from both home and abroad flock to this beautiful little hill station for a holiday.

Ooty abounds in tourist spots. The most prominent among them is the Botanical Garden, which was established in 1847. A variety of exotic and ornamental plants adorn this garden. The chief attraction of the garden is a fossil tree trunk which is 20 million years old.

A small lake runs through the garden. The government organises a flower festival in May every year. About 10 kilometers away is Daddabetta Peak, which is the highest point in the Nilgiris. It offers a beautiful view of the surrounding hill ranges.

The Hindustan Photo Film Company's factory is situated in the picturesque Wenlock Downs. From here, one can get a view of the tea estates of Ooty and the fields of Coimbatore.

Description of a Process

Here there is a process description. It is about "How to apply blue in a piece of cloth?"

At first add the required drops of Robin Liquid Blue to half a bucket of water. Then swirl and mix it well. After that dip the washed cloth in the blue water and let it soak for a while. Now squeeze it and put it to dry.

Exercise:

Describe the following birds, animals, etc.

i)   a tiger
ii)   a snake
iii)   a crow
iv)   a kingfisher
v)   preparing tea
vi)   preparing *dalma*
vii)   a computer
vii)   a bike
viii)   a cell phone
ix)   a laptop
x)   a bicycle
xi)   preparing coffee
xii)   a Hindi film actor
xiii)   a college student
xiv)   preparing rice
xv)   polishing shoes
xvi)   a table
xvii)   Cuttack
xviii) Bhubaneswar
xix)   an old woman

"The world is a country which nobody ever yet knew by description; one must travel through it one's self to be acquainted with it."

– Lord Chesterfield

CHAPTER 19

TELEPHONIC CONVERSATION

MAKING AND RECEIVING A PHONE CALL

Learning how to communicate well on the telephone is one of the top priorities for many students who need to use English at work. Learning the common phrases or word-groups that are used on the telephone helps students know what to expect.

Word-Groups Used while Making a Phone Call:

❖ Hello? Is that (the HDFC Bank)?
❖ Can I speak to (the manager), please?
❖ Can I have extension 801?
❖ Could I speak to . . . ? (Can I—more informal / May I—more formal)
❖ Is George in? (Informal idiom meaning: Is George in the office?)
❖ I'd like to speak to (Miss Alice)
❖ I'm calling to ask about . . .
❖ I'd like to ask about/inquire/know if . . .
❖ Can/Could you give any information about/on . . . ?
❖ I'd appreciate it if you could give me some information on . . .
❖ I wonder if you could tell me about . . .
❖ I was wondering if you could help me . . .
❖ I'd like to know . . .
❖ I'd like to speak to . . .
❖ Could I speak to someone who . . .
❖ Could you put me through to Mr. Jones, please?
❖ Can/Could you tell me . . . ?

- ❖ Sorry to trouble you, but . . .
- ❖ Do you have any idea when/what/where . . .
- ❖ Hello is this Dr John's office?

If you are answering the phone on behalf of the company, e.g. as a receptionist would, it is normal to say 'Hello' and give the name of the company. If you are answering your own phone, you would normally say 'Hello' and give your full name. For example: "Hello, David Abraham". If you don't do that the caller can easily become confused.

It's a good idea to write down someone's name at the beginning of a call. If you miss the name, do ask again. Say 'I'm sorry I didn't catch your name'. If you want somebody to spell the name, do ask too—say 'Would you mind spelling your name please?'

Word-Groups Used for Receiving a Phone Call:

- ❖ Good morning / afternoon / evening, Jackson Enterprises, Silvia Jones speaking.
- ❖ This is . . . speaking
- ❖ How can I help you?
- ❖ How may I help you?
- ❖ Could you speak up, please?
- ❖ Who's speaking, please?
- ❖ Excuse me, who is this?
- ❖ Can I ask who is calling, please?
- ❖ Am I speaking to . . . ?
- ❖ Could you spell that please?
- ❖ Who would you like to talk to sir/ madam?
- ❖ One moment please, I'll see if Mr. John is available
- ❖ Hello / This is (23476356)/(Simpson's Ltd)
- ❖ Who's speaking, please?
- ❖ Who's calling?
- ❖ Excuse me, who is this?
- ❖ Can I ask who is calling, please?
- ❖ Speaking.
- ❖ This is Kate.
- ❖ Kate speaking.

❖ This is (me) speaking.
❖ Hold on/Hang on.
❖ I'll call him/I'll get him.
❖ I'll put you through/I'll connect you.
❖ Goodbye.

Putting Someone on Hold:

❖ Just a moment, please.
❖ Hold on, please.
❖ Hold the line, please.

Asking Someone to Call Back:

❖ Thank you for waiting. I'm afraid Mr. Jones is not in at the moment.
❖ I'm sorry, Mr. Jones is in a meeting.
❖ Can/ Could you call back later in the day?
❖ I'm afraid he is not available at the moment.
❖ The line is busy . . . (when the extension requested is being used)
❖ Mr. Jackson isn't in . . .
❖ Mr. Jackson is out at the moment . . .

When someone is unavailable, you can use:

❖ I'll wait/I'll hang on.
❖ When can I ring him back?
❖ Well, please find him/please interrupt him.
❖ Will you please make sure (he) rings me back?
❖ Where is he?
❖ When will he be in?
❖ Where can I find him?

As you finish your telephone conversation, there are some appropriate and courteous statements that should always be made. You should:

❖ Thank the customer for calling.
❖ Let the customer know you appreciate his or her business.
❖ Provide assurance that any promises will be fulfilled.

❖ Leave the customer with a positive feeling.

Courteous Closing Statements:

❖ "Thanks for calling. We appreciate your business."
❖ "Thanks for your order"
❖ "Please call us anytime."
❖ "I enjoyed talking to you,"
❖ "Thank you for your patience. I am glad we could resolve your concern."
❖ "It was a pleasure talking with you."
❖ "If you have additional questions, please call again."
❖ "I know you had to wait a long time. Thank you for being so patient."
❖ "My apology about the mix up. We do appreciate your business."
❖ "Thanks for placing your order with us."
❖ "Goodbye, and thanks for calling."

Closing Phrases for Telephonic Conversations:

❖ Listen, I can't talk now.
❖ Someone's just come in.
❖ Someone wants to speak to me.
❖ There's someone on the other line.
❖ I've got some people here right now.
❖ There are dinner guests here.
❖ Hang on, I can hear something boiling over.
❖ I can hear the doorbell.
❖ I'll have to go.
❖ Well, I'd better let you go.
❖ Well, I don't want to use/run up your phone bill.
❖ Well, thanks for calling/returning my call.
❖ I'm really glad you called.
❖ I appreciate your calling.
❖ It was nice of you to call.
❖ I'll get back to you on that.
❖ I'll Talk to you later.
❖ Well, It's been good talking to you.
❖ I've really got to run.

Problems:

- ❖ I'm sorry, I don't understand.
- ❖ I cannot hear you very well
- ❖ You must have dialed the wrong number.
- ❖ I've tried to get through several times, but it's always engaged.
- ❖ Sorry, wrong number
- ❖ Wrong number/you've got the wrong number. This is (6453), you should dial again.
- ❖ Can I leave a message?
- ❖ I'll ring back later. When's the right time? Can you ask (him) to call me?
- ❖ Can I take a message?
- ❖ Could you ring back in half an hour?
- ❖ Shall I get him to ring you back?
- ❖ I've been trying to get (12363576).
- ❖ It rings engaged all the time.
- ❖ I was cut off.

Tips for Telephoning:

Telephoning in a language, which is not your own, is not easy. You should be aware that the person you are speaking to may have difficulties too. Therefore, keep the following points in mind:

- ❖ Speak clearly. Use clear articulation and avoid difficult words and long sentences if it is not necessary to use them.
- ❖ Do not speak too fast. Keep in mind that many people tend to speak too fast when they are nervous. Hardly anyone ever speaks slowly.
- ❖ Ensure that you have got everything right. This is especially important if the other person gives addresses or dates.
- ❖ Be polite. Start and end the conversation politely. Try to avoid being too direct. In English this is often done by using 'would'. Compare: I want some more information—I would like to have some more information.
- ❖ Be efficient. Make sure that you are well prepared for the call and know what you want to say and how you want to say it in advance.

❖ Get familiar with the telephone alphabet. This is particularly important if you have to spell names and addresses.
❖ Get familiar with frequently used expressions.
❖ Listen carefully so that you don't need to ask the other person to repeat information.

Exercise:

Real Life Situations—Businesses are always interested in telling you about their products. Find a product you are interested in and research it over the telephone. You can . . .

❖ Call a store to find out the prices and specifications.
❖ Ring the company representative to find out details on how the product works.
❖ Telephone a consumer agency to find out if the product has any defects.
❖ call customer service to find out about replacement parts, etc.

Telephonic Conversation in the Spoken English Class:

❖ Place two chairs facing each other at the front of the classroom.
❖ Let the students in pair come up to these chairs to perform Telephonic Conversation.
❖ The students should do it as a role play and the situations should be given in advance.
❖ Students should hold cell phones during the role play for making it realistic.

"People used what they called a telephone because they hated being close together and they were scared of being alone."

– Chuck Palahniuk

CHAPTER 20

Body Language

Body language refers to non-verbal and usually unconscious communication through the use of postures, gestures and facial expressions. It is one of the most important aspects of an interview as first impression lasts long. The interviewer wants to see a confident candidate who is capable of taking initiatives, of finding solutions to problems and of picking out important details.

Posture

Posture refers to the structure of a body in a particular position. In other words, it is the way we sit or stand or lie down. The way people sit or stand speaks a lot about their attitude. Slouching while sitting or standing indicates weakness, lack of knowledge or confidence, nervousness, etc. Sitting back expansively, on the other hand, may suggest authoritativeness. Sitting and standing straight, without stiffening the body is the ideal posture.

Gesture

Gesture includes headshakes, hand and leg movements, shoulder movements, etc. Exaggerated gestures are same as lack of gestures. One should use gestures in a controlled way to an extent that will help communicating in a more meaningful way.

Facial Expressions

The face is the most expressive part of the human body probably because it receives quick attention. Smiling, eye movements, frowning, lip movements are together called facial expressions.

More on Postures, Gestures and facial expressions:

<u>EYES</u>

By observing the eyes and in what way a person looks at things we can understand much about him. Let us consider various types of looking:

1. The direct look:
    This is when a person looks at the other directly with wide open eyes. This shows undivided attention, genuine interest and sincere respect for the other person.
2. The sidelong glance:
    This is also called the stolen look. The observer looks sideways rather than directly. This shows that one is suspicious, doubtful, or distrusting of the other person.
3. The concentrated gaze:
    Here the eyelids are lowered to focus them on some interesting object. The stare means to look fixedly at a person. It is a sign of disrespect, so we generally avoid doing so.
4. The blank stare:
    This shows boredom. The person stares blankly into space with an unfocussed look in his eyes.
5. Blinking:
    Research shows that the frequency of blinking (meaning how often a person blinks) shows how worried a person is. Lack of blinking shows that a person is hostile or bored.
6. Rubbing the eye:
    This gesture is made when a person is in doubt or telling a lie.

<u>HANDS</u>

We will look at some hand signals and see what they mean. Let us consider various types of hand signals:

1. Limp hands:
   A limp or hanging hand shows boredom, restlessness or tiredness. It can also show disgust or frustration.
2. Relaxed hands:
   If a person is calm, confident and self-assured, his hands will rest easily and move little.
3. Restless hands:
   If a person is uneasy or nervous, his hands will be active and restless.
4. Clenched hands:
   To clench means to close together tightly or grasp firmly. This has a number of meanings.
   a. It can show fierce determination.
   b. It can show tension, frustration or anger.

FINGER MOVEMENTS

1. Pointing the index finger:
   The pointing finger is often used by parents, people in authority, preachers, and politicians while scolding, demanding discipline or driving a point home. People dislike being the target of a pointing finger. Do not point your finger in an interview.

2. Steepling:
   Some people join their fingertips and form what is called a church steeple. This shows that a person is very sure of what he is saying. It is a very positive gesture.

3. Thumb gesture:
   Men sometimes put their hands in their pockets and let the thumbs stick out. Dominant and aggressive women also make this gesture. Do not use this gesture during an interview.

4. Cracking of knuckles:
   This shows anxiety, nervousness, boredom, restlessness and a confused mind. Do not do this during an interview.

ARMS

1. Crossed or folded arms:
   This gesture is used worldwide to show defensiveness. It can also show a closed mind.

2. Arm gripping:
    Here the hands hold the arms tightly. This shows a negative or suppressed attitude.
3. Arms behind the back:
    This is a gesture of self-control. It shows that a person is having inner conflict.

OTHER GESTURES

1. Rubbing the Nose:
    Rubbing the nose can be a gesture of rejection or of doubt. It can be used by the speaker to hide the fact that he is lying or by the listener if he doubts the speaker's words.
2. Putting the hand on the Cheek:
    When a person puts his hands on his cheek and his eyes blink, it shows that he is thinking deeply. It could also indicate attention and interest.
3. Palms covering Cheeks:
    When a person presses his palms flat against his cheek it suggests that he is being patient, or resigned, or feeling helpless.
4. Stroking the Chin:
    People make this gesture when they are going through a decision making process or evaluating something or when they are thinking deeply.
5. Head in Hand:
    The head supported at the cheeks by one or both hands can signify despair, loss, prolonged thinking, or boredom. When a person supports his forehead with his palms it may show that he is in deep thought or in a desperate situation.
6. Hands behind the Head:
    Professionals or people who are feeling confident, dominant or superior commonly use this gesture.

MORE ON BODY LANGUAGE

NONVERBAL BEHAVIOR → means → INTERPRETATION
Brisk, erect walk → Confidence
Standing with hands on hips → Readiness, aggression
Sitting with legs crossed, foot kicking slightly → Boredom
Sitting, legs apart → Open, relaxed
Arms crossed on chest → Defensiveness
Walking with hands in pockets, shoulders hunched → Dejection

Hand to cheek → Evaluation, thinking
Touching, slightly rubbing nose → Rejection, doubt, lying
Rubbing the eye → Doubt, disbelief
Hands clasped behind back → Anger, frustration, apprehension
Locked ankles → Apprehension
Head resting in hand, eyes downcast → Boredom
Rubbing hands → Anticipation
Open palm → Sincerity, openness, innocence
Pinching bridge of nose, eyes closed → Negative evaluation
Tapping or drumming fingers → Impatience
Steepling fingers → Authoritative
Patting/fondling hair → Lack of self-confidence; insecurity
Tilted head → Interest
Stroking chin → Trying to make a decision
Looking down, face turned away → Disbelief

Stage Fearing? Try This.

A young preacher was shy and afraid of talking in public. After having been encouraged, he was told to deliver his sermon to pumpkins that grew in abundance in his garden. He tried and was quite satisfied. His instructor remarked, "Well today you preached to pumpkins as if they were men, and you scored well. Tomorrow you will preach to men as if they were pumpkins, and you will score better.

CHAPTER 21

GROUP DISCUSSION

FAQ's ABOUT GD

1. **What is a GD?**

   Ans.: GD is a discussion by a group of people which involves an exchange of thoughts and ideas. Group Discussions are largely used by institutes where there is a high level of competition.

2. **What is evaluated?**

   Ans.: GD is a means to assess one's overall personality and different skills. The skills evaluated are:

   ⇨ INTERPERSONAL/PERSONALITY SKILL
   ⇨ KNOWLEDGE/CONCEPTUALISATION SKILL
   ⇨ PROBLEM-SOLVING SKILL
   ⇨ COMMUNICATION SKILL
   ⇨ PERSUASIVE SKILL
   ⇨ LEADERSHIP SKILL

   An Examiner can easily make an assessment of candidates on above parameters in a GD. All that one observes in a GD can be categorized into two broad areas: the Content and the Process. The content is all about the 'matter' (or the 'what') spoken in the GD; whereas, the process refers to the 'how', 'when' and 'why' of the GD. Both are equally important and need adequate attention at all stages.

3. **How does a GD take place?**

   Ans.: A Group of 6-15 candidates are made to sit in a circular or a semi-circular (U Shaped) fashion so that they can see each other and take part in the discussion easily. Roll Numbers may be allotted to participants for easy recognition. Before the GD, the examiner (observer) announces the topic for discussion and informs candidates about the time-limit. He may also draw attention towards the etiquette, rules and regulation, procedure to be followed. The individuals of the group might be given some initial time to put down their thoughts on the topic. The examiner observes the proceedings of the discussion from a distance without directly interfering into it.

4. **Are the topics decided on the basis of the academic background of the participants?**
    Ans.: No, the grouping of members and the topics is done by the institute's admission team. Academic background is rarely asked.

5. **Can a definite stand be taken?**
    Ans.: If you have complete conviction on your stand TAKE IT, (esp. in case of ethical topics)—It is important to be true and fair first to yourself and then to others. But, at the same time appreciate others' point of view and evaluate their judgment without bias.

    Taking one side of the topic initially and then moving to another or oscillating between the two sides during the GD shows signs of indecisiveness. Remember, managers are effective decision makers.

    In most groups, you would find close to a 50:50 situation for and against a topic. Even if you are a minority take the stand.

6. **What is the right time to enter to ensure I am heard?**
    Ans.: If the order is preset by the examiner then you will have your chance as per your turn. The opportunities to enter are First Member, Last Member and the Middle Member. The best time to enter is in the first so that you maintain uniqueness of your points, but at the risk of losing out on others' points which you could build on. If you find it uncomfortable to be the first to take the plunge, listen out others and then enter along with the middle/last members. Frankly, there is no right or wrong time to enter or not. Just make sure that you speak out your points in the initial round of discussion.

7. **How necessary is it to use examples for illustrating an idea?**
    Ans.: Using an example simplifies the understanding of your point to the group. Substantiation is like putting a seal of authenticity to your

statement. Try and use relevant facts/figures wherever possible. Use an example or two for a point that you wish to project.

8. **What is summarization?**

   Ans.: Converting the entire discussion into 4 or 5 points without any bias to fully represent the thoughts of the group. In some cases, everyone might be asked to summarize so you must form a habit of summarizing.

9. **What should you do if one member is very stubborn and aggressive?**

   Ans.: Don't get into an argument with the member—"Don't let his virus infect you". Objectively and calmly present your point of view vis-à-vis his. You could ask other group members to comment (to break the deadlock) and take the discussion forward.

10. **How do you participate when the noise level is high?**

    Ans.: Every group has a High—when most people are talking—This is when you should listen and your mind should think and evaluate the plethora of others' thoughts. You can interject when the group is on a low (You will be able to observe it if you are alert.)—Then present your evaluation of others' thoughts and perhaps take the discussion on to a more positive platform. This would show a clear structure in your thinking. Sometimes you can bring the group to a refocus, when the group digresses from the topics. These are all positive traits of a manager and naturally give you plus points.

11. **What is the normal duration of a GD?**

    Ans.: A GD is generally of 15-20 minutes duration.

12. **How many panel members are there to evaluate?**

    Ans.: There are usually 3-4 panel members to evaluate.

13. **Is there time given for preparation after the topic is given and before starting the GD?**

    Ans.: Usually some time (2-5 minutes) is given to collect one's thoughts, but there could be instances when this does not happen, so it is best not to bank on this.

14. **Should I address the panel or the group members?**

    Ans.: Don't ever make the mistake of addressing the panel members. The GD is between you and the other members, not the panel members. You must avoid even looking at the panel members while the GD is in progress. Just ignore their existence.

15. **What is the seating arrangement like?**

    Ans.: It could be semi-circular, or circular, or seating alongside a rectangular table, depending upon the venue. It is best not to bother about trivial issues like this, which you have no control over.

16. How should I address the other group members?

Ans.: If you are initiating the discussion, you could do so by collectively addressing the group as "Friends". Subsequently, you could use names (if the group has had a round of self-introduction prior to starting the discussion and you remember the names) or simply use 'speaker-1', 'speaker-2', etc.

17. Suppose I have a lot to say on the topic, should I say all of it?

Ans.: You would not be looked upon favourably if you kept speaking all the time and did not listen to anyone else. Contrary to the misconception, the person who talks the most is not necessarily the one who is judged the best. The quality and not the quantity of your contribution is the success factor.

18. Should I encourage others to speak up?

Ans.: Do not directly put someone who is consistently silent on the spot by asking him/her to speak up. If someone has been trying to speak and has a good point but is cut off constantly, you may encourage him/her to continue with her point as you would like to hear her out.

19. Are the group members supposed to keep track of the time or will the panel keep track?

Ans.: It would be good if you are conscious of the time, but not to the point of getting so distracted looking at your watch that you do not contribute to the discussion.

20. What are the types of GD's?

Ans.: GDs can be topic-based or case-based. Topic based GDs can be classified into three types like Factual Topics, Controversial Topics and Abstract Topics.

1. Factual Topics:

Factual topics are about practical things, which an ordinary person is aware of in his day-to-day life. Typically these are about socio-economic topics. These can be current, i.e. they may have been in the news lately, or could be unbound by time. A factual topic for discussion gives a candidate a chance to prove that he is aware of and sensitive to his environment.

Ex.: Democracy is a Luxury in India, Indian Railways, and State of the Aged in the Nation.

2. Controversial Topics:

Controversial topics are the ones that are argumentative in nature. They are meant to generate controversy. In GDs where these topics are given for discussion, the noise level is usually high, there may be tempers flying. The idea behind giving a topic like this is to see how much maturity the candidate is displaying by keeping his temper in check, by rationally and logically arguing his point of view without getting personal and emotional.

Ex.: Reservations should be removed, GDs as a means of selection by the IIMs are a farce, Women make better managers, Religion and Politics, etc.

3. Abstract Topics:

Abstract topics are about intangible things. These topics are not given often for discussion, but their possibility cannot be ruled out. These topics test your lateral thinking and creativity.

Ex.: When red meets red, Twinkle twinkle little star, Virtue has its own reward, The number 1, etc.

Case-based GD:

Another variation is the use of a case instead of a topic. The case study tries to simulate a real-life situation. Information about the situation will be given to you and you would be asked as a group to resolve the situation. In the case study there are no incorrect answers or perfect solutions. The objective in the case study is to get you to think about the situation from various angles.

IIM's and IIM's have a case-based discussion rather than topic-based discussion in their selection procedures.

SKILLS EVALUATED IN A GD

Here is a sample list of skills assessed during a group discussion:

Leadership skills:

Ability to take leadership roles and ability to lead, inspire and carry the team along to help them achieve group's objectives.

Example:
To be able to initiate the group discussion, or to be able to guide the group especially when the discussion begins losing relevance or try to encourage all members to participate in the discussion.

Communication skills:
The participating candidates will be assessed in terms of clarity of thought, expression and aptness of language. One key aspect is listening. It indicates a willingness to accommodate others' views.

Example:
To be able to use simple language and explain concepts clearly so that it is easily understood by all. You actually get negative marks for using esoteric jargons in an attempt to show-off your knowledge.

Interpersonal skills:
It is reflected in the ability of the individual to interact with other members of the group in a brief situation. Emotional maturity and balance promotes good interpersonal relationships. The person has to be more people centric and less self-centered.

Example:
To remain cool even when someone provokes you with personal comment, ability to remain objective, ability to empathize, non-threatening and more of a team player.

Persuasive skills:
Ability to analyze and persuade others to see the problem from multiple perspectives without hurting the group members.

Example:
While appreciating someone else's point of view, you should be able to effectively communicate your view without overtly hurting the other person.

Problem solving skills:
Ability to come out with divergent and offbeat solutions and use one's own creativity.

Example:
While thinking of solutions, don't be afraid to think of novel solutions. This is a high-risk, high-return strategy.

Conceptualizing skills (Knowledge):
The ability to grasp the situation, take it from the day to day mundane problem level and apply it to a macro level.

Example:
At the end of the discussion, you could probably summarize the findings in a few sentences that present the overall perspective.

Do's and Don'ts of G.D.

DO's
⇨ Listen to others. It is not absolutely necessary to initiate a Group Discussion.
⇨ Initiate the discussion if you are familiar with the topic.
⇨ Intervene if the discussion is turning out to be hostile. It reflects your leadership.
⇨ Speak to the point without repeating.
⇨ Back your points with facts and figures.
⇨ Be gentle with your presentation.
⇨ Be natural, calm and maintain your composure.
⇨ Be participative and reciprocative.
⇨ Say 'Thank You' before ending your presentation.
⇨ Think before you speak.
⇨ Say what you feel, without going in "Favour"/ "Against".

DON'Ts
⇨ Do not be loud or aggressive.
⇨ Do not go overboard with enthusiasm if you are familiar with the topic.
⇨ Do not interrupt other speakers.
⇨ Do not deprecate other speakers.
⇨ Do not speak first if you are unfamiliar with the topic.
⇨ Do not change your opinions.
⇨ Do not ask irrelevant questions.
⇨ Do not stop abruptly.

➡ Do not get nervous if the previous speakers have presented their points in a better way.

➡ Do not exhibit your emotions.

Tips

➡ Always be the initiator and concluder of the Group Discussion than being a participant.

➡ But if you are participant always try to be the most key participant.

➡ Put points firmly and always try to get others support too.

➡ If you find that the discussion is going off the track, bring it back to stream to get better score.

➡ Try to keep latest information on the topic.

➡ Be very polite, people may try to provoke you to get more points but try to keep cool.

➡ Most important, don't wait for your turn to speak when discussion is on. Interrupt politely if you want to put forward your points.

➡ Last but not the least, keep a tab on the time given for discussion. Score points by wrapping up the discussion if you feel that the discussion is heating but the time is going to be over.

➡ During conclusion, do end with the conclusion note. That shows your leadership quality.

THE GD PROCESS

In a Group Discussion the candidates are divided in groups of 8 to 10 and each group is tested by a panel of Judges. Usually topics of general interest are given by the panel to the group and the group is asked to proceed with discussion. Every candidate is supposed to express his opinion and views on the topic given. The time for discussion is approximately 20 minutes. During the discussion, the panel of Judges quietly observes the performance and behavior of the candidates and makes his own assessment. A group discussion can be categorically divided into three different phases:

    i.   Initiation/ Introduction

    ii. Body of the group discussion

    iii. Summarisation/ Conclusion

Let's stress on the initiation and summarisation:

i. Initiation Techniques

Initiating a Group Discussion is a high profit-high loss strategy. If you can make a favourable first impression with your content and communication skills after you initiate a Group Discussion, it will help you sail through the discussion. But if you initiate a Group Discussion and stammer/ stutter/ quote wrong facts and figures, the damage might be irreparable. If you initiate a Group Discussion impeccably but don't speak much after that, it gives the impression that you started the Group Discussion for the sake of starting it or getting those initial kitty of points earmarked for an initiator!

When you start a Group Discussion, you are responsible for putting it into the right perspective or framework. So initiate one only if you have in depth knowledge about the topic at hand.

There are different techniques to initiate a Group Discussion and make a good first impression:
1. Quotes
2. Definition
3. Questions
4. Shock statement
5. Facts, figures and statistics
6. Short story
7. General statement

Quotes:

Quotes are an effective way of initiating a Group Discussion. If the topic of a Group Discussion is: Should the Censor Board be abolished?, you could start with a quote like, 'Hidden apples are always sweet'. For a Group Discussion topic like, Customer is King, you could quote Sam (Wal-mart) Walton's famous saying, 'There is only one boss: the customer. And he can fire everybody in the company—from the chairman on down, simply by spending his money somewhere else.'

Definition:

Start a Group Discussion by defining the topic or an important term in the topic. For example, if the topic of the Group Discussion is Advertising is a Diplomatic Way of Telling a Lie, why not start the Group Discussion by defining advertising as, 'Any paid form of non-personal presentation and promotion of ideas, goods or services through mass media like newspapers, magazines, television or radio by an identified sponsor'?

For a topic like The Malthusian Economic Prophecy is no longer relevant, you could start by explaining the definition of the Malthusian Economic Prophecy.

Questions:

Asking a question is an impactive way of starting a Group Discussion. It does not signify asking a question to any of the candidates in a Group Discussion so as to hamper the flow. It implies asking a question, and answering it yourself. Any question that might hamper the flow of a Group Discussion or insult a participant or play devil's advocate must be discouraged. Questions that promote a flow of ideas are always appreciated.

For a topic like, Should India go to war with Pakistan, you could start by asking, 'What does war bring to the people of a nation? We have had four clashes with Pakistan. The pertinent question is: what have we achieved?'

Shock statement:

Initiating a Group Discussion with a shocking statement is the best way to grab immediate attention and put forth your point.

If a Group Discussion topic is, The Impact of Population on the Indian Economy, you could start with, 'At the centre of the Indian capital stands a population clock that ticks away relentlessly. It tracks 33 births a minute, 2,000 an hour, 48,000 a day, which calculates to about 12 million every year. That is roughly the size of Australia. As a current political slogan puts it, 'Nothing is impossible when 1 billion Indians work together'.

Facts, figures and statistics:

If you decide to initiate your Group Discussion with facts, figure and statistics make sure to quote them accurately. Approximation is allowed in macro level figures, but micro level figures need to be correct and accurate.

For example, you can say, approximately 70 per cent of the Indian population stays in rural areas (macro figures, approximation allowed). But you cannot say 30 states of India instead of 28 (micro figures, no approximations). Remember stating wrong facts works to your disadvantage.

For a Group Discussion topic like, China, a Rising Tiger, you could start with, 'In 1983, when China was still in its initial stages of reform and opening up, China's real use of Foreign Direct Investment only stood at $636 million. China actually utilised $60 billion of FDI in 2004, which is almost 100 times that of its 1983 statistics."

Short story:

Use a short story in a Group Discussion topic like 'Attitude is Everything'.

This can be initiated with, 'A child once asked a balloon vendor, who was selling helium gas-filled balloons, whether a blue-coloured balloon will go as high in the sky as a green-coloured balloon. The balloon vendor told the child, it is not the colour of the balloon but what is inside it that makes it go high.'

General statement:
Use a general statement to put the Group Discussion in proper perspective.

For example, if the topic is, Should Sonia Gandhi be the prime minister of India?, you could start by saying, 'Before jumping to conclusions like, 'Yes, Sonia Gandhi should be', or 'No, Sonia Gandhi should not be', let's first find out the qualities one needs to be a good prime minister of India. Then we can compare these qualities with those that Mrs. Gandhi possesses. This will help us reach the conclusion in a more objective and effective manner.'

ii. **Summarisation Techniques:**
❖ Most Group Discussions do not really have conclusions. A conclusion is where the whole group decides in favour or against the topic.
❖ But every Group Discussion is summarised. You can summarise what the group has discussed in the Group Discussion in a nutshell. Keep the following points in mind while summarising a discussion:
❖ Avoid raising new points.
❖ Avoid stating only your viewpoint.

❖ Avoid dwelling only on one aspect of the Group Discussion.

❖ Keep it brief and concise.

❖ It must incorporate all the important points that came out during the Group Discussion.

❖ If the examiner asks you to summarise a Group Discussion, it means the Group Discussion has come to an end. Do not add anything once the Group Discussion has been summarised.

Mistakes in GD

Wise men learn from others' mistakes, while the less fortunate, from their own. Here's a list of the most common mistakes made at group discussions.

Emotional outburst:
Rashmi was offended when one of the male participants in a group discussion made a statement on women generally being submissive while explaining his point of view. When Rashmi finally got an opportunity to speak, instead of focussing on the topic, she vented her anger by accusing the other candidate for being a male chauvinist and went on to defend women in general.

What Rashmi essentially did was to:
❖ Deviate from the subject;
❖ Treat the discussion as a forum to air her own views;
❖ Lose objectivity and make personal attacks.

Her behaviour would have been perceived as immature and demotivating to the rest of the team.

Quality Vs. Quantity:
Gautam believed that the more he talked, the more likely he was to get through the GD. So, he interrupted other people at every opportunity. He did this so often that the other candidates got together to prevent him from participating in the rest of the discussion.

❖ Assessment is not only on your communication skills but also on your ability to be a team player.

❖ Evaluation is based on quality, and not on quantity. Your contribution must be relevant.

❖ The mantra is "Contributing meaningfully to the team's success." Domination is frowned upon.

Egotism/Showing off:

Krishna was happy to have got a group discussion topic he had prepared for. So, he took pains to project his vast knowledge of the topic. Every other sentence of his contained statistical data—"20% of companies; 24.27% of parliamentarians felt that; I recently read in a Jupiter Report that . . ." and so on. Soon, the rest of the team either laughed at him or ignored his attempts to enlighten them as they perceived that he was cooking up the data.

❖ Exercise restraint in anything. You will end up being frowned upon if you attempt showing-off your knowledge.
❖ Facts and figures need not validate all your statements.
❖ Its your analysis and interpretation that are equally important—not just facts and figures.
❖ You might be appreciated for your in-depth knowledge. But you will fail miserably in your people skills.

Such a behavior indicates how self-centered you are and highlights your inability to work in an atmosphere where different opinions are expressed.

Get noticed—But for the right reasons:

Srikumar knew that everyone would compete to initiate the discussion. So as soon as the topic—"Discuss the negative effects of India joining the WTO"—was read out, he began talking. In his anxiety to be the first to start speaking, he did not hear the word "negative" in the topic. He began discussing the ways in which the country had benefited by joining WTO, only to be stopped by the evaluator, who then corrected his mistake.

❖ False starts are extremely expensive. They cost you your admission. It is very important to listen and understand the topic before you air your opinions.
❖ Spending a little time analyzing the topic may provide you with insights which others may not have thought about. Use a pen and paper to jot down your ideas.
❖ Listen! It gives you the time to conceptualize and present the information in a better manner.

Some mistakes are irreparable. Starting off the group discussion with a mistake is one such mistake, unless you have a great sense of humor.

Managing one's insecurities:
Sumati was very nervous. She thought that some of the other candidates were exceptionally good. Thanks to her insecurity, she contributed little to the discussion. Even when she was asked to comment on a particular point, she preferred to remain silent.

❖ Your personality is also being evaluated. Your verbal and non verbal cues are being read.

❖ Remember, you are the participant in the GD; not the evaluator. So, rather than evaluating others and your performance, participate in the discussion.

❖ Your confidence level is being evaluated. Decent communication skills with good confidence is a must to crack the GDs.

❖ Focus on your strengths and do not spend too much time thinking about how others are superior or inferior to you. It is easy to pick up these cues from your body language.

GD TOPICS

POLITICAL
1. Election means wastage of money.
2. USA—the biggest threat to world peace.
3. It's all politician's fault.
4. Democracy is the dictatorship of a group.
5. Democracy is the root of all evils.
6. Compulsory higher education for all politicians.
7. If Laloo becomes the PM?
8. Should business houses finance elections?
9. China, a superpower.
10. Coalition politics, a new trend in India.
11. Politicians and industialists' nexus
12. Presidential form of Government for India
13. Students should not take part in politics
14. Retirement age for politicians
15. India should adopt bi-party system.
17. Should Sonia Gandhi be made the PM?

18. Reserving seats for women in Panchayat has not only been a farce but has distracted from developing a more genuine voice of women.
19. Voters, not, political parties are responsible for the criminalisation of politics.
20. The voters are required to be well informed and educated about their candidates so that they can elect the right aspirant by their own assessment.

ECONOMIC
1. The concept of Swadeshi is an obstacle to economic growth.
2. Public sector should be disinvested.
3. Privatisation in Agriculture
4. Economic Reform
5. Globalisation is bad for the Indian Companies.
6. Is plastic money harming the economy?
7. Income tax should be abolished.
8. Public sector in India is vital for economic development.
9. Is India able to compete in the global market?
10. Import is essential for economic development.
11. India as you visualise in the year 2020.
12. Economic Liberalisation—a critical assessment
13. Privatisation is necessary in every sector.
14. Unemployment in India.
15. Inflation as you know it.
16. BPO's in India.
17. Governmant's contribution to IT
18. Is china a threat to indian industry?
19. 36.Is Swadeshi relevant for India today?
20. The future lies with glocalisation.
21. Is the consumer really the king in India?.
22. Globalisation versus nationalism
23. Conditional access system for cable TV watchers: boon or bane?
24. What we need to reduce scams is better regulatory bodies.
25. Trade can help the poor?

EDUCATIONAL
1. Privatisation of higher education.
2. Teachers' assessment by the students.
3. Students and politics
4. More primary schools than IIT's

5. Reservation in Educational Institutes
6. Reservation policy in promotion
7. TV—a means of education for children.
8. Adding 'C' to 3R's
9. History should be deleted from the school syllabus.
10. Educational Institutes for farmers.
11. Say 'YES' to private tuition.
12. English as the compulsory medium of instruction in schools.
13. Say 'NO' to public schools.
14. Right to Information
15. Girls make better teachers than boys.
16. The education system needs serious reforms.
17. Our Culture is Decaying.
18. A Gandhian State selling liquor is an anomaly.
19. Commercialisation of health care: Good or Bad?
20. Are women as good as men or inferior?

ENVIRONMENT
1. Noise Pollution
2. Environment Pollution
3. Afforestation
4. Deforestation
5. Social Forestry Programme
6. Urbanisation and Environment
7. Industrialisation and Environment.
8. Waste Management
9. Economic Development and Growth of Slum
10. Is plastic better than paper?
11. Developed countries are damaging the ecosystem.
12. Pollution is the price of economic development.
13. Smoking should be banned.
14. Over attention on ecological issues slows down development.
15. Genetically modified crops.
16. Environment Management.
17. One man, one tree
18. Water pollution
19. Pollution Control

ETHICS AND LAW

1. Ethics in politics
2. Business ethics is a contradictory term.
3. Is greed a key to business success?
4. Common sense is more important than being a genius for business.
5. Corruption performs an economic function.
6. Politics and ethics can't coexist.
7. Mercy killing should be legalised.
8. Say 'NO' to capital punishment.
9. Gandhian philosophy is irrelevant today.
10. Corruption has become a way of life.
11. Our Culture is Decaying
12. Business and ethics go hand in hand, or do they?

TECHNOLOGY

1. The internet is for the benefit of the Indian middle class.
2. Computers: boon or bane?
3. India needs microchips, not potato chips.
4. Computers cause unemployment.
5. Importance of e-commerce.
6. Impact of computers on business
7. Technological advancement and India's backwardness
8. Is China better than India in software?
9. Dot com or doubt com?
10. Technology: the Ism' of the new millennium?

MBA RELATED

1. Good managers—born or made?
2. Women can't manage both home and work.
3. Women make better managers than men.
4. India needs managers, not leaders.
5. The role of managers in tomorrow's liberalised world.
6. Are MBA's overpaid?
7. Management education is a luxury in a poor country like India
8. Management graduates are more interested in salaries than management.
9. Everybody is a manager.
10. If I were the CEO of Pepsi Co.?
11. Balance between professionalism and family

12. Do you think MBAs are useful in the manufacturing and production department?
13. Indians perform better as individuals rather than in groups.
14. MBA in India is highly overrated.

SOCIAL
1. Is population a blessing?
2. Corruption in India
3. AIDS test should be made compulsory.
4. Equality of sexes
5. The next generation is a generation of rebels.
6. An Indian woman—a better homemaker or a better business woman?
7. Beauty contests should be banned.
8. Love marriages are better.
9. Is advertising a waste?
10. Advertising should be banned.
11. T.V. addiction and its consequences.
12. Be Indian and buy Indian.
13. Joint family or nucleus family?
14. Hindi films are the strongest integrating force.
15. Causes of disintegration of joint families.
16. Effect of cinema on Youth
17. What is the effect of movies on youth? (Is it good or bad?)
18. The impact of MTV on our psyche.
19. Media is a mixed blessing / How ethical is media?
20. To fight AIDS, stop being coy about sex education.

SPORTS
1. Future of sports in India
2. Cricket should be our national game.
3. Test matches should be abolished.
4. Should betting in cricket be legalised?
5. Fifty—50 or Twenty—20?
6. Our cricketers are not to be blamed for match fixing.
7. Six billion and one bronze!
8. India—more players, less audience.
9. More money for prize and less for the preparation.
10. Should gambling be a game?

INTERNATIONAL AFFAIRS
1. US war on Iraq-justified or not.
2. Role of UN in peacekeeping.
3. 'UN's peace activities" and "America's war on Iraq".
4. How to deal with international terrorism?
5. Should we pursue our policy of dialogue with Pakistan?
6. Is India a Soft Nation?

ABSTRACT
1. Catch them young.
2. Dead yesterday—unborn tomorrow
3. What about me?
4. Dreams can happen.
5. We are being watched.
6. Life after death
7. Is love just a four-letter word?
8. When I woke up in the morning, I saw . . .
9. Necessity is the mother of all inventions.
10. The ends justify the means.
11. Time is money.
12. Your name
13. Black is beauty.
14. The third eye
15. The last few lines
16. Just as we have smoke free zones, we should have child free zones.
17. Marriage is a social trap.
18. All work and no play makes Jack a dull boy.
19. Age and Youth: Experience and Young Talent

Some Sample Group Discussions

Topic 1: 'Succeeding in Group Discussions' (For the Beginners):

Aditi, Bijoy, Charu, Daisy and Ehsan are waiting for their group discussion to start. They do not have a topic yet and are waiting for the moderator to make everybody comfortable. There, the moderator looks at the clock and announces: "You have 5 minutes for this group discussion. And your topic is 'How to Succeed in Group Discussions.' Please start."

The Discussion:

Bijoy:	This should be interesting. A GD on GD! I suggest we should discuss the importance of a GD first. I mean, why have a GD at all?
Charu:	I find this very strange. How can you have a GD on GD? We should be discussing some current topic to test our knowledge.
Ehsan:	I agree that this is rather unusual. At the same time, our job is to conduct a meaningful discussion regardless of the topic. Bijoy has suggested we start with the importance of GD. Today, GD is a very important part of various selection procedures.
Aditi:	GD is all about teamwork. That's all.
Bijoy:	Management is all about working with people. I suppose GD is one way of establishing one's ability to work with others. How we are able to lead and be led.
Charu:	(Laughs) You are using some impressive management jargon, my friend! I don't think GD has anything to do with leading or being led. At the most, a GD may give an idea about how a business meeting is held. Otherwise it is only about sharing your knowledge with others.
Bijoy:	(Visibly irritated) Looks like you are very sure about your knowledge. Perhaps there is no need for a group or even a discussion?
Ehsan:	We have some interesting points here. Leadership and sharing knowledge. Perhaps, a GD is a good tool to assess how well you are able to function within a group.
Daisy:	I want to . . .
Aditi:	I don't think any discussion is meaningful unless everyone has the same level of knowledge.
Daisy:	I want to say something. Pardon if I make any wrong. I am from vernacular medium . . .
Aditi:	Don't waste our time talking about your background. The topic is GD. Talk about that.
Bijoy:	Every subject has various angles. So, many heads can raise many ideas.
Charu:	Also, too many cooks spoil the broth (laughs).
Ehsan:	Yes, a group makes it possible to brainstorm any issue. Perhaps Daisy has something to add to this thought . . .

Daisy: Thanks for giving me chance. A GD is good for 'consensus.' It is always better everybody agree. Otherwise only one person is there.

Charu: (Leaning forward and pointing to Daisy) I think the correct word is consensus. Don't use a word unless you know what you are talking about.

Bijoy: Consensus is fine. But is it necessary that everyone should have the same viewpoint?

Ehsan: That is an interesting thought. Yes, Daisy is right that a GD is about consensus but there can still be differences. A GD provides an opportunity to discuss various aspects of an issue and weigh merits and demerits of different approaches.

Charu: Agree to disagree.

Bijoy: But the question is how to succeed in GDs. I think the first prerequisite is patience. Some of us must learn to shut up and let others talk (looks directly at Charu).

Aditi: If everyone follows that we will only have silence and no discussion.

Ehsan: I suppose the point is to participate and give others also a chance to participate.

Daisy: Please can I speak?

Aditi: Come on! You don't have to beg for permission to speak!

Daisy: I said that because I thought someone might have wanted to speak before me. Anyway, is it not possible to only listen?

Charu: (Smirks) I don't know how the moderator will rate your profound silence!

Bijoy: But Daisy, no one can read your mind. Unless you speak, how do you contribute?

Ehsan: I think a GD is very much like a business meeting. Every participant may present an individual point of view but the thinking about that point of view is collective.

Aditi: I don't think you can compare a GD to a business meeting. In a meeting, there is usually a chairman whose job is to control the meeting.

Bijoy: A GD may not have a chairman but I suppose one person usually emerges as the leader and guides the discussion.

Charu: I suppose someone fancies himself to be a leader. This is so boring!

Moderator: Your time is up. Thank you everyone.

Analysis:
Ehsan shows leadership skills and the ability to hold a group together. He appears to have a good grasp of the subject though on the whole the GD failed to do justice to the core subject of how to succeed. Bijoy also has some interesting ideas but is prone to being provoked easily. Charu is too sure and too full of herself to be able to contribute to a group. Aditi is guilty of intolerance and rude interruptions. Daisy needs to work on her language and her confidence, though she may have the right concepts.

Topic 2: 'The Extension of the Retirement Age'

Background Information:
A group discussion consisting of eight participants is being held. The candidates are seated in a closed circle. The examiner makes a brief speech welcoming candidates and wishing them success. He announces the topic and allots 20 minutes for the discussion.

The Discussion:
With the departure of the examiner, candidates start murmuring and whispering. Suddenly No. 1 raises his voice in a commanding tone, and begins, "Listen chaps, this is a damn stupid topic. I don't think any young person can welcome a thing like the extension of the retirement age. I was the president of my college union for a long time. I fully understand what today's youth wants. At best this is an old man's game. I can speak on the topic for hours . . ." He is interrupted by No. 3, "You loud mouth! Don't pose as a Mr. Know All. Don't you have manners enough to refer to old people? I can also speak for hours and can shut your mouth with equally indecent words."

No. 4 steps in and in a sober but assertive tone addresses both No. 1 and No. 3, "Dear friends, I appreciate the views both of you have expressed and I value your opinion, but we should spell out the implication of a significant decision by the government in the right perspective. It is not a question of old versus young; we have to evaluate the pros and cons of the decision. I hope both of you understands, and the rest of our friends will also appreciate that we are here with a mission. We have to complete our discussion within the stipulated 20 minutes and therefore, I suggest that we should go for two rounds. In the first, each of us will take one and a half minute to express his views and the second round will be for the discussion. May I further suggest starting with No. 1 and then go on to No. 2, No. 3, and so on?"

Candidate No. 6:	Thank God. Here's a sensible man. I support you.
Candidate No. 7:	Yes, I also do.
Candidate No. 8:	I also agree, but I would like to make a suggestion. If anybody other than No. 1 is desirous to open the game, he is welcome.
Many of them:	"No, No. It is quite appropriate to begin with No. 1. Let us stick to it."
Candidate No. 1:	I strongly oppose this move by the government. It is a stab on the back of the youths of India who will be thrown into the stinking pool of unemployment. All political parties have promised a better and larger job opportunity for the youth, but they have back-tracked most shamelessly. Will there be any jobs in the coming two years? What will we do? Should we turn into smugglers, criminals, drug peddlers, or terrorists? No, no, I want the government to scrap the decision at the earliest. It is a very stupid and callous decision. I am not going to accept it.
Candidate No. 2:	Well friends, in fact, I am not ready now. I would like to speak at the end after having listened to your views. However, I am definitely sure that this move is going to affect our job prospects and in the near future we shall have great hassles in life. I hope our other friends will make more interesting points.
Candidate No. 3:	Thank you No. 2. I totally disagree with No. 1 who has used high-flown words and has poured venom against the government and has also displayed a contemptuous attitude to the senior members of the society. Has he forgotten that we are the children of our elders? Does he want his parents to sit idle and starve and feel the pangs of futility while he gets all the fruits in his share? As long as a person is physically and mentally fit, he should continue in his/her job. This is indeed a bonanza for our elders. I hope, No. 1 will use his mind and see that he develops a right perspective. All of us know that our country is passing through an economic crisis,

particularly, after the nuclear explosions. And this is a right step to manage revenue gains. I hope, No. 1 will surely revise his obstinate and foolish opinion.

Candidate No. 4: Dear friends, I do appreciate the points made by the previous speakers. I also understand the fervour of their feeling. I only suggest them to be more friendly and warm in their behaviour. It is quite relevant that our country needs money to tide over the economic peril which has suddenly assumed dangerous proportions due to sanctions imposed by the U.S., Japan, and other countries. But, the revenue gain is a shortsighted step. The dangers on the other hand are much more alarming. This extension of the retirement age for central government employees is like opening the Pandora's Box. The public sector has already consented and banking organizations are following suit. The state governments are under great pressure and will have to give in. It will hamstring job opportunities, compelling a very large number of youth to embrace violence, terrorist activities, smuggling, and anti-social and criminal offences. Kashmir and Punjab are the two burning examples where life has been brought back to normalcy only after adequate employment opportunities were provided. New Kashmirs and Punjabs will emerge on the national scene. Brain-drain, which is already a painful and sad reality in our country, will spread because large chunks of youth will run away to other countries in search of jobs. So far we had brain-drain only at the qualitative level, but this move by the government will lead to a quantitative exodus as well. And ethically speaking, it is against the manifestoes of all political parties, which had promised during the elections, enhanced job packages for the youth. It is at best a Machiavellian political move, in sharp contrast to the Gandhian philosophy of the right means for the right end.

Candidate No. 5: Thanks No. 4, but I would like to dispute you. Every sensible citizen has to help the government in a crisis. However, I am sure that it is going to affect our job prospects in the near future. I hope, our other friends will make more interesting point. External threats can be counter-balanced by maintaining economic restraint, displaying complete solidarity, and achieving self-reliance. This step is a worthy endeavour in this direction. It would be unwise to accuse the government of betrayal, as the country needs our support and sacrifice at this critical hour. Moreover, the country will be able to utilize the expertise of senior and mature scientists, teachers, defence officers, and other persons engaged in research and other developmental works.

Candidate No. 6: Thanks No. 5, I agree with you. While I really appreciate and value the arguments put forward against the decision by my friends here, particularly No. 1 and 4, I would like to pose a question to ourselves— Why did the government take this decision after all? I draw your attention to the fact that this specific recommendation of the government will bring in a gain of Rs. 5,200 crore annually for two years which will stand in good stead at this perilous time.

Every significant policy has a rationale behind it. The retirement age is linked with the average life span. In view of the improved medical facilities, expanding health awareness among people, and a healthy life style, the average Indian life-span has increased. Thus it is quite natural to raise the retirement age. After all, we must take into account the changes in life span and give more chance to people to show their worth and excellence. It is quite in the fitness of things, that the country will get and should avail itself of the skill, expertise and knowledge of senior, qualified, competent persons in certain sectors like defence, scientific research and development, teaching, and judiciary.

Candidate No.7: Thanks friends, I am both surprised and pleased to hear such interesting points from the speakers. I don't think I have anything else to add. I would like to pass it on to the next participant.

Candidate No. 8:   Dear friends, thank you all for your nice observations. Being the last speaker I have strong points, both in favour of and against the move. To me, it is a mixed bag—both a boon and a bane. Many economists are apprehensive of a collapse of our economy. Immediate financial boost gained from withholding retirement benefits like pension, gratuity, leave encashment, etc. shall help a long way in tiding over inflation and the imminent debt trap. This policy is a positive recognition of the increased life span and provides for useful exploitation of mature human experience, particularly in specific fields. Nevertheless, it is quite difficult and will also be a dishonesty to close our eyes to the dangers it brings in its trail. It will create an extensive employment problem resulting in a mass of frustrated youth.

Intelligent hands will cross the borders for greener pastures and quite a number will join hands with anti-social elements. I am afraid that Buddha's land of peace may run into a wasteland of smouldering flames of hatred and violence.

I hope you all will appreciate my idea that the government should have devised some other economic strategy to generate revenue enhancement. After all, the youth of the country are the makers of the golden millennium, a better, happier, more glorious India. We cannot run the race with props. Let the young people with energy, zest and dynamism take the command. The elderly citizens may be honoured by the youth seeking their advice in the relevant contexts. The man at the driving seat must have full potential and alertness. I, therefore, reiterate that the decision needs a serious reconsideration. I wish it is scrapped at the earliest, much before it is too late.

Analysis:

The participants of the group discussion reflect varying degrees of suitability. Candidate No. 1 is aggressive, intolerant, and arrogant. His language is full of indecent and unseemly words. When he speaks he makes one or two relevant points but his tone is excited and his language reflects anger and a lack of control or balance. He is rejected. He needs to improve on all counts.

Candidate No. 3 shows initiative and assertiveness. On the count of knowledge he has a point to make, he does not show depth or range or analytical ability. His language is good but he reacts with anger and uses some unhappy words. He needs to improve his information level and show a warmer response and a greater sense of team spirit. With some sincere labour and improvement in personality he can come to the mark and can get selected.

Candidate No. 4 is a good, deserving candidate. He shows a balanced temperament; his gestures are friendly. He displays good understanding of the given topic, analyses problems critically and organises his ideas coherently. He also reveals the ability to listen to different speakers with patience and puts his points across with force, fluency, and effectiveness. Above all, he possesses admirable qualities of leadership in terms of initiative, team spirit, endurance, and assertiveness. He is the best candidate of the group. He could, however, add tonal variations and style to his speech for still better effect.

Candidate No. 5 shows an average response to the whole situation. He makes some relevant points but fails to organise them coherently. The effect of his arguments is, thus dissipated. Moreover he does not care to take the initiative or show team spirit or other leadership qualities. He needs to improve on these points. If he improves his leadership traits and the ability to analyse and organise his points coherently, he can come up to the mark.

Candidate No. 6 is also an admirable candidate. He has a balanced and positive personality and shows good knowledge and understanding of the topic. He can make his points lucidly and leave a good impression on his listeners. Though he does not show as much of initiative or team spirit as does No. 4, yet he is not deficient in these qualities either. His approval of No. 4 shows his potentiality. This candidate requires improving his leadership traits.

Candidate No. 7 is a poor candidate; he lacks initiative, confidence and knowledge and cuts a very sorry figure. He can be rejected outright. He needs to practise hard to be able to get through a group discussion.

Candidate No. 8 is also a positive and balanced personality. He makes his points logically and leaves a good impression. His understanding of the topic is balanced and rational. His language is clear as well as powerful. His choice of words are appropriate and appealing. Though he does not manifest obvious leadership qualities, his rational stand does give a hint of such qualities and when he makes an exit he leaves behind a happy impression. He needs to improve his leadership traits to become a stronger candidate.

Hence, candidate Nos 4, 6, and 8 are selected.

Topic 3: 'Success of Public Sector in India'

Background Information
A group of eight selected candidates assembled together to participate in a group discussion. The examiner announced the topic and left. Immediately, the candidates started whispering. Gradually, the noise in the group increased and a chaotic scene reigned.

The Discussion:

Candidate No. 5: Friends, I appeal most earnestly to all of you to stop side talk and take the given assignment seriously. We are all responsible candidates who have gathered here to accomplish a task with the best of our abilities and decency. Though we are free to exchange our opinions we need not quarrel or clash. We have been given 25 minutes. Let us use five minutes for preliminary work of reaching an understanding among ourselves. In my opinion, we should go for two rounds. In the first round, each of us will speak for a minute and a half starting from the participant No. 1 to the last. The second round will be open for free interaction. I wish each of us must express his or her opinion. Friends, please come forward with your ideas.

Candidate No. 3:   Great God! who is this self-styled leader pretending to be a good Samaritan. Are we here to listen to his sermons? Why doesn't he join a college if he is so enamoured of lecturing? Well, chaps tell him, Group Discussion is an open battlefield; everybody is at liberty to fix one's gun the way one likes. We don't need any guidance.

Candidate No. 7:   (He raises his voice in a decent manner to catch the attention of the group.) Well, friends, let us be honest. We must appreciate the very relevant suggestion made by No. 5. Let us not delay any longer; we should begin with No. 1 and make discussion lively, useful and enjoyable without being unpleasant to anybody.

Candidates No. 1, 4 and 8: Yes, yes, he is very right. Let us not poke one's nose; it's already getting late.

Candidate No. 3:   What a shame! Are all of you hopeless bugs? Can't you assert yourselves?

(Almost all participants speak at a louder pitch and ask No. 3 to stop.)

Candidate No. 4:   (He becomes a little restless, raises his voice and directs his finger towards No. 3.) We are not hopeless bugs, but you are definitely a spoilt brat, mindless and discourteous. You seem to a social misfit. Better quit our company lest something unpleasant might happen. I warn you, behave yourself.

(There is silence for some moments; candidates look towards one another.)

Candidate No. 5:   I am really sad at this unhappy turn of the situation. After all, we are here for a short meeting. Let us not depart with a bitter taste in our mouth. I reiterate my stand and request all of you to keep cool and take things sportingly. Any deviation will cause unnecessary hurdles in the smooth process of our discussion. Let us take the given competition with an open mind without any ill feeling for anybody. I call upon No. 1 to initiate the discussion.

Several candidates: Right, very right; we are all willing to listen to No. 1. He is most welcome; he must begin now.

Candidate No. 1:   Thank you, friends, for giving me a chance to be the opening speaker. Public sector may not be a great success in India, but it would not be fair to say that they have not contributed to our economic growth at all. We should not forget that our national goal is to achieve economic growth with social justice. This involves equal opportunities and the narrowing of the gap between the rich and the poor. It is true that private sector can achieve faster and higher economic growth but it may lead to suffering, ill-health and exploitation of the masses. Such has been the case with the industrialised countries of the West which gained economic growth and breakthrough in the wake of the Industrial Revolution. Even today the gap between the rich and the poor in the U.S. is alarming.

The private sector is primarily concerned with profit. It will invest only in such areas and industries as it can expect maximum profit in the minimum time and with minimum capital. Consequently industries will be started by the private sector only in locations where all facilities are available. Thus already developed regions will be flooded with industries and backward regions will be ignored. But the government has to develop all the regions and better the lot of the people whether they live in cities, villages, or backward areas.

Further, the private sector has a tendency to combine into monopolies and cartels to impose their will, with regard to products and prices. The government also has the right to protect consumers from such monopoly houses and institutions. The banks, the insurance industry, the air transport had to be nationalised so that the profits earned through these are not misused by a few to enhance their power. Therefore, since we cannot do away with public sector in the welfare state, it is essential that we learn to operate them efficiently and profitably to ensur economic growth and social welfare.

Candidate No. 2: Thank you, No. 1. You have explained the subject well and have made several relevant points. However, I have a different point of view. I think the domestic economy of a developing country depends a lot on both the public and the private sectors. But in our country the public sector has not been performing up to expectations. It has always been treated as an extension of the government rather than as an instrument of growth. In fact it has been a pasture land of corrupt bureaucrats and politicians, a drain on the national exchequer and a total failure.

Public sector in India largely represents the philosophy of a mixed economy in the country. The philosophy, as enshrined in successive industrial policy resolutions, laid heavy reliance on the public sector because of problems such as low per capita income, over-dependence on agriculture, high population growth, unemployment, uneven distribution of income and wealth, lack of technical know-how, poor infrastructure, and low industrial growth that reared their heads soon after independence. The management of public sector units is suffering from zero accountability and red-tapism. Political intervention in the day-to-day working makes things more hopeless. Bureaucrats treat their top positions in public sector enterprises as good retiring posts. Political influence sometimes leads an organisation to remain headless for years as has been in the case of National Hydel Power Corporation which has an investment of Rs. 5,000 crores and was till recently headless for about two years. The quality of services offered by the public sector, irrespective of the huge capital investment, is pathetic. Air India flights are notoriously unpunctual and have poor safety records. The food served in Indian Tourism Development Corporation hotels is unpalatable. Bad roads, poor supply of water, and erratic supply of electricity are common phenomena. Almost all the big names in public sector suffer from labour and personnel problems. The loss suffered by public sector undertaking is phenomenal. Financial irregularities, faulty payments, fake accounts, and poor repayment of loans are resulting in new scams in public sector banks. Keeping in view the above inflictions of public sector and its overall performance till date, I am left with no alternative, but Hobson's choice to declare the public sector a wounded horse rather than a bouncing tiger.

Candidate No. 3: Gentlemen, the subject is a known fact. I wonder what there is to discuss about it. We have wasted crores of rupees on the public sector and it has all gone down the drain. Can any of you name a single public sector enterprise which has proved to be a success and which gives profits? Every public sector unit is inefficient. They keep dragging their feet, proving to be a great burden on our economy. Public sector only means one thing and that is concentration of power and patronage in the hands of politicians. Hence there is this tendency to take over every profit-making private industry as a government institution in the guise of nationalisation.

Candidate No. 4: Friends, economic growth can come about only if we compete successfully with advanced countries in quality, cost, and innovation. Unfortunately, these things cannot be expected under a controlled economy in the public sector as the basic motivation is lacking there. We need some driving force to achieve results. In China, it is force and fear that worked. In America and Japan, it is the lure of profit. In India, we have neither. Hence the public sector has been a failure. We can't have compulsion and force in a democracy; the best thing is to abolish the public sector.

Candidate No. 5: Dear fellow participants, I do agree that public sector has become a cesspool of waste and corruption. But we cannot dismiss it; it is vital for our economy. Over the years, the public sector has been hijacked by opportunist bureaucrats. It has suffered in the hands of nasty politicians. It also suffers from a glaring lack of innovation, dynamism and work culture. It has to falter and fumble at every step, as it always had depended on the budgetary support. The net result is that from the 'commanding heights', the public sector has been reduced to the 'dismal depths'. In fact, waste and corruption feed on each other and form a vicious circle, because most of the public sector undertakings are run like charitable institutions or private fiefdoms of the government.

The honeymoon with socialism is over in most parts of the world. Amid the buzz of globalisation and a free-market economy, the role of the public sector has been dwindling. More than a decade back, during the Thatcher era, Great Britain kicked off the process of privatisation on a large scale by privatising giants like British Telecom. With slight variations, the idea caught on in countries like China, Mexico and, of late, even Pakistan. However, I definitely do not subscribe to the view that everything public is bad and everything private is good. "That government is the best which governs the least", is a misleading statement. In fact, waste and corruption are as much a problem in the private sector as in the public sector. The only way out of this mess is realisation of the fact that business and philanthropy can never go together. The government should stop making the public sector a scapegoat of its 'welfare objectives'. The 'social sector' should not be confused with the 'public sector'.

Candidate No. 6: Gentleman, I see there are supporters as well as detractors of the public sector in this group. From what I have heard, each side has some merits. I, therefore, want to be neutral. I feel and, what I feel is normally right, that both public sector and private sector should be given their due and no partisan attitude should be adopted.

Candidate No. 7: Friends, I am really surprised and also happy to observe that all of you are so widely aware of the Indian economic situation and that you have put forward cogent and valid arguments on the role of the public sector in our country. To my mind public sector is neither all black nor all white. It is a necessary instrument of growth for the Indian economy. In fact the public sector was initially required to strengthen infrastructure and to establish areas such as electricity generation and heavy engineering where huge capital investment and high risk were involved. It has also played a major role in welfare activity by providing facilities like drinking water, sanitation, roads, and railways. It has rendered invaluable service in the development sectors like tourism, mines, and traditional craft industries. It has entered fields where private sector has shown no interest because there is no profit to be had there. In brief, the public sector in India has played a vital role in developing the economy. Its purpose is not merely profit-making but providing services to the common man. Despite the flak which the public sector undertakings are currently facing, it has to be borne in mind that many of them such as Bharat Heavy Electricals Limited (BHEL), Hindustan Aeronautics Limited (HAL), and Indian Space Reserach Organisation (ISRO) have added feathers in the nation's cap and have justified the rationale behind setting them up.

But in the current global economic scenario, privatisation has become the buzz word. Zero accountability, red-tapism, political interference, poor service, labour and personnel problems, corruption, and malpractices are some of the evils that affect the public sector now. Therefore, privatisation has become a Hobson's choice. However, privatisation is not the required panacea. A research paper by an eminent economist points out that the introduction of privatisation by Margaret Thatcher in England has brought negligible gains. Therefore, it is advisable to adopt a two-fold policy. The public sector should be granted more autonomy, and infused with professionalism and technical advancement. At the same time slow and controlled privatisation with definite limit, proper fixing share prices, and evaluation systems should be introduced. A synchronised approach is the only relevant remedy for the Indian economy.

Candidate No. 8: Fellow participants, I have given a patient hearing to your arguments and counter arguments. Most of you have painted the public sector in black and have blown it up as a dangerous devil. But I hold a contrary opinion that public sectors are of vital importance and tremendous relevance for the growth and development of our country. The private sector, has after all, played a second fiddle in building of the basic infrastructure and key sectors of our socio-economic life.

The public sector has succeeded in achieving the commanding heights of controlling our economy. It lays down the framework of supply, demand, and pricing policy for the private sector. It has helped the country's industrialisation by assuming responsibility for providing the infrastructure and in establishing the basic and key industries. The market forces and the private sector alone would not have made this possible.

The public sector undertakings employ a large number of persons. They also have a multiplier effect on the growth of employment through the growth of ancillary industries, distribution and marketing channels, and so on. The public sector undertakings have helped achieve this by facilitating capital accumulation, attaining a certain amount of balanced growth, developing infrastructural facilities, and acting as a regulatory leverage.

Analysis:

In the group of eight participants Nos. 2, 4, 5, 7, and 8 are poor performers and they need improvement on all counts; they need regular, rigorous practice and continuous interaction with people to develop the right kind of personalities. They should also pay more attention to reading newspapers and magazines to improve their awareness of general happenings. No. 1 is an average candidate and can make improvements. Nos. 3 and 6 are competent candidates and selected.

Candidate No. 1 is an average candidate. He has some points to make and he puts them across to others with clarity but needs to be more analytical, forceful, and persuasive. He also needs to develop leadership skills though he is not utterly lacking in them. With some effort he can come up to the mark.

Candidate No. 2 may be presentable to look at but he lacks other virtues of personality. He has a bad temper. He knows little. His communication skills are average. He is deficient in leadership qualities. He is rejected. He needs rigorous, all round training and much practice.

Candidate No. 3 is a very good candidate. He has an attractive personality, he is knowledgeable and he has the necessary communication skill and leadership qualities. He needs to work more on his strengths so that he becomes a brilliant candidate, ready to make his mark everywhere.

Candidate No. 4 is a candidate whose performance is below average. Though he has a pleasant personality, his gestures are indecent, his knowledge is limited, his communication skill is average, and leadership qualities almost nil. He is rejected. He needs much practice and training

Candidate No. 5 is also a poor performer. His personality is average, knowledge poor, communication skill below average, and leadership quality, at best, ordinary. He is rejected. He needs to improve his knowledge, communication skill, and improvement in leadership qualities.

Candidate No. 6 is a good candidate. Though he is ordinary to look at, his overall personality is impressive. He is knowledgeable, has effective communication skills but in leadership he is just better than average. He is the best candidate amongst the eight. He needs to improve his leadership qualities to become unbeatable.

Candidate No. 7 is a candidate with poor personality, limited knowledge, little communication skill, and near-zero leadership qualities. He is rejected. He needs to work hard for long.

Candidate No. 8 is also a pretty poor candidate with an average personality, zero knowledge, ordinary communication skill, and absolutely no leadership trait. He is rejected. He too needs to work hard.

ASSESSMENT OF PERFORMANCE IN A GD

SCORE SHEET FOR A GROUP

PURPOSE OF DISCUSSION

| Unachieved | 1 2 3 4 5 | Achieved |

EMOTIONAL CLIMATE

Listless	1 2 3 4 5	Animated
Tense, Hostile	1 2 3 4 5	Friendly atmosphere
Dogmatic, Uncooperative	1 2 3 4 5	Very Cooperative

THOUGHT

Little use of information	1 2 3 4 5	Adequate information
Frequently off the subject	1 2 3 4 5	Relevant
Superficial	1 2 3 4 5	Thought, depth
Aimless, Confused	1 2 3 4 5	Methodical; group has sense of direction

BEHAVIOUR

| Often interrupt each other | 1 2 3 4 5 | Orderly, Attentive |
| Long contributions | 1 2 3 4 5 | Brief contributions |

SCORE SHEET FOR A CANDIDATE

ASSESSMENT	O	A+	A	B+	B	C+	C
PERSONALITY							
Appearance	5	4	3	2	1	0	-1
Temperament	5	4	3	2	1	0	-1
Gesture	5	4	3	2	1	0	-1
Mental State	5	4	3	2	1	0	-1
Overall Impression	5	4	3	2	1	0	-1
Total:	**25**	**20**	**15**	**10**	**5**	**0**	**-5**
KNOWLEDGE							
Depth	5	4	3	2	1	0	-1
Range	5	4	3	2	1	0	-1
Analytical Ability	5	4	3	2	1	0	-1
Organisation of ideas	5	4	3	2	1	0	-1
Overall Impression	5	4	3	2	1	0	-1

Total:	**25**	**20**	**15**	**10**	**5**	**0**	**-5**
COMMUNICATION SKILL							
Listening Skills	5	4	3	2	1	0	-1
Fluency	5	4	3	2	1	0	-1
Language	5	4	3	2	1	0	-1
Phonetic Ability	5	4	3	2	1	0	-1
Overall Impression	5	4	3	2	1	0	-1
Total:	**25**	**20**	**15**	**10**	**5**	**0**	**-5**
LEADERSHIP							
Initiative	5	4	3	2	1	0	-1
Team Spirit	5	4	3	2	1	0	-1
Endurance	5	4	3	2	1	0	-1
Decision Making	5	4	3	2	1	0	-1
Overall Impression	5	4	3	2	1	0	-1
Total:	**25**	**20**	**15**	**10**	**5**	**0**	**-5**
Grand Total:	**100**	**80**	**60**	**40**	**20**	**0**	**-20**

Legends: O = Outstanding, A+ = Very Good, A = Good, B+ = Average, B = Poor, C+ = Very Poor, C = Avoidable

"Group discussion is very valuable; group drafting is less productive."

– Jon Postel

CHAPTER 22

CASE STUDY

The case study tries to simulate a real-life situation. Information about the situation will be given to you and you would be asked as a group to resolve the situation. In the case study there are no incorrect answers or perfect solutions. The objective in the case study is to get you to think about the situation from various angles. IIM's and IIT's have a case-based discussion rather than topic-based discussion in their selection procedures.

What is a case study?

A case study provides a simulated management situation through which theoretical concepts and approaches can be applied and the feasibility and suitability of any recommendations assessed. Through the case study an approach to greater insights into management issues can be provided. The approach seeks to identify issues, analyze problems, and develop solutions to these problems and to assess implementation challenges arising from these solutions. The case study method is based on real-life (realistic) practical problems and as such seeks to make the issues come alive for the student.

SKILLS TO SUCCEED IN A CASE STUDY

Comprehension: Students need to grasp the detail of the case, often with limited time available, and to differentiate between relevant and irrelevant information.

Analysis: Students need to break the case study into its constituent parts and examine the relationship between the parts.

Problem diagnosis: Often it is unclear what the problem is and why it is a problem and, indeed, who it is a problem for.

Problem solution: Case studies often require the generation and evaluation of different options. A key question is often 'What would happen if X did this?'

Application of theory: Often a case involves the application of general managerial or ethical concepts or theory to a specific example.

Use of quantitative tools: A case may encourage the application of quantitative data so that students can understand how such data can be used

Presentation skills: A case should be presented with a lot of discipline. The presentation part should not be dominated with body language, rather with knowledge and its application.

Team-working skills: It is rare that managers work in isolation and most managers' work in teams for at least part of the time.

PREPARING FOR CASE STUDY

❖ Students read and analyze the different dimensions of the case. Subgroups can examine a particular issue covering finance, the external environment, people, processes and so on before reporting back to the main group. It is important, however, that in subdividing the case, students do not lose sight of the overall picture.

❖ The case will pose a number of problems that need addressing and students will need to identify major and minor problems and prioritize their importance. Alternate solutions may be generated and evaluated. Typically, cases require a decision and an implementation plan involving short-term, medium-term and long-term solutions.

❖ Students adopt particular roles in seeking to understand the feelings, opinions and values of key stakeholders. Such role-playing can lead to a very lively discussion.

❖ Case studies rarely have right or wrong answers; answers may be more or less appropriate depending upon the strength of the supporting arguments and the use that is made of the available information. All this can, of course, be very frustrating, but managing involves making decisions with limited information, limited time and limited resources.

Sample Case 1:

In a department of a college, the principal of the college announces in a function that Mrs. Nair would be the next head of the department. Now this comes as a shock to Mrs. Nair, because she was not taken into confidence and she just liked teaching. The retiring head Mrs. Johnson was a capable head and although Mrs. Nair did help her in her duties, yet she did not want to be tied to that position. The reason why Mrs. Nair was made head was because there was a policy of the department that the senior most teacher is made the next head, which obviously Mrs. Nair satisfied. Now Mrs. Nair leaves the function and goes back to her house thinking about the whole thing.

Question: What should Mrs. Nair do?

Sample Case 2: Production Vs. Personnel (with the Answer)

Background Information:
Khandari Hotels International Ltd. is situated near the sea coast in Visakhapatnam. It is a five star hotel and one of the biggest hotels in India. It is a prestigious name in Visakhapatnam. Almost all the foreigners who visit Visakhapatnam stay and dine at the Khandari Hotels. There are four major departments in the hotel viz. Production, Marketing, Personnel and Finance. Mr. Chandan is the head of Production Department. Mr. Dayanand is the Head of the Personnel Department. Mr. Sabaran was selected three years back as an Assistant Cook in the Production Department. After getting the job training for a month, he was placed on the job of Assistant Cook— Western Foods. He has been actually doing the job with the help of nearly 15 assistants in his section. But Mr. Chandan, the Production Manager has received nearly twenty complaints regarding tastes, varieties, degree of boiling, roasting etc., regarding Western Foods in a month. After scrutinising all these twenty complaints received in a month, Mr. Chandan has written to the General Manager of the Company to terminate the services of Mr. Sabaran. Immediately the General Manager has written about Mr. Chandan's letter to Mr. Sabaran and Mr. Dayanand and convened a meeting next day. On the other hand, Mr. Dayanand is the Head of the Personnel Department opines that Mr. Sabaran is innocent.

Question: What should be done with Mr. Sabaran?

Presentation and Role Play:

It is the General Manager's room. The following persons were present in the meeting in the room:

General Manager (GM), Production Manager, Personnel Manager, Mr. Sabaran, Mr. Kishore, Personnel Assistant to the General Manager.

Production Manager attends the meeting with a file containing the complaints received by him against Mr. Sabaran. Mr. Sabaran appears to be somewhat depressed. The following discussion takes place among them.

G.M.	:	Good Morning everybody.
All Others	:	Good Morning Sir.
G.M.	:	You know very well the purpose of this meeting.
All Others	:	Yes Sir.

(Facing the G.M., immediately Mr. Dayanand reacts and says.) Mr. Dayanand: Sir, it is quite unfortunate to receive complaints against a competent and well experienced man like Mr. Sabaran.) (Immediately Mr. Chandan responds facing towards Mr. Dayanand.)

Chandan	:	Mr. Personnel Manager, how can you say that Sabaran is competent? Are you supervising his work?
Dayanand	:	Mr. Chandan, of course. I am not supervising his work, but I am the head of the Personnel Department. I know the competence of most of the employees in the organisation including you.
Chandan	:	(Sarcastically) Including me! Then why do not you manage every department?
G.M.	:	Don't create rift between yourselves. We shall discuss the main problem in this meeting.
Dayanand	:	Sir, What I said about the competence of Mr. Sabaran is true as his performance appraisal reports for the past three years spell the same. All those reports were given by Mr. Chandan.
G.M.	:	What is your reaction to this, Mr. Chandan?

Chandan	:	Sir, of course. I have done it based on the reports submitted by the Deputy Production Manager.
G.M.	:	Mr. Chandan, then shall we check it up with the Deputy Production Manager?
Chandan	:	Not necessary Sir. The complaints I received themselves are enough to evaluate his performance of deciding upon the termination of his services.
Dayanand	:	(Immediately reacts) Sir, he (Mr. Chandan) is not the man either to recommend for termination or concluding on the complaints.
Chandan	:	Then, are you the right person?
Dayanand	:	Yes, certainly. It is the Personnel matter and Personnel Department enquires in the case and submits the facts of the case and sends the recommendations to the General Manager.
Chandan	:	Never. You can't enquire into the matter of my department and recommend to the General Manager.
Dayanand	:	No, Mr. Chandan. You are the Manager of Production but not Personnel. My department is meant for personnel management and resolving issues relating to personnel issues. So Mr. Sabaran's issue falls within the purview of Prsonnel Department but not Production Department.
G.M.	:	(Addressing Messers Chandan and Dayanand) Why do you unnecessarily dispute between yourselves about the authority over the issue? First let us concentrate on the performance of Mr. Sabaran during the last three years.
Dayanand	:	(Addressing the G.M.) Sir, refer the case to our department. I will enquire into the matter and submit all the facts.
Chandan	:	Sir, It is my work, Mr. Sabaran is my subordinate. You believe me. You treat the information supplied by me as facts and take necessary action. I do hope that you will cooperate with me to maintain quality of our food stuffs and run my department effectively.
G.M.	:	What do you mean by it, Mr. Chandan? I would like to finalise the case sympathetically as it involves the life of Mr. Sabaran. It does not mean we spoil the image of your department.
Sabaran	:	Sir, you please consider my case on humanitarian grounds. Further my performance was rated as 'excellent' by my superordinate during the last three years.

G.M.	:	I know it. I got the information.
Sabaran	:	Sir, I got my degree and P.O. Diploma from a reputed Institution in the relevant field.
Dayanand	:	It is true Sir.
G.M.	:	I see.
Sabaran	:	Sir, I worked in Ashoka Hotels for five years as Officer, Western Foods and one year in the capacity of Assistant Manager, Western Foods. My performance was rated as excellent.
G.M.	:	I see.
Dayanand	:	It is also true Sir.
G.M.	:	In such a case, what is wrong with you now?
		(Sabaran tries to say something, but in the meanwhile Mr. Chandan says.)
Chandan	:	Sir, all might be true just on the paper. I also give certificates to the outgoing employees as 'Outstanding'. It does not mean that actual performance on the job is outstanding.
G.M.	:	Is it so? What compels you to give such a certificate?
Chandan	:	It is the practice with most of the Production Managers.
G.M.	:	I see.
Chandan	:	Yes Sir.
G.M.	:	Then do you feel that your rating regarding Mr. Sabaran during the last three years was also false?
Chandan	:	I can't exactly say. But I feel it is false as I have done final rating based on the rating done by the Deputy Manager.
G.M.	:	In such a situation, the case must be enquired into.
Dayanand	:	It is what I exactly feel Sir.
G.M.	:	Mr. Kishore
Kishore	:	Yes Sir.
G.M.	:	Telephone to Mr. Nayanar, Deputy Manager, Production and ask him to come over immediately.
Kishore	:	Yes, Sir.

(Kishore telephones and asks Mr. Nayanar, Deputy Manager, Production, to come over to General Manager's room. In a few minutes Mr. Nayanar, Deputy Manager, Production, attends the meeting).

Nayanar	:	Good Morning to you all.

All	:	Very good morning.
Nayanar	:	(Addressing the General Manager) What is the matter, Sir.
G.M.	:	Mr. Nayanar, what is your opinion regarding the performance of Mr. Sabaran?
Nayanar	:	He is competent in his work. He is friendly with people in his section. He is quite obedient to his super-ordinates.
G.M.	:	I see.
Nayanar	:	Yes, Sir.
G.M.	:	Mr. Nayanar, Mr. Dayanand says his performance was rated 'excellent' during the last three years.
Nayanar	:	It is true Sir. I appraised his performance during the last three years Sir. Indeed, our Production Manager, Mr. Chandan also knows this fact.
G.M.	:	I see. Mr. Nayanar, Thank you very much for this information.
Nayanar	:	What for this information, Sir.
G.M.	:	You see Mr. Nayanar, Mr. Chandan reported against Mr. Sabaran and recommended for the termination of his services.
Nayanar	:	What happened Sir?
G.M.	:	Mr. Chandan says, he received 20 complaints against Mr. Sabaran's performance during the last month.
Nayanar	:	It is quite surprising. Chandan: But it is true.
G.M.	:	But Mr. Dayanand says his performance was rated excellent. So what shall we do now?
Nayanar	:	As you please Sir.
G.M.	:	Mr. Kishore, request Mr. Kuldeep Singh, the Finance Manager and Mr. Narayana Rao, Marketing Manager to be present here.
Kishore	:	Yes Sir.

(Mr. Kishore telephones and informs the matter both to Mr. Kuldeep Singh and Narayana Rao. Both enter the room.) Both of them: Good Morning to you all.

All	:	Very good morning.
G.M.	:	Mr. Singh and Mr. Rao, I have an issue to discuss with you all before the final action is to be taken.
Singh & Rao	:	What is it Sir?

G.M.	:	You know Mr. Sabaran. He is with us for the last three years in our Production Department. His performance was rated as excellent during the last three years. But Mr. Chandan says he received 20 complaints against his performance during the last one month. Hence he recommends termination of his services. But Mr. Nayanar, Mr. Dayanand say his performance is excellent. (All of them think for a while.)
G.M.	:	In view of this contradicting information, Mr. Dayanand says the issue should be enquired into.
Singh & Rao	:	It would be better.
G.M.	:	Mr. Chandan, you please give me the file relating to complaints against Mr. Sabaran. (Mr. Chandan gives the file to G.M.).
G.M.	:	feel it would be better that the case should be enquired by Mr. Dayanand.
Chandan	:	It is not wise Sir. The case of Production Department should not be enquired by the Personnel Manager.
Singh & Rao	:	What Mr. Chandan said is correct Sir.
Dayanand	:	It is the personnel problem, but not the production problem.
Singh & Ram	:	Even then, Mr. Sabaran is working in Production Department. So it is the problem of Production Department.
Dayanand	:	You are functional heads, you deal with functional problems. My job is to solve the personnel problem. Mr. Sabaran's case is a personnel problem but not a production problem.
G.M.	:	Mr. Dayanand will enquire into the matter. Chandan, Singh & Rao: It is OK, Sir.

"Case studies of failure should be made a part of the vocabulary of every engineer so that he or she can recall or recite them when something in a new design or design process is suggestive of what went wrong in the case study."

– Henry Petroski

CHAPTER 23

PERSONAL INTERVIEW

THE CONCEPT

The word 'interview' is derived from *intrevue* meaning 'sight between'. It is a meeting between two persons with a specific purpose. However, an interview situation may consist of one interviewee and several interviewers and vice versa.

An interview demands direct and dynamic interaction. By its very nature the process involves an assessment of one participant by another. Sometimes one of the participants represents an organisation or a group whereas the other participates in his individual capacity. One of the purposes of the interview is to elicit information which is not available from the written records or other sources.

TYPES OF INTERVIEWS

There are various types of interviews ranging from the one conducted by a journalist for newspaper reporting to that by a psychiatrist with a patient. The purpose defines the types of interview. The interview broadcast and telecast on the radio and television is on issues of current interest to people or to educate the public on a matter of general importance. Such interviews have the semblance of privacy but we all know that they are meant for public consumption. Similar is the case with a journalistic interview, only that it is made public after a time-lag. Then there are situations where interview takes the forms of a series of probing questions with a view of discovering the truth, for example, the kind of interrogation that is done by the police. Another type of interview termed as counseling interview is conducted to provide guidance and psychological support to the interviewee. In large professional organisations and educational institutions provision may exist for the conduct of such interviews.

Here we are interested only in the employment interview and nothing else.

EMPLOYMENT INTERVIEW:

The term 'employment interview' refers to the interview of a candidate for a job in a particular organisation. Promotion interview and annual interview are conducted in respect of the employees who are already in service. The former is arranged when a proposal for promotion of an employee is under consideration. The latter is a routine annual feature; its purpose is to assess through personal interaction the contribution and progress made by an employee during the year under review. But both these types of interview are not common in India. We shall therefore discuss only the employment interview in some detail. It is clear that several fundamental points in this discussion are relevant for not only promotion and annual interviews but also for data collection interview. Obviously the discussion of any employment interview is from the viewpoint of the interviewee.

PLANNING FOR AN EMPLOYMENT INTERVIEW BY A PROSPECTIVE CANDIDATE

Planning the interview, whatever be its type, demands adequate and careful prior preparation. How should one plan to appear in an interview of this sort? Surely each applicant wants to be successful, to be offered the job even if he may ultimately decide not to accept it. Failure in an interview certainly injures the ego of a person temporarily. You should therefore pay close attention to the following, if you wish to achieve success. The planning for an Employment Interview is discussed under the following three heads:
1. Before the Interview
2. During the Interview
3. After the Interview

Before the Interview:

Do's

* Do some homework and learn something about the organization—how it runs, the services it provides, its specialty etc.
* Find out the route to reach the venue beforehand. Reach the place half-an-hour before so that you get time to relax and compose yourself.
* Keep your documents and publication ready so that you don't fumble at the last moment.
* Rehearse and have a mock interview with your friend with all the possible questions that you think are important.
* Read your CV again and try answering the straight questions from it like your interests and the meaning of your name.
* Some organizations have a dress code, many others do not. A small start-up computer company would tend to dress more informally than a multinational bank. There is nothing universally true here but better to be on the safe side, i.e. slightly more formal than informal.
* Certainly everything should be neat, clean and pressed, and footwear polished. If an organization representative has given you a briefing, from his or her dress you will get some idea. A visit to the organization before the interview or a talk with a member of the organization should indicate what is appropriate.

Don'ts

* Do not keep any religious marks or symbols with you that distinguish you as a member of a particular section or community like a cross or crescent or swastika.
* Do not use a strong perfume, use a very mild perfume which will conceal your body odour and may not be repulsive to the sensitive interviewer as well.
* Avoid overdressing, e.g. a coat, vest, and tie would seem to be excessive in most Indian situations; coat and tie would seem to be enough even when the company culture is rather formal. Avoid also under-dressing: jeans, t-shirt and rubber chappals.

Getting Ready with Questions you may be asked at the Interview:

It is difficult to visualise the questions that may be asked at an interview. However, we give below a sample of questions that could be asked at an employment interview.

A. Educational Background:
(i)   Give a brief resume of your educational career.
(ii) Why did you decide to offer Economics in your M.A.?
(iii) Have you studied some books in this field other than those prescribed?
(iv) Apart from Economics which field of knowledge interests you?

B. Co-curricular Activities:
(i)   You have produced a number of plays during your educational career. Tell us how you got interested in drama.
(ii) Do you think your interest in drama affected your studies?
(iii) What work did you do as a member of the editorial board of your college newsletter?
(iv) Do you think this kind of work has added something to your academic experience?

C. Extra-curricular Activities:
(i)   How is it that, although you played badminton throughout your college career, you never participated in any worthwhile tournament?
(ii) Apart from physical exercise, does this game impart any other qualities to the player?
(iii) What is the size of the badminton court?
(iv) Do you play any other games?

D. Experience:
(i)   Describe the specific work that you were doing in the production department.
(ii) What new things have you learnt?
(iii) What are the ways of maximising production?
(iv) In what way will your experience help our organisation?

E. General Knowledge:

(i) What is your opinion about the new industrial policy announced by the Government of India?

(ii) What are the main causes of inflation in India?

(iii) Do you think deficit financing should be stopped? Why?

(iv) Comment on the Sports Culture of India.

F. Miscellaneous:

(i) What do you understand by team-spirit?

(ii) Do you think it can be cultivated? If yes, how?

(iii) What are the qualities of an efficient manager?

(iv) Do you think you possess these qualities?

During the Interview:

a. Taking care of the Body Language

Do's

- ❖ Look the interviewer in the eye. This shows honesty and confidence. Looking away suggests you are unsure and uncomfortable. If you are talking to a group don't fix to one person, keep roaming your eyes at everyone.
- ❖ If the interviewer wants to shake hands give a warm and firm handshake not a crushing or weak one.
- ❖ Smile frequently but it should be genuine and not artificial.
- ❖ Sit straight in an attentive position.
- ❖ Plan your personal appearance. Dressing and grooming are equally important.
- ❖ Ask permission before entering the room. Greet everyone present there with a smile and a "good morning" or preferably a "Namaste" with folded hands.
- ❖ Use hand gestures. This shows that you're attentive, alert and energetic.
- ❖ While leaving the room, leave confidently with a smile and politely thanking them.

Don'ts

- ❖ Do not chew gums or other things.
- ❖ Do not play with objects on the desk or constantly move your fingers. These are signs of nervousness.
- ❖ Voice Modulation: Don't be loud—be clear and firm.

❖ Do not grin or laugh aloud.

❖ Do not sit unless they tell you to and thank while sitting. Do not stoop.

❖ Do not have an air of overconfidence or lack of confidence.

❖ Fold your arms or slouch.

❖ Gnaw your lip or drum your fingers.

❖ Fidget in the chair.

❖ Look glum.

❖ Twist your handkerchief or/ the like in your hands.

b.   <u>While Answering the Questions</u>

Do's

❖ Listen carefully to the questions asked. Pause briefly and then answer wisely.

❖ Be positive. You'll be judged for your attitude too! Try developing a positive attitude. This is surely reflected in your interaction.

❖ If you come from a distant place and you are asked "how was the journey?" say "it was pleasant" or "quite comfortable" rather than complaining about the delay of the train/ plane, etc.

❖ Be honest. If you do not know the answer of a question, admit it politely without getting panicky or confused. Say, "I'm sorry, I don't know. Could you please enlighten me on this?"

❖ See that you use simple no threatening language without lots of jargon and the right kind of expressions. While arguing for a case, be polite and non-aggressive.

❖ If invited to ask questions, ask one or two questions regarding the organization but not about holidays and salary.

❖ If the interviewer initiates the discussion about salary, say that you expect to receive the standard salary given for that position.

❖ Emphasize your skills and say how they are relevant to the job and can contribute to the organisation.

Don'ts

❖ Do not grumble and complain about your environment or situation.

❖ Don't speak derogatorily about your previous employer.

❖ Don't use slang or informal language like "you know", "thanks", "yeah", etc. Instead use "thank you", "yes" etc.

❖ Cough before answer.

❖ Avoid eye contact.

❖ Don't play 'hard to get.'
❖ Don't be thrown off if the interviewer takes notes during the interview.

c. <u>Factors that hurt prospects of candidates</u>

One survey of recruiters listed the following factors as disqualifiers:

1. Has poor personal appearance: wrong or ill-fitting clothes, unpolished footwear, unruly hair, unclean nails.
2. Is overbearing, over aggressive, conceited, has a 'superiority complex', seems to 'know it all'.
3. Is unable to express self clearly, has poor voice, diction, grammar.
4. Lacks knowledge or experience.
5. Is not prepared for the interview.
6. Has no real interest in the job.
7. Lacks planning for career; has no purpose/goals.
8. Lacks enthusiasm; is passive and indifferent.
9. Lacks confidence and poise.
10. Shows insufficient evidence of achievement.
11. No participation in extra-curricular activities.
12. Overemphasizes money, is interested only in the best monetary offer.
13. Has poor academic record; just got by.
14. Is unwilling to start at the bottom; expects too much, too soon.
15. Makes excuses.
16. Is evasive; hedges on unfavourable factors in record.
17. Lacks tact.
18. Lacks maturity.
19. Lacks courtesy; is ill-mannered.
20. Condemns past employers.
21. Lacks social skills.
22. Shows marked dislike for schoolwork.

One survey work against an interviewee:

1. Comes late for the interview.
2. Fails to talk.
3. Says or presents something that is not true.

4. Has left a job without providing adequate notice.
5. Accepts salary terms and then tries to increase them.
6. Demands that the organization match another offer.
7. Can't supply verifiable references.
8. Reveals confidential information.

To summarize, candidates who seem to be overly interested in benefits, candidates who criticize their former bosses, candidates who have unrealistic goals: these weaken their chances of selection. Needless to say, any falsification in documents presented would eliminate a candidate. Also, it is wise to avoid the topics of politics or religion.

d. Employer's Expectations

We may classify the information which an employer seeks while considering a person for a job, into the following sub-headings:

(i)   State of health: Every organisation desires its employees to be in a healthy state. Apart from judging at the interview, the organisation requires a new entrant to undergo a medical examination, the standards of which differ from profession to profession.

(ii) Attainments: A probe is made through searching questions to verify what is written by the candidate in the bio-data and to assess the nature and quality of his achievements.

(iii) Intelligence: A close observation is made of the reflexes and responses of the interviewee to discover the extent of his grasp and confidence.

(iv) Aptitude: Certain questions are directed merely to find out the candidate's aptitude for the job he has applied for.

(v)   Interests: An attempt is made to understand the other dimensions of the personality of the candidate by encouraging him to speak about his intellectual or social pursuits.

(vi) Disposition: A vital piece of information that all employers would like to have is whether the candidate has the ability to work with others.

(vii) Circumstances: A peep into the interviewee's previous environment and family circumstances may give some clue to the candidate's capacity to work.

After the Interview:

After the interview, there are two things one may wish to do. The first is that one may write to the employer thanking him or her for the chance to have an interview and reminding him or her of one's interest and suitability for the post. Sometimes this results in another interview or better.
Here there is a sample letter:

> *Dear Mr. (or Mrs.)*_____ *,*
>
> *Thank you for the opportunity to meet you on Tuesday. The position sounds challenging and I believe it fits well with my abilities and experience. I believe I can make a significant contribution.*
>
> *If you need any additional information, please contact me at 0674-4321*
>
> *Sincerely yours,*
>
> _____

The second thing is that one may look forward. With people changing jobs and employers more frequently than in the past, it is a good thing to reflect on one's behaviour at the interview just held to learn from it for possible future interviews. Most likely one will have to face more interviews in the future and it is good to profit by the experience. Keep growing by reflecting on your experience.

APPEARING FOR AN INTERVIEW

The following points must be kept in mind when presenting yourself for an interview.

Sense of Time:
You must make sure that you are punctual. You must report at the venue of the interview at least half an hour before the given time. Punctuality creates a good impression and if you are on time you will be calm, unruffled, and confident. In case you find that you are going to be late for the interview, try to inform the concerned office so that the interview can be rescheduled.

Be polite to everyone you meet both before and after the interview. The nicer you are to people, the more they will help you retain your equilibrium.

Appearance:

First impressions are largely formed by our appearance even before we begin to speak. Research shows that people form 90% of their opinion of you within a minute and a half of meeting you. Since it is difficult to correct impressions during an interview, it is necessary to gain as much as possible through a smart, pleasant appearance. It is important to be well dressed and well groomed. Sociological studies have shown that all other things being equal, a well groomed person is credited with greater intelligence and achievement as compared to one who is not. Very few people care to discover the true worth of a person hidden beneath an untidy appearance, inappropriate clothes, and sloppy mannerisms.

Your clothes must look neither too casual nor conspicuously formal. They must be clean and ironed. Footwear should feel comfortable and be polished. Women should wear minimum jewellery.

Body Language:

A candidate's body language speaks a lot about his personality. Stooping shoulders and rounded back are placatory signals and indicate a dangerous lack of confidence. You should walk into the room with your back straight and maintain the posture while sitting down. Seek permission to sit with a request, "May I sit down?" Shake hands with a firm grip while maintaining eye contact and a smile. Your handshake is a basic gesture of friendliness. Therefore, a domineering handshake will antagonise the interviewers who will subconsciously feel threatened. On the other hand, if your handshake is limp, you could be dismissed as a weakling.

A soft pleasing expression with a hint of a smile enhances your personality. A frowning, tired, or harsh expression can put off the interviewer consciously or unconsciously. You must appear cheerful and confident.

Good listening skills are vital if one wants an interaction to be fruitful because, without exception, people love to talk to those who listen to them attentively.

You must also remember the following points.

1. Do not loll in your chair in a relaxed way.
2. Do not get too close to the interviewer.
3. Do not put your hands in your pocket.
4. Do not cross your arms.
5. Do not place your hands or fingers over your mouth when you speak.
6. Do not evade eye contact with the interviewer.

Communication Skill:

Delivery
Delivery refers to your tone, voice, and choice of words and phrases—in short, the art of speaking. A candidate can make a good impression if he modulates the pitch of his voice.

Enthusiasm
A candidate can win more attention from the interviewer if he displays an enthusiasm in whatever he says.

Brevity
Good communication does not imply speaking in a flowery language. True communication means speaking with brevity in clear, unambiguous terms. A garrulous person is often dismissed as a gossip monger.

Careful Listening
Most often people do not have the patience to listen to others; they are in a hurry to speak or express themselves. Listening carefully to the interviewer not only pleases him, it also generates unconsciously a positive feeling in you.

Honesty
Never make any attempt to bluff the interviewers. If you do not know the answer, it is better to acknowledge it. The interviewer will respect your integrity and honesty. You can tactfully make the interviewers ask you about areas known to you.

Selling Yourself
It is always useful to keep the interest of the interviewer alive. An element of salesmanship is always helpful in facing an interview. You must find out what

interests the interviewer and talk about it. If the interest of the interviewer seems to flag, you can reawaken his interest by effecting a change in your tone, by lowering or raising your voice, or by speaking faster or slower.

THE INTERVIEW PROCESS

STEP 1: INITIATION OF THE INTERVIEW

The interviewer's task is not to trick or trap the candidate but to get the best out of him. Normally, therefore, the interview begins with encouraging, lively questions. There are several methods of initiating an interview. Some of them are discussed below.

1. Initiation from the Candidate's Background:
    You belong to Himachal Pradesh and have studied in a public school in Shimla. Do you find any special advantage in locating the public schools in hill stations?

2. Initiation Based on the Candidate's Interests and Hobbies:
    How do you reconcile your two hobbies like reading and outdoor activities?

3. Initiation Based on General Awareness:
    Today everybody is talking of e-commorce. What is that?

4. Initiation through Academic Topics:
    You are a student of Economics. Please tell us what is 'Say's Law of Market'.

5. Initiation Based on Odd Questions:
    Which is your favourite newspaper?

STEP 2: EXPLORING THE MATRICES OF BEHAVIOUR

Since an interview is an assessment of the total personality of the candidate, it is imperative on the part of the interviewer to explore the implications of the behavioural pattern of the candidate right from the moment of his entrance in the interview hall, his way of walking, his way of sitting, and his manners during the interview to his final exit from the interview hall. The dialogues between the members of the interview board or the chairperson and the candidate also reveal many facets of the latter's personality.

STEP 3: ASSESSING THE CANDIDATE'S KNOWLEDGE AND AWARENESS

This is a very important aspect of the interview process. The board evaluates the candidate's general knowledge, his study of specific subjects, his understanding of current affairs, his interest in and critical awareness of all that is happening around him. The candidate's ability to apply his knowledge to a given situation or social problem is also tested. His ability to organise ideas and information into a coherent concept or approach is also evaluated. Candidates must make an in-depth study of their specific subjects and be up-to-date on topics of current affairs. For this they should read editorials and important articles published in magazines, and newspapers and go through their analyses either in newspapers or in television programmes.

STEP IV: ASSESSING INTERPERSONAL AND SOCIAL QUALITIES

In most cases the questions asked at different stages of an interview themselves reveal the social aspects of the personality of the candidate like his sense of responsibility, cooperation, adaptability, integrity, group sense, and persuasiveness. However, the interview board may also ask specific questions which will reveal the above qualities of the candidate.

STEP V: SUMMING UP

In this last stage of the interview, the board makes a final impression of the candidate. Therefore some questions may get repeated to guage whether the candidate is consistent and firm in his attitude. The candidate's answers must be the same all along the interview. The chairperson may give a hint when the interview is over. A candidate must thank the chairperson and other members of the interview board and leave the hall with confidence, without looking back. The door of the interview room must be shut quietly while leaving.

Some Sample Interviews

Interview 1 (for IAS):

Background Information
Sneha is a tall, very fair complexioned, beautiful candidate who is fully at ease, quite relaxed and confident in the company of other candidates. Dressed in an almond coloured silk sari which goes well with her nicely tailored blouse, she gives an elegant look. She has selected a simple makeup and hair style with immaculate care, which leaves the right impact on others. Her sweet voice and impeccable pronunciation makes her pleasant and endearing. Her etiquette and manners add to her style. She speaks with confidence in a soft voice, shows courage and initiative, and articulates herself well while talking to fellow candidates in the waiting hall and later during the interview.

Four candidates are waiting in the hall; one of them is seated in corner and is busy reading a book. The rest three are sitting close to one another and are discussing something seriously.

Sneha enters and says "Hello everybody, good morning," (The man in the corner does not react at all, but the rest three respond.)

Sneha	:	You seem to be discussing something interesting. May I join you?
		(She sits close to them. Batra, Singh and Satyanarayan—all three welcome her.)
Batra	:	You are most welcome.
Singh	:	Please join us.
Satyanarayan	:	We shall greatly enjoy your company and will benefit from mutual discussion. In fact, we are trying to identify what exactly is the purpose behind an interview. What is the board looking for among the candidates? My friend, Batra, says that an interview or a personality test is a farce, a mere eyewash.
Singh	:	I also have my own doubts though I cannot dismiss them outright as ridiculous. By the way, what's your opinion?
Sneha	:	Friends, I have an opinion contrary to that of yours. I believe in the functionality of an interview as a suitable

instrument to assess the personality of a candidate. Personality does not mean mere outward appearance but, mental alertness, knowledge, analytical ability, communicative skill, sense of judgment, sense of decision, cooperation, team spirit, and other interpersonal abilities. Talking to a candidate for half an hour or so may reveal his personality.

Batra   : Pardon me, Ms Sneha, how is this possible?

Sneha   : Of course, it's possible. Suppose, a member of the board asks a candidate as to how will he/she react to India going for nuclear tests at Pokharan, candidate No. 1 may say, "Sir, I think it depends on how you take it," whereas candidate No. 2 might respond as "Sir, it is not good. I think it will cause a grim situation for India." Candidate No. 3 might say, "Sir, this is a very right step," and candidate No. 4 might respond as "Sir, in my opinion this is a fully justified step. India has to safeguard her security as she is presently vulnerable to nuclear attacks from China and Pakistan. India should also resist nuclear blackmailing from superpowers like America, France, and the U.K. The economic sanctions against us by these superpowers will have only a short-term impact; in the long-run it will free us from excessive foreign dependency".

Now you see, the first candidate lacks confidence and clarity. The second candidate has given his opinion but does not sound convincing because he has missed the chance to show his information level, his analytical approach to a situation, his sense of firmness, or his sense of judgment. The third candidate just gives an opinion without giving causes and thus, he is also like the second one. The fourth candidate gives a firm opinion, shows analytical ability, his sense of evaluating the international scenario, his view on and an understanding of what will happen in the future.

All these reveal several aspects of their personality. If one simple question can elicit so much, a half-an-hour session can fully explore a candidate's personality. Is it not so?

All other candidates murmur in agreement "Hmm, yes it is right."

Batra   : Thank you Miss Sneha; you have taken off a lot of
                 confusion from my mind. I wish you the best of luck.
Sneha   : Thank you, friends.

(A messenger comes in and calls the name of Miss Sneha. She goes along,
taps the door, opens it, seeks permission to enter and moves with a firm,
elegant posture to the chair.)

Sneha   : (Standing near the chair meant for the candidate, and
                 smiling cheerfully): Good morning to you all, Sirs.
Chairperson : Good morning. Miss Sneha, please sit down. Let me first
                 introduce myself and the other board members to you
                 before we briefly go through your bio data.
Sneha   : Thank you, Sir (She takes her seat and remains attentive,
                 slightly bowing to each board member who are being
                 introduced to her by the chairperson).
Chairperson : According to your bio data you are now in the medical
                 profession, which is noble, respected, full of scope for
                 future, and well-paid. Could you, therefore, tell us why do
                 you wish to switch over to the IAS, which is hazardous and
                 very demanding?
Sneha (smiling): I want to choose a challenging and exciting career which
                 offers full scope for selfless service to people, and where I
                 can do full justice to my talent and equip myself well for
                 such challenging and demanding duty. Not that the medical
                 profession is not exciting and challenging, but the IAS is
                 more so. I do agree with you that the IAS is a hazardous as
                 well as challenging and demanding job. I would like to take
                 on this challenge and prove successful.
Chairperson : Why do you feel that the IAS is hazardous and demanding?
Sneha (smiling again): An IAS officer has to look after the welfare of the
                 people who are the citizens or guests of India and also to
                 attend to the politicians, both in power and even those out
                 of it. I presume nothing could be more demanding and
                 challenging.

Chairperson	:	You also stated that your ambition is to render selfless service to people. Can you explain how this service would enable you to realise this goal?
Sneha	:	An IAS officer remains in direct contact with the people at every level and every strata of the society. For example, a collector is responsible for the total well-being of all the people of his district. He has to implement successfully the various social, economic, and other developmental programmes. He has to cope up with natural calamities like floods, droughts, earthquakes and mitigate their hardships. Averting communal clashes, linguistic riots, inter-caste conflicts and the like is also his responsibility. As one gains experience and assumes greater responsibility like the office of the Chief Secretary of a state or Secretary of a ministry at the Centre, one will be required to look after the welfare and interests of all the people in the country as a whole.
First Member	:	Do you favour the creation of an all-India judicial service on the lines of the IAS and IPS?
Sneha	:	The idea of having an all-India judicial service has been in circulation for over two decades now. The Law Commission has favoured it and the 42nd Amendment to the Constitution provides for the creation of Indian Judicial Service to cover all judicial officers for the rank of additional district Judge and above. However, the recommendation has not so far been implemented as the states, in general, are opposed to it. They feel that the creation of such a service would curtail the state autonomy. Even state High Courts are opposing the creation of an all-India judicial service since, it would mean losing their hold on the subordinate courts under them in the state. But, I feel, for the purpose of national integration and having a merit-based cadre, an all-India judicial service should come into being immediately. In fact, we should also have an all-India educational service on such lines. To be frank, I am in favour of anything that will promote national integration and would simultaneously give weightage to merit and performance.
2nd Member	:	Well, Miss Sneha, you will agree with me that price rise is a big menace. How would you react to it?

| Sneha | : | With the spectra of unprecedented price-rise of essential commodities staring at us and making big holes in the pockets of all, it is time the 'power-that be', both in the states as well as at the Centre, woke up and took some stern and serious steps to stem the escalation. There is no gainsaying the fact that the worst affected segments of the society are those with fixed income, daily wage earners, migrant labourers and the like. The only way out to check the spiralling prices is to adopt a two-pronged strategy. Going in for imports in the short-run and augmenting production on a long-term basis, along with a scrupulous ban on wasteful and unproductive expenditure can certainly have a salutary effect on the run-away price-rise. |

Strong political will to book all those who indulge in hoarding and black-marketing can prove the bonafides of the government, both at the Centre as well as in the states. That the government of the day means business, should be apparent by its actions and not only in tall claims and silly statistics. Revamping of the public distribution system, introduction of more mobile shops for the weaker and vulnerable sections of the society can go a long way in arresting the menace of price rise.

3rd Member	:	With the collapse of communism in the former Russia, would you say communism would meet the same fate in China, North Korea, Vietnam, and other parts of the world where it is currently in vogue?
Sneha	:	Yes, Sir. The collapse of communism in Russia will have its fallout, and even China is under pressure to grant freedom of expression and dissent to its citizens.
3rd Member	:	Would you say that with the collapse of communism in Eastern Europe and Russia, only democracy will prevail and the days of dictatorship have ended?
Sneha	:	Sir, if you would permit me, I wish to submit that the issue 'Democracy vs. Dictatorship' should be considered independent of communism. Communism is not necessary for a dictatorship to appear and thrive. Other factors can give rise to dictatorship as in the case of Nazi Germany. All I can say is that, democracy is becoming increasingly popular at this point of time. If democratic governments

fail to deliver the goods to their people, other forms of government may arise, as has happened in ancient Greece and Rome.

2nd Member	:	What is the future of communism in India?

2nd Member : What is the future of communism in India?

Sneha : It was attempting to get a foothold in our country and so far it could not make much impact except in Bengal and Kerala. Poverty and political awareness could be fertile grounds for philosophies like communism to take root. With the failure of the Russian experiment, it may lose its appeal in India.

3rd Member : What in your view is most vital for democracy to thrive?

Sneha (Smiles): Sir, it all depends on circumstances, local situation, leadership, etc. but I would say freedom of expression, which includes a free press and other media like TV and radio, is very vital.

2nd Member : Well Miss Sneha, we have heard your view on several problems and, in fact, I myself have really enjoyed listening to you. These days I hear a lot about journalists joining politics, I think journalists, like judge, should not join politics. What is your opinion?

Sneha : I understand and appreciate the fact that everybody should have the freedom to choose or to change to a profession of his or her choice, but then there are certain ethical implications in changing a profession. In my opinion, journalists should not join politics. The eminent English writer, Dr. Johnson, said long back that 'politics is the last resort of a scoundrel'. Now it has become the first priority and an easy passport to power and prestige for any citizen. If, like the legendary Ali Baba, the Indian journalists keep a watchful eye over the misdemeanour of our politicians and shun the temptation of joining politics, the heavens will not fall.

Chairperson : Well said, Miss Sneha, but I would like you to apprise us how the journalists justify the relevance of their profession.

Sneha : Sir, journalists are a class committed to upholding certain values that politicians generally consider impractical or inconvenient. Journalists play a very responsible role in the society. The recent scams have come to light or are being investigated only because the journalists persistently

focused on them in their writings. They have developed
public awareness or governmental response to situations
of atrocities on women or weaker section of the society,
natural calamities, the need for preservation of species that
are becoming extinct, or handicrafts, art and culture of
specific communities. Thus, they should voluntarily stay
away from the mire of politics to keep those indulging
in unholy nexus with criminals on their tenterhooks.
The glitter of power politics is too strong to resist, but
with the courage of conviction, journalists can rise to the
occasion and stem the emergence of a culture of sycophancy
and death of qualitative and investigative journalism,
by religiously sticking to their rigorous role of being an
upholder of the truth rather than becoming a suspect of
people's trust.

Chairperson : Well, Miss Sneha, it was really enjoyable talking to you on
such varied problems. Thank you very much indeed.

(She takes the hint that the interview is now over. She leaves the chair, stands
and addresses all the members.)

Sneha   : Thank you Sirs and good day to all of you. (She makes a
smart, graceful exit.)

Analysis:

The scores reveal that Sneha is a deserving candidate. The background
information apprises us that she is beautiful but not haughty. She has a
pleasant bearing, a good sense of clothes and style, she is affable. She has
sound manners exhibited in her conduct in the waiting hall as well as
during the interview. Her posture is graceful. She is cheerful, energetic,
and optimistic. Her intelligence is revealed in her talk with the chairperson
right at the initial stage when she convinces him about her stand on the civil
services. Her intelligence is also revealed in her opinion about the Indian
Judicial Service and her views on an All-India Educational Service. She also
hints about her interest in national integration and her belief in merit and
performance.

The range of her knowledge is quite wide. She is able to make an in-depth
analysis of the problem of price rise, the collapse, of communism and its

impact, and the concept of democracy. She gives an up-to-date information about the proposed Indian Judicial Service. She demonstrates that she can apply her knowledge to real situations. Her thoughts are coherent and consistent.

That she can converse easily and does not fumble for words is exhibited the way she explains to fellow candidates, the usefulness of an interview. She is clear, logical, and consistent in all of her answers. Her language is correct. She also displays the leadership qualities of being able to mix easily, a group sense, organisational ability, and the guts to accept a challenging and demanding job. She shows moral strength in her answers. She shows her quick but correct decision-making power in her answer on why she would like to join the civil services and in her opinion on why journalists should not join politics.

Thus, Sneha is selected without any reservations on the part of any member of the interview board.

Interview 2 (for IAS):

Background Information
Rajiv Chaddha is a tall, healthy young man with an attractive face, but he seems to be careless and casual about his appearance. He sports a pair of blue jeans with a deep red coloured shirt and a black jacket over it. Though he has shaved his beard, his overall look is slightly dishevelled. His face reflects either arrogance or lack of concern. He seems to avoid mixing with people. He is sitting in a corner, smoking a cigarette and is engrossed reading a book which he flaunts before his face. There are four other candidates, including a lady, who are sitting close to one another. One of them goes near Rajiv, bids him hello invites him to join the group.

Rajiv Chaddha : I am sorry; I am busy reading the last part of an
                 interesting novel.

(A messenger comes in and calls Rajiv's name. Rajiv gets ready to go for the interview. The other four fellow candidates wish him good luck to which he hardly reacts. He enters the room without seeking permission, walks with a stooping left shoulder to the chair meant for the interviewee.)

Chairperson	:	*He is engrossed in reading some papers spread before him on the table. The creaking sound of the chair displaced roughly, draws his attention and he looks at Mr. Rajiv,* Are you Mr. Santosh Narang?
Rajiv	:	No Sir, I am Rajiv Chaddha.
Chairperson	:	I am sorry gentleman, in fact, we were awaiting Mr. Narang, and perhaps he is absent.
Rajiv	:	But sir, your messenger called my name and I rushed to the room.
Chairperson	:	Did you listen to him carefully? He might have requested you to keep in readiness.
Rajiv	:	Oh, I did not bother about these details.
Chairperson	:	But I think you have to bother about each detail if you intend to be exact.
Rajiv	:	In fact, sir, I was reading a novel.
Chairperson	:	Oh, I see, that's fine. What was that novel? Was it by Lawrence or by Hemingway?
Rajiv	:	Oh no, I do not read literary novels. It is a thriller. In fact, I do not like literature at all; it is a sheer waste of time. I have been a science student. Literature is just fancy and romance and no more. There is no scope for these things now.
Chairperson	:	I have this idea that literature deepens human awareness and enhances man's finer sensibility. Literature also reflects the culture of a society. Am I mistaken, Mr. Rajiv?
Rajiv	:	I cannot say so sir, but please ask me questions on my subjects.
Chairperson	:	But Mr. Rajiv, we are not interviewing you for lectureship. Are we supposed to be subject-specific? Anyway, your bio-data shows that you have opted for political science as one of your subjects for the main examination. I hope you have a comprehensive understanding of the national and international political scenario. What is your opinion about President Bill Clinton's visit to India?
Rajiv	:	Sir, I do not think Mr. Clinton's visit could be of any real significance. We Indians were unnecessarily lyrical and overenthusiastic in our reception. Are the Americans so zealous about receiving an Indian Prime Minister?

Chairperson	:	He looks towards other members and says) Well, would you like to converse with him?
A Member	:	Well, gentleman you say, you are a science student. How will you explain the functioning of the Internet to a layman?
Rajiv	:	The Internet is just an addition to a computer. It is becoming very popular. Very soon it will come down to the common man. It is an electronic revolution.
Another Member:		Well, Mr. Rajiv, I hope you are fully aware about the Kargil episode. In the light of this event, many people are of the opinion that only superior military power and might can contain Pakistan from launching further attacks on India. There is no scope for any dialogue or any other kind of peaceful means. What is your opinion?
Rajiv	:	I do not really understand why do people make a mess of everything? The only solution is to inflict a war against Pakistan. As you know, offense is the best defence. We must teach Pakistan a good lesson and humble it down for all times to come.
Another Member	:	Well gentleman, these days we have had a lot of furore over organised and induced religious conversions. What is your opinion on this crisis?
Rajiv	:	Sir, in my opinion religion is the opium to the people. Rather, this is what Marx said, and I fully agree with him. In Russia and China, religion has been practically banned. It is only in the Indian subcontinent that we give too much importance to religion. I think the right thing to do is to ban all religious activities in public. All religious funds should be taken over by the State. Then all problems will disappear. That is all.
Chairperson	:	Thank you Mr. Rajiv, we can call it a day now.

(Rajiv gets up from the chair, says "Thank you sirs," and makes an exit.)

Analysis:

Mr. Rajiv Chaddha is a poor candidate. He lacks dress sense and a sense of grooming. Moreover, he seems unconcerned about everything. His personality score is very low. He does not appear very intelligent nor does he grasp the real intention behind a question.

His knowledge is limited. His responses are confused. His information on the Internet is shallow. His communication skill is also below average. Though his language is correct and clear, his opinions are unclear and unconvincing. He cannot analyse a situation. He has no idea of literature and his answer to the question on the Kargil episode is reflective of obstinacy and a lack of understanding of the matter. His answer to the question on conversion also shows that he is neither informed on the subject nor can he analyse the subject.

He is unsocial, ill-mannered, arrogant, and devoid of a group sense, organisational skills, and integrity of character. Therefore he scores badly in leadership qualities.

Rajiv Chaddha is rejected. He needs to improve on all counts.

THE SUPER 16

Candidates preparing for PI must be aware of the following 16 points.
1. Short Self-Introduction
2. Job Objective
3. Nativity
4. Family Background
5. Academic Background
6. Hobby
7. Strength
8. Weakness
9. Opportunity
10. Threat
11. Work Experience
12. Industry profile
13. Job Profile
14. Current Affair
15. Salary Negotiation
16. Query for the HR

Proper Attire: a Positive Image

How important is proper dress for a job interview? Well, the final selection of a job candidate will rarely be determined by the attire. However, first-round candidates for an opening are often quickly eliminated by inappropriate dress. Image is often as important as content; in fact, studies have shown that at least 65% of the conveyed message is nonverbal! First impressions—often made within the first 15 seconds—are lasting impressions.

What your clothes say about you?

❖ In an interview your attire plays a supporting role.
❖ Your conduct, your interpersonal skills and your ability to articulate intelligent and well thought out responses to questions are the most important elements.
❖ Be aware that in some industries, customer contact and image presented to the customer is critical. In such industries, your attire will be judged more critically.
❖ Your attire should be noticed as being appropriate and well-fitting, but it should not take center stage.
❖ If you are primarily remembered for your interview attire, this is probably because you made an error in judgment!
❖ Dressing nicely and appropriately is a compliment to the person you meet, so if in doubt, err on the side of dressing better than you might need to.
❖ Even if you are aware that employees of an organization dress casually on the job, dress up for the interview unless you are specifically told otherwise by the employer.
❖ Never confuse an interview or business function with a social event. Don't dress for a party or a date.

Grooming Tips for Everyone

❖ Hair:
Should be clean and neat.
❖ Shoes:
Should be in polished condition. Make sure heels are not worn.
❖ Details:

No missing buttons, no lint; and don't forget to remove external tags and tacking stitches from new clothes.

❖ Hands:
   Clean fingernails.
❖ Fit:
   Clothes should be clean, neatly pressed, and fit properly.
❖ Smell:
   Perfume or cologne should be used sparingly or not at all. No odors in clothes. Don't smell like smoke.
❖ Pad folios:
   Preferred over a bulky briefcase. A small briefcase is also appropriate. But if you have no reason to carry a briefcase, don't; you risk looking silly.
❖ Book bags:
   Leave it at home for an on-site interview. For an on-campus interview, you can leave it in the waiting area.

Men's Interview Attire

❖ Suit (solid color—navy or dark grey)
❖ Long sleeve shirt (white or coordinated with the suit)
❖ Belt
❖ Tie
❖ Dark socks, conservative leather shoes
❖ Little or no jewelry
❖ Neat, professional hairstyle
❖ Limit the aftershave
❖ Neatly trimmed nails
❖ Portfolio or briefcase

Women's Interview Attire

❖ Suit (navy, black or dark grey)
❖ Long suit skirt for sitting down comfortably
❖ Coordinated blouse
❖ Conservative shoes
❖ Limited jewelry
❖ No jewelry is better than cheap jewelry
❖ Professional hairstyle
❖ Neutral pantyhose

- ❖ Light make-up and perfume
- ❖ Neatly manicured clean nails
- ❖ Portfolio or briefcase

Assessment of Performance in a PI

An interview is essentially an evaluation of the total personality of a candidate. Personality does not mean mere outward appearance or intelligence or the ability to prevail in a situation; it is a blend of different qualities of mind, body, and spirit. Personality can be grouped under four heads: 1. disposition, 2. knowledge, 3. communication skill, and 4. leadership traits. These four heads can be further classified as given below:

ASSESSMENT   O   A+   A   B+   B   C+   C
1. Disposition
    a. Appearance
    b. Social manners
    c. Dynamism
    d. Mental power
    e. Overall impression

2. Knowledge/Qualification
    a. Range of knowledge
    b. Depth of knowledge
    c. Application of knowledge to real situations
    d. Coherence of thought
    e. Overall impression

3. Communication skill
    a. Language
    b. Voice, tone, rhythm
    c. Clarity and logic
    d. Convincing power
    e. Overall impression

4. Leadership traits
    a. Initiative
    b. Organisational skill
    c. Deciding power

    d. Character
    e. Overall impression

N.B.: Each basic head is allotted 25 marks, with 5 marks for each sub-division. Negative marking may also be done.

Legends: O = Outstanding, A+ = Very Good, A = Good, B+ = Average, B = Poor, C+ = Very Poor, C = Avoidable

SOME COMMON INTERVIEW QUESTIONS

Q.   Introduce yourself.
Ans.: I am XXX from Cuttack. At present I am pursuing my PG in YYY (name of your subject) at Ravenshaw University, Cuttack.
Q.   Tell something about your family.
Ans.: My father, Mr. . . . is a . . . and my mother Mrs . . . is a housewife. We are . . . brothers and . . . sisters.
Q.   Why do you want to join MBA / our Company?
Ans.: For it provides the best opportunity to grow in life and let others grow simultaneously.
Q.   Why you are not interested to pursue your career in XYZ?
Ans.: A career in MBA provides better opportunity than XYZ.
Q.   What are your hobbies?
Ans.: Singing songs . . . (Prepare yourself accordingly)
Q.   What are your weaknesses?
Ans.: I easily believe people and therefore sometimes become a victim of the treachery of the crooked ones.
Q.   What is your strength?
Ans.: My confidence is my strength. It helps me to face tough challenges.
Q.   You are a student of Arts do you think it will be a problem in your MBA study?
Ans.: I don't think so. Rather it is my plus point as an arts student is more socialized and loves to work with people.
Q.   Tell about your work experience.
Ans.: No work experience. But I shall give my cent percent given the opportunity to shoulder responsibility.
Q.   Where do you see yourself after 10 years?
Ans.: The GM of a top-ranking multinational firm.
Q.   Do you think you will be a good manager?

Ans.: Sure. That has been the dream throughout my life. I shall take any trouble to achieve the qualification of a good manager.

Q. Tell about your role model.

Ans.: Indra Nooyi (born October 28, 1955 in Chennai, Tamil Nadu, India) is the Chairman and CEO of PepsiCo, the world's fourth-largest food and beverage company. On August 14, 2006, Nooyi was named the successor to Steve Reinemund as Chief Executive Officer of the company. She was effectively appointed as CEO by PepsiCo's board of directors on October 1, 2006. According to the polls Forbes magazine conducted, Nooyi ranks fifth on the 2007 list of the World's 100 Most Powerful Women. Nooyi has been named the number one Most Powerful Woman in Business in 2006 and 2007 by Fortune magazine. Now she is a model for thousands of Indian women.

Q. Why are you not interested to follow your father's profession?

Ans.: It has no scope to grow (socially, economically and also limited within the world of books.)

Q. What is the biggest turning point in your life?

Ans.: The day I wanted to be an MBA

Q. What is the biggest achievement in your life?

Ans.: My successful preparation for MBA.

Q. Tell something about your academic career?

Ans.: XXX

Q. Tell something about your home town?

Ans.: Cuttack is the old capital of Orissa and a historic city. It's an area which is locked by the rivers Mahanadi and Kathajodi. Cuttack is well known for its filigree works in silver, ivory and brass works. The silk and cotton sarees of Cuttack known as 'Katki' is also very famous.

According to the 2001 Census, Cuttack has a population of 535,139. Males constitute 53% of the population and females comprise 47% of the population. Literacy rate of the city is quite high at 75% with the average literacy rate at 59.5%. The female literacy rate is 69% and the male literacy rate is 80%

Q. Why is Odisha a poor state?

Ans.: Misutilisation of natural resources and lack of adequate human resources, poor and inefficient in administration.

Q. Tell something about Odisha.

Ans.: It is a state located on the east coast of India. Odisha is a littoral state of India with a long coastline and a storehouse of mineral wealth. Because of its mineral wealth and strategic location it attracts foreign investment in steel, aluminum, power, refineries, and infrastructure. Odisha is also emerging as a player in the outsourcing IT (Information Technology) and IT services industry.

Odisha has several popular tourist destinations. Puri, with the Jagannatha's temple near the sea, and Konark, with the Sun Temple, are visited by thousands of tourists every year. The Lingaraja Temple of Bhubaneswar, the Jagannatha Temple, the Sun Temple of Konark and the Barabati Fort of Cuttack are important in the archaeological history of India.

Q.   What do you mean by management?
Ans.: Handling man, money and time judiciously to get maximum benefit out of it.
Q.   Why should we select you?
Ans.: To see the success of your organization touching new heights.
Q.   How are you different from others around you?
Ans.: It is my attitude to solve problem happily without showing any excuse.
Q.   What does success mean to you?
Ans.: It means continuously working for doing things in a better way.
Q.   What qualities should a good manager have?
Ans.: He should be a good motivator and visionary.
Q.   Do you have these qualities?
Ans.: I hope so.

MORE QUESTIONS WITH ANSWER GUIDES

Q.   : What is your long-range objective?
AG. : The key is to focus on your achievable objectives and what you are doing to reach those objectives.
     For example: "Within five years, I would like to become the very best accountant your company has on staff. I want to work towards becoming the expert that others rely upon. And in doing so, I feel I'll be fully prepared to take on any greater responsibilities which might be presented in the long term. For example, here is what I'm presently doing to prepare myself . . ."

Then go on to show by your examples what you are doing to reach your goals and objectives.

Q. : How has your education prepared you for your career?

AG. : This is a broad question and you need to focus on the behavioral examples in your educational background which specifically align to the required competencies for the career. An example: "My education has focused on not only the learning the fundamentals, but also on the practical application of the information learned within those classes. For example, I played a lead role in a class project where we gathered and analyzed best practice data from this industry. Let me tell you more about the results . . ."

Focus on behavioral examples supporting the key competencies for the career. Then ask if they would like to hear more examples.

Q. : Are you a team player?

AG. : Almost everyone says yes to this question. But it is not just a yes/no question. You need to provide behavioral examples to back up your answer.

A sample answer: "Yes, I'm very much a team player. In fact, I've had opportunities in my work, school and athletics to develop my skills as a team player. For example, on a recent project . . ."

Emphasize teamwork behavioral examples and focus on your openness to diversity of backgrounds. Talk about the strength of the team above the individual. And note that this question may be used as a lead in to questions around how you handle conflict within a team, so be prepared.

Q. : What qualities do you feel a successful manager should have?

AG. : Focus on two words: leadership and vision.

Here is a sample of how to respond: "The key quality in a successful manager should be leadership—the ability to be the visionary for the people who are working under them. The person who can set the course and direction for subordinates. The highest calling of a true leader is inspiring others to reach the highest of their abilities. I'd like to tell you about a person whom I consider to be a true leader . . ."

Then give an example of someone who has touched your life and how his impact has helped in your personal development.

Q : Why did you leave your last job?

AG. : Stay positive regardless of the circumstances. Never refer to a major problem with management and never speak ill of supervisors, co-workers or the organization. If you do, you will be the one looking bad. Keep smiling and talk about leaving for a positive reason such as an opportunity, a chance to do something special or other forward-looking reasons.

Q   : What experience do you have in this field?

AG. : Speak about specifics that relate to the position you are applying for. If you do not have specific experience, get as close as you can.

Q   : Do you consider yourself successful?

AG. : You should always answer yes and briefly explain why. A good explanation is that you have set goals, and you have met some and are on track to achieve the others.

Q   : What do you know about this organization?

AG. : This question is one reason to do some research on the organization before the interview. Find out where they have been and where they are going. What are the current issues and who are the major players?

Q   : Why do you want to work for this organization?

AG. : This may take some thought and certainly, should be based on the research you have done on the organization. Sincerity is extremely important here and will easily be sensed. Relate it to your long-term career goals.

Q   : What kind of salary do you need?

AG. : A loaded question. A nasty little game that you will probably lose if you answer first. So, do not answer it. Instead, say something like, That is a tough question. Can you tell me the range for this position? In most cases, the interviewer, taken off guard, will tell you. If not, say that it can depend on the details of the job. Then give a wide range.

Q   : Are you a team player?

AG. : You are, of course, a team player. Be sure to have examples ready. Specifics that show you often perform for the good of the team rather than for yourself are good evidence of your team attitude. Do not brag; just say it in a matter-of-fact tone. This is a key point.

Q   : How long would you expect to work for us if hired?

AG. : Specifics here are not good. Something like this should work: I'd like it to be a long time. Or as long as we both feel I'm doing a good job.

Q   : Explain how you would be an asset to this organization

AG. : You should be anxious for this question. It gives you a chance to highlight your best points as they relate to the position being discussed. Give a little advance thought to this relationship.

Q   : Why should we hire you?

AG. : Point out how your assets meet what the organization needs. Do not mention any other candidates to make a comparison.

Q : Tell me about a suggestion you have made

AG. : Have a good one ready. Be sure and use a suggestion that was accepted and was then considered successful. One related to the type of work applied for is a real plus.

Q : Tell me about your dream job.

AG. : Stay away from a specific job. You cannot win. If you say the job you are contending for is it, you strain credibility. If you say another job is it, you plant the suspicion that you will be dissatisfied with this position if hired. The best is to stay genetic and say something like: A job where I love the work, like the people, can contribute and can't wait to get to work.

Q : Why do you think you would do well at this job?

AG. : Give several reasons and include skills, experience and interest.

Q : What kind of person would you refuse to work with?

AG. : Do not be trivial. It would take disloyalty to the organization, violence or lawbreaking to get you to object. Minor objections will label you as a whiner.

Q : What is more important to you: the money or the work?

AG. : Money is always important, but the work is the most important. There is no better answer.

Q : What would your previous supervisor say your strongest point is?

AG. : There are numerous good possibilities: Loyalty, Energy, Positive attitude, Leadership, Team player, Expertise, Initiative, Patience, Hard work, Creativity, Problem solver, etc.

Q : Tell me about a problem you had with a supervisor

AG. : Biggest trap of all. This is a test to see if you will speak ill of your boss. If you fall for it and tell about a problem with a former boss, you may well below the interview right there. Stay positive and develop a poor memory about any trouble with a supervisor.

Q : What has disappointed you about a job?

AG. : Don't get trivial or negative. Safe areas are few but can include not enough of a challenge. You were laid off in a reduction Company did not win a contract, which would have given you more responsibility.

Q : Tell me about your ability to work under pressure.

AG. : You may say that you thrive under certain types of pressure. Give an example that relates to the type of position applied for.

Q : Do your skills match this job or another job more closely?

AG. : Probably this one. Do not give fuel to the suspicion that you may want another job more than this one.

Q   : What motivates you to do your best on the job?

AG. : This is a personal trait that only you can say, but good examples are: Challenge, Achievement, Recognition, etc.

Q   : Are you willing to work overtime? Nights? Weekends?

AG. : This is up to you. Be totally honest.

Q   : How would you know you were successful on this job?

AG. : Several ways are good measures: You set high standards for yourself and meet them. Your outcomes are a success. Your boss tells you that you are successful.

Q   : Would you be willing to relocate if required?

AG. : You should be clear on this with your family prior to the interview if you think there is a chance it may come up. Do not say yes just to get the job if the real answer is no. This can create a lot of problems later on in your career. Be honest at this point and save yourself future grief.

Q   : Are you willing to put the interests of the organization ahead of your own?

AG. : This is a straight loyalty and dedication question. Do not worry about the deep ethical and philosophical implications. Just say 'yes'.

Q   : Describe your management style.

AG. : Try to avoid labels. Some of the more common labels, like progressive, salesman or consensus can have several meanings or descriptions depending on which management expert you listen to. The situational style is safe, because it says you will manage according to the situation, instead of one size fits all.

Q   : What have you learned from mistakes on the job?

AG. : Here you have to come up with something or you strain credibility. Make it small, well intentioned mistake with a positive lesson learned. An example would be working too far ahead of colleagues on a project and thus throwing coordination off.

Q   : Do you have any blind spots?

AG. : Trick question. If you know about blind spots, they are no longer blind spots. Do not reveal any personal areas of concern here. Let them do their own discovery on your bad points. Do not hand it to them.

Q   : If you were hiring a person for this job, what would you look for?

AG. : Be careful to mention traits that are needed and that you have.

Q : Do you think you are overqualified for this position?

AG. : Regardless of your qualifications, state that you are very well qualified for the position.

Q : How do you propose to compensate for your lack of experience?

AG. : First, if you have experience that the interviewer does not know about, bring that up: Then, point out (if true) that you are a hard working quick learner.

Q : What qualities do you look for in a boss?

AG. : Be generic and positive. Safe qualities are knowledgeable, a sense of humor, fair, loyal to subordinates and holder of high standards. All bosses think they have these traits.

Q : Tell me about a time when you helped resolve a dispute between others.

AG. : Pick a specific incident. Concentrate on your problem solving technique and not the dispute you settled.

Q : What position do you prefer on a team working on a project?

AG. : Be honest. If you are comfortable in different roles, point that out.

Q : Describe your work ethic.

AG. : Emphasize benefits to the organization. Things like, determination to get the job done and work hard but enjoy your work are good.

Q : What has been your biggest professional disappointment?

AG. : Be sure that you refer to something that was beyond your control. Show acceptance and no negative feelings.

Q : Tell me about the most fun you have had on the job.

AG. : Talk about having fun by accomplishing something for the organization.

Q : How do you react in a situation where you need to take an immediate decision? What process will you follow for decision making in such a critical situation?

AG. : Candidate should show that they have patience and the good judgment to identify problems first, then prioritize, and plan well in solving problems.

Q : Have you ever faced a situation when you had to take a decision, which did not fall within in your area of responsibility? What decision did you make and how?

AG. : Candidate's answer should show that they know how to take responsibility, that they can make a decision to meet the needs of clients, and that they can make innovative decisions.

Q : Have you ever tried to delay any decision-making? What were the consequences of this on both your company and customers?

AG. : You want to hear that the applicant does not like to delay decision-making, they can make quick decisions, and they can implement decisions in a timely manner.

Q : Do you always make decisions on your own without the help of others? In which situations do seek other's help for decision-making?

AG. : Candidate should show that they have the presence of mind and sensibility to judge any situation and make a decision independently, if required. You should hear that in critical situation candidate will seek advice and guidance to reach correct decision.

Q : Describe one experience when you had to lead a team.

AG. : Applicant may not have had experienced a leadership role, but they should be able to display leadership skills and abilities.

Q : How do you keep each member of the team involved and motivated, while keeping morale high? What steps do you need to take to achieve this?

AG. : Applicant should work hard to develop respect for each member of the team and try to makes team members feel important. Mutual respect is vital to success.

Q : In what situations do you prefer to use your leadership skills? Can you give me some examples?

AG. : Applicant should have ideas about where their skills would work best. They should show that they create solutions to tricky and unexpected situations when extraordinary leadership skills are needed.

Q : Do you like to praise team members in public? How do you express your appreciation of them?

AG. : Job seeker should be open-minded enough to appreciate the efforts and achievements of every member of the team.

Q : Have you ever tried to act as a mentor to a colleague? Was it worth it from a professional point of view?

AG. : Applicant should enjoy assisting others in their personal development as it helps to achieve common goals. They should understand that helping people increases morale.

Four guys, from Harvard, Yale, Oxford and IIM, Delhi were to be interviewed for a prestigious job. One common question was asked to all four of them.

Interviewer : "Which is the fastest thing in the world?"

Yale Guy : "It's LIGHT; Nothing can travel faster than light."

Harvard Guy : "It's the THOUGHT; because thought is so fast it comes instantly in your mind."

Oxford Guy : "Its BLINK, you can blink and it's hard to realize you blinked."

IIM Guy : "Its LOOSE MOTION."

Interviewer : (Shocked to hear the reply and asked) "Why"?

IIM, Guy : "Last night after dinner, I was lying in my bed and I got the worst stomach cramps, and before I could THINK, BLINK, or TURN ON THE LIGHTS, it was over!!!"

So there is no such model answer for any specific interview questions. You should mix up your experience with truth and answer.

CHAPTER 24

SWOT ANALYSIS

SWOT Analysis is a powerful technique for understanding your Strengths and Weaknesses, and for looking at the Opportunities and Threats you face. Used in a business context, it helps you carve a sustainable position in your market. Used in a personal context, it helps you develop your career in a way that takes best advantage of your talents, abilities and opportunities.

Strengths:
* What advantages do you have as a person which make you special and different from others?
* What do you do better than anyone else?
* What do people in your circle see as your strengths?

Consider this from an internal perspective and from the point of view of your employers and people whom you know in your circle. If you are having any difficulty with this, try writing down a list of your characteristics like loyalty, positive attitude, leadership, patience, problem solver, etc.

Weaknesses:
* What could you improve?
* What should you avoid?
* What are people in your circle likely to see as weaknesses?

Again, consider this from an internal and external basis: Do other people seem to perceive weaknesses that you do not see? Are your competitors doing any better than you? It is best to be realistic now, and face any unpleasant truths as soon as possible. You can write down a list of your negative characteristics: indecisiveness, ignorance, arrogance, short-temperedness, etc.

Opportunities:
- ❖ Where are the good opportunities facing you?
- ❖ What are the interesting trends you are aware of?

Useful opportunities can come from such things as:
- ❖ Changes in technology and markets on both a broad and narrow scale
- ❖ Changes in government policy related to your field
- ❖ Changes in social patterns, population profiles, lifestyle changes, etc.
- ❖ Local Events

A useful approach to looking at opportunities is to look at your strengths and ask yourself whether these open up any opportunities. Alternatively, look at your weaknesses and ask yourself whether you could open up opportunities by eliminating them.

Threats:
- ❖ What obstacles do you face?
- ❖ What are your competitors doing?
- ❖ Are the required specifications for your job, products or services changing?
- ❖ Is changing technology threatening your position?
- ❖ Do you have bad debt or cash-flow problems?
- ❖ Could any of your weaknesses seriously threaten your business?

Carrying out this analysis will often be illuminating—both in terms of pointing out what needs to be done, and in putting problems into perspective.

Strengths and weaknesses are internal to your personality or organization. Opportunities and threats relate to external factors. For this reason the SWOT Analysis is sometimes called Internal-External Analysis and the SWOT Matrix is sometimes called an IE Matrix Analysis Tool. You can also apply SWOT Analysis to your competitors. As you do this, you'll start to see how and where you should compete against them.

A start-up small consultancy business might draw up the following SWOT matrix:

Strengths:

- ❖ We are able to respond very quickly as we have no red tape, no need for higher management approval, etc.
- ❖ We are able to give really good customer care, as the current small amount of work means we have plenty of time to devote to customers.
- ❖ Our lead consultant has strong reputation within the market.
- ❖ We can change direction quickly if we find that our marketing is not working.
- ❖ We have little overhead, so can offer good value to customers.

Weaknesses:

- ❖ Our company has no market presence or reputation.
- ❖ We have a small staff with a shallow skills base in many areas.
- ❖ We are vulnerable to vital staff being sick, leaving, etc.
- ❖ Our cash flow will be unreliable in the early stages.

Opportunities:

- ❖ Our business sector is expanding, with many future opportunities for success.
- ❖ Our local council wants to encourage local businesses with work where possible.
- ❖ Our competitors may be slow to adopt new technologies.

Threats:

- ❖ Will developments in technology change this market beyond our ability to adapt?
- ❖ A small change in focus of a large competitor might wipe out any market position we achieve.
- ❖ Is there any change in Government's policy regarding your favourite profession?

CHAPTER 25

SRT

Situation Reaction Test (SRT) is a test of general intelligence i.e. common sense. SRT is conducted by SSB in order to unearth the candidate's attributes of psychology i.e. perception, cognition and behaviour which in turn are used by the psychologist to assess the OLQ's (Officer Like Qualities) of the candidates. In SRT, a candidate is required to solve 60 Situations (questions) in 30 minutes.

SOME SITUATIONS WITH ANSWERS

Situation : You are in train and lost your purse with money. You . . .

Reaction : I will use the money which I kept safely in my luggage for emergency situation and will file an FIR later. (OR) I dint lose it. It is in my bag

Situation : In his train compartment, two gunmen force passengers to give their belongings. You . . .

Reaction : Those gunmen are nothing but RPF jawans checking up as a part of security.

Situation : You got a marriage proposal from a sexually harassed girl who is struggling for justice. You . . .

Reaction : I will politely let her know that I have a girl friend and I am already committed to her and help her as much as I can in her fight against injustice.

Situation : You were standing in a ticket queue. There 2 persons with gun came from last and asked you to give them space. You . . .

Reaction : They are police men for security. I would cooperate with them.

Situation : You went to bathroom; saw a king cobra, no stick nearby, door closed? You . . .

Reaction : Put the towel on it and quickly open the door and escape, inform others. (OR) Invert the bucket on it to lock it. Inform others.

Situation : You are moving across the road on a scooter when you observe that two boys on a bike snatch a lady's gold chain and ride away. You . . .

Reaction : I'll follow them, note the number of their bike, then contact the police. (OR) I shall follow them quickly, catch hold of them and retrieve the chain to return.

Situation : You find that the person whom you call your friend has been cheating you. You . . .

Reaction : Let him realize his mistake and then make him feel guilty in his own eyes.

Situation : You are living in the college hostel. The dal served to you in the mess has a lot of stones. You . . .

Reaction : Inform the mess maintenance department.

Situation : While travelling in a train, you notice a man from the coach behind yours fall off the train. You . . .

Reaction : Pull the chain and inform the guard.

Situation : He has some other plans in life but his parents are forcing him to join Indian Defence Services. He . . .

Reaction : Sticks to his plan, makes his parents proud one day with his success.

SOME SITUATIONS FOR PRACTICE

1. He was appointed captain of basketball team but other players revolted against his appointment. He . . .
2. While traveling by train he goes to toilet. On his return to his seat he finds his briefcase missing. He . . .
3. He receives conflicting orders from his two superior officers. He . . .
4. While he discusses his view point others do not listen to him carefully. He . . .
5. An epidemic has spread in the village due to poor hygiene condition. He . . .
6. He notices a car moving with high speed running over a child on the road. He . . .
7. A fellow passenger has fallen from a running train. He . . .
8. He makes a silly mistake and his friends point it out. He . . .

9. His parents want him to marry a wealthy and less educated girl, but he has already found a suitable educated girl for himself. He . . .

10. He hears his neighbours screaming "thief-thief" at mid night. He . . .

11. A fellow passenger in the train objects to his smoking being an offense in public place. He . . .

12. He reached home from office and saw his house on fire. He . . .

13. While he was going up in a lift the electric power supply failed. He . . .

14. He was going to Delhi for an interview but realized after one hour that he has boarded a wrong train. He . . .

15. While he was hosting a dinner to his friends in a hotel, he realized that he has forgotten his wallet at home. He . . .

16. His friends came to borrow the book from which he was preparing for next morning paper. He . . .

17. He was appointed to supervise evening games in the college but he was staying far away. He . . .

18. He proposed to invite a political leader to preside over the annual day celebration but others were against it. He . . .

19. His parents were insisting on his early marriage but he wanted to take a job. He . . .

20. He had undergone a major surgical operation but there was no one to look after. He . . .

21. He realizes that his seniors were giving step motherly treatment to him. He . . .

22. He was going to attend the SSB interview. On reaching the railway station he noticed that his suitcase has been stolen with his original certificates needed at SSB. He . . .

23. Hearing an unusual sound at night he woke up and found a thief jumping out of his window. He . . .

24. He went to college but rowdy students told him to boycott the class. He . . .

25. While he was traveling on his scooter, someone at gunpoint demanded his purse. He . . .

26. His father has a dispute with his uncle on landed property. He . . .

27. He wanted to borrow money for his sister's marriage. The relative who assured him, declined to lend him at the time of marriage. He . . .

28. He went to buy a ticket to travel by rail. On getting the ticket he found that his purse was missing. He . . .

29. He was going on a bicycle in thick jungle. It was already dark and his destination was 10 Km away. His cycle got punctured. He . . .

30. While he was in jungle in Nagaland, he saw six Nagas with *lathies* rushing to him. He . . .

31. He did not do well in written test of SCO Commission. His friends advised him not to venture. He . . .

32. He was appointed Langar Commander. The Dal has often been having stones which were complained by the dining members. He . . .

33. He was traveling in a train on reserved seat. A fellow passenger claimed to have the same seat on his reservation ticket. He . . .

34. His two school going children frequently miss the classes. He . . .

35. He wins a lottery of rupees one lakh. He . . .

36. He was going to the market and he noticed a car and a *tonga* collide with each other. He . . .

37. He was asked to organize a picnic to a nearby historical place. He . . .

38. On returning to his barrack from the firing range, he finds that his friend had brought 20 rounds of 7.62 mm SLR. He . . .

39. A helicopter crashes in the vicinity of his unit. He . . .

40. He sees a rifle disc lying in the football field of his company. He . . .

41. A speedy motor truck runs over a man as he happens to pass by. He . . .

42. He was on a boat and he noticed mid stream water entering in the boat. He . . .

43. He and his sister are passing through a thick forest on a scooter. The scooter is stopped at gun point for ransom. He . . .

44. He is called upon to organized a variety entertainment show in aid of jawan's welfare in his unit. He . . .

45. Due to financial difficulty his father cannot support him for further studies after he passes matric examination. He . . .

46. Demand of a loan from his closed relative is urgent whereas he needs the same money for his sons hostel admission. He . . .

47. He enters in the bathroom and notices a black cobra hanging from the ceiling of the roof. He . . .

48. Recently his younger brother has become arrogant. He . . .

49. While he was watching cinema he suddenly noticed smoke coming out of cinema hall. The viewers started running causing stampede. He . . .

50. His father had borrowed some money for his higher studies which he could not pay back. He . . .

51. While passing through a mountainous track he was challenged by two persons with weapons in their hands. He . . .

52. He has to appear in an exam. On reaching the city, he noticed that curfew has been clamped. He . . .

53. He was the captain of basketball team and his team was about to lose in the final. He . . .

54. After marriage, his in-laws forced him to leave the job. He . . .

55. His parents often irritated him with their orthodox ideas about the role of women in a society. He . . .

56. At the time of interview, he found that his certificates were missing. He . . .

57. When he observed that his friend was having some suspicion on him. He . . .

58. His colleagues advised his to be tactful with his boss. He . . .

59. He happens to be present at a bus stop, when a child who was with his mother was hit by a speeding motorbike and was injured seriously. He . . .

60. He has already decided to vote for a particulars candidate, whereas his friends wanted his commitment for the other candidate. He . . .

"When we are no longer able to change a situation - we are challenged to change ourselves."

– Viktor E. Frankl

CHAPTER 26

WRITING RESUMES

A resume is a document by which you 'sell' yourself. It should emphasize your strengths. While there is no single way of writing a resume, here are some tips that you may find useful.

1. State your career objective and include all training, experiences and skills that are in line with it.
2. Sell yourself. Emphasize your education, skills, and levels of responsibility attained; all this however, without exaggeration.
3. Put first things first. The important items belong at the top. Within each item arrange the information with your career goal in mind.
4. Use reverse chronological order. When items are listed by date, put the most recent first.
5. Write in an action-oriented style. Use action verbs to highlight what you have done.
6. Make it brief. Omit unnecessary words and phrases: "I", "my duties consisted of", etc. Do not use serial numbers.
7. Be accurate. No mistakes in spelling or grammar.
8. Make it spotless and attractive; well centred and no crowding.

POINTS IN A RESUME

Here are the points. If certain categories are not applicable for you, leave them out. If you have additional information which does not fit into a suggested section, create a new one; e.g. "Related Qualifications" can be changed to "Skills and Abilities".

1. **Career Objectives:**
   Employers prefer candidates who have stated goals. Your job hunt will be more effective if you clarify your job target.
   Example:
   - Position of responsibility in an NGO utilizing my background and experience in rural development.
   - Position in labour relations area at shop floor level with professionally managed concern.

2. **Education:**
   A brief description of your diplomas or degrees, noting aspects linked with your career objective.
   Example:
   - B.A., St. Xavier's College, Ranchi, 1994.
   Major in Sociology with emphasis on social analysis, rural sociology and social research.

3. **Related Qualifications:**
   Focus on skills, areas of knowledge, and demonstrated abilities that support your career bjective. Mention three, at least.
   Examples:
   - Demonstrated public speaking skills
   - Strong research and writing abilities
   - Solid fluency in three regional languages.

4. **Other Training: Focus on relevant seminars, workshops, apprenticeships.**
   Example:
   - Training in Group Entrepreneurship, Pune, 2010.

5. **Related Work Experience:**
   List (in reverse chronological order) and describe your work experience including volunteer, unpaid positions, as well as paid positions. Use action words to describe main responsibilities.
   Example:
   - Administrative Assistant, LIFE Water, Chaibasa, Bihar, June 1997 to present.
   - Conduct needs survey.
   - Prepare audio-visuals.

6. **Additional Experience:**
   Significant experiences not related to career objective.
   Example:
   - Field Investigator, Leprosy Survey, HLC, 1991.

7. **Publications:**
   Mention any publications of significant length and quality that pertain to your objective.
   Example:
   - "Why Primary Health Centres?" Focus, May, 1999.

8. **Honours / Awards:**
   Mention any recognitions you have received.
   Example:
   - Outstanding College Debater, 1996.

9. **Extracurricular Activities:**
   List past and present activities in which you participated. If the experience supports your career objective, you should describe what you did.
   Example:
   - Member, Global Education Associates; organized three local chapters in Bihar.

10. **Professional Memberships:**
    Present or past
    Example:
    - Indian Society for Training and Development

11. **Personal:**
    - Include interests or other details
    Example:
    - Interests include trekking, football, painting References: Let employer know that references are available if desired.

TYPES OF RESUME

1. Chronological Resume

In a chronological resume you have to list your job experience in date order, starting with the most recent first. The sections of a chronological resume are—Job Objective, Career and Related Accomplishments, Work Experience, Professional Affiliations and Interest, References, etc. You'll need to highlight your job experience. This type of resume is the best when you are applying for traditional jobs, especially positions within government entities or private institutions. In fact, this should be preferred by the experienced candidates only. So these types of resumes are:

❖ for Professionals;
❖ for Government, or
❖ for Traditional Jobs.

Chronological Resume Sample:

PRADIP KUMAR SINHA
206/Uday Marg
P.O. Barauni
Begusarai-851114
Bihar
Telephone: 0338769087
email: uday@gmail.com

Job Objective	: A management track position in a private corporation utilizing my administrative, research and accounting skills.
Education	: PG. Dip. in Management, 1995 XLRI, Jamshedpur Specialization: Finance B.Sc. (First Class), 1989 Presidency College, Calcutta.
Work Experience	: September, 1991 to June, 1993—Computer salesman, HCL, Calcutta. September, 1990 to July, 1991—Computer operator, DPS, Jamshedpur.

Extracurricular and Volunteer Activities:
General Secretary, XLRI (1993-94);

Planned and coordinated the major campus social and cultural events (an elected position)
Asha Niketan for handicapped (1991-92).
Led record fund raising drive through city-wide Kabaddi competition.

Personal   : Born 2-8-1969; married;
                          Languages: Hindi, Bengali, Odia.

References available upon request.

2. Functional Resume

Functional resumes are best used in situations where specific skills and accomplishments gained through experience or academic qualifications will demonstrate the candidate's competency. Your skills should be listed in order of their importance. The categories are based on: Career Objectives, Different Functional Skills (must), Interest, References, etc. The functional resume is ideal if you are looking for a complete career change. This resume is ideal for students who have no previous work experience and are applying for their first job. Avoid the functional resume when you are applying for traditional jobs, especially positions within government entities or private institutions. So these types of resumes are:

❖ For Freshers;
❖ For Career Change, and
❖ For Completely New Jobs.

Functional Resume Sample:

NIRMALA JOSEPH
14 Moyenville Lane
Langford Town
Bangalore-15
Phone: 0128769087
email: fsdrt@yahoomail.com

Job Objective   : Entry level management position in advertising
                           company.
Education   : Stella Maris, B.A. 1996, Major—English Honours
Related Qualifications   : Broad liberal arts background.

Excellent planning, organizing, and administrative skills.

Strong communication skills including writing and speaking.

Functional Skills

Administration   : Activities Chairperson, an elected position, organized seven off-campus events. Planned and coordinated liberal arts career day, involving 20 career professionals and 400 students.

Communication   : Delivered talks to business and community groups for aid to Jyoti Niketan, home for the blind.

Edited monthly newsletter.

Research   : Conducted studies on images of women in Karnatic literature, consumer preferences in Bangalore city.

References available upon request.

"Resume: a written exaggeration of only the good things a person has done in the past, as well as a wish list of the qualities a person would like to have."

– Bo Bennett

CHAPTER 27

BRAINSTORMING

Brainstorming is a problem-solving technique. It is a way of getting a large number of new ideas from a group of people in a short time. There are three steps in brainstorming:

Step One: Statement of the problem
The session leader should get a statement of the problem to the participants before the session, if possible, giving the essential facts relevant to the problem. This gives time for ideas to incubate and develop.

For about five or ten minutes at the beginning of the session, participants should try to restate the problem in different ways, always beginning with the words: "How to . . ." This forces people to see it from different angles, something we rarely do.

Step Two: Brainstorming (Getting Idea)
1. The leader, taking the best restatement of the problem, puts it before the group with the words: "In how many ways can we . . . ?"
2. Participants then call out at random any possible solution that occurs to them or modifications of others' solutions. No reasons are given. One person with notebook or at blackboard quickly writes all solutions offered. This step, the key one, continues for 20-25 minutes.

Step Three: Evaluation and screening
A small group is appointed to select the more promising ideas from the list for further consideration.

Practice Items

Here are some areas to practise with. You can add your own.

1. A programme Doordarshan or AIR should introduce.
2. Sushil lives in a town of over 100,000 people. He has a good computer, and an Internet connection. What are possible business opportunities for him?
3. A social project in the neighbourhood.
4. A new gadget for the home.
5. Employment possibilities in the area for school drop-outs.
6. Better traffic control along the main road of your town or city or at the railway station.
7. Economic possibilities of two acres of land at the outskirts of your town or city.
8. Projects for faculty-student groups during holidays.

THE PROCESS

❖ Participants who have ideas but are unable to present them are encouraged to write down the ideas and present them later.

❖ The idea collector should number the ideas, so that the chairperson can use the number to encourage an idea generation goal, "We have 44 ideas now, let's get it to 50."

❖ The idea collector should repeat each idea in the words he or she has written to confirm that it expresses the meaning intended by the originator.

❖ When more participants are having ideas, the one with the most associated idea should have priority. This is to encourage elaboration on previous ideas.

❖ During a brainstorming session, managers and other superiors may be discouraged from attending, as it may generate unusual ideas.

EVALUATION

Brainstorming is not just about generating ideas for others to evaluate and select. Usually the group itself will, in its final stage, evaluate the ideas and select one as the solution to the problem proposed to the group.

❖ The solution should not require resources or skills the members of the group do not have or cannot acquire.

- ❖ If acquiring additional resources or skills is necessary, that needs to be the first part of the solution.
- ❖ There must be a way to measure progress and success.
- ❖ The steps to carry out the solution must be clear to all, and amenable to being assigned to the members so that each will have an important role.
- ❖ There must be a common decision making process to enable a coordinated effort to proceed, and to reassign tasks as the project unfolds.
- ❖ There should be evaluations at milestones to decide whether the group is on track towards a final solution.
- ❖ There should be incentives to participation so that participants maintain their efforts.

"I've always loved brainstorming with other writers, and I consider having my work critiqued a part of that brainstorming."

– Jay Asher

CHAPTER 28

Mock Seminar

A seminar refers to the discussion on a small group in which the result of original research or advanced study is presented through oral or written reports. Generally one person presents a lead paper incorporating his findings and there is an in-depth discussion on the material presented. Seminar is a research technique for higher studies. **But here we are concerned with mock-seminar only.**

In the context of *ELT classes* the students should be allowed to develop the four language skills (LSRW) by taking part in seminars. Therefore, much importance should not be given on the factual and academic matters related to the topic. Rather the teacher should see that all the students participate in the discussion on their own. They should write their own seminar papers, read them aloud before others, listen others' seminar topics and discuss on them. Therefore, the term 'mock' has been used here.

A Sample Mock Seminar: Types of Newspapers in India

Newspapers in India are classified into two categories according to the amount and completeness of information in them. Newspapers in the first category have more information and truth. Those in the second category do not have much information and sometimes they hide the truth. Newspapers in the first category have news collected from different parts of the country and also from different countries. They also have a lot of sports and business news and classified ads. The information they give is clear and complete and it is supported by showing pictures. The best know example of this category is the Indian Express. Important news goes on the first page with big headlines, photographs from different angles, and complete information. For example, in 1991, the Indian Prime Minister, Rajive Gandi, was killed by a terrorist using a bomb. This newspaper investigated the situation and gave information that helped the CBI to get more support. They also showed diagrams of the area where the prime minister was killed and the positions of the bodies after the attack. This helped the reader understand what happened. Unlike newspaper in the first category, newspapers in the second category do not give as much information. They do not have international news, sports, or business news and they do not have classified ads. Also, the news they give is not complete. For example, the newspaper Hindi gave news on the death of the prime minister, but the news was not complete. The newspaper didn't investigate the terrorist group or try to find out why this happened. Also, it did not show any pictures from the attack or give any news the next day. It just gave the news when it happened, but it didn't follow up. Therefore, newspapers in the first group are more popular than those in the second group.

Sample Questions for Discussion:
1. How many types of newspapers are there in India?
2. What are the types of newspapers in India?
3. When was Rajiv Gandhi killed?
4. How did CBI get more support for Rajiv's killing?
5. Which category of newspapers does not give much information?

"It might be an idea for all literary critics to read the books they analyse aloud - it certainly helps to fix them in the mind, while providing a readymade seminar with your audience."

– Will Self

CHAPTER 29

PICTURE READING

Picture Reading is the extraction of meaningful information from a given picture.

Example: Life is a race. One, who wins, wins others' heart and life gives him all the joy. But one, who loses, hides his face. Life becomes a burden for him. But one should not quit easily. It's because, quitters never win and winners never quit.

Look at the first picture here. Ravi and Gopal are good friends. Ravi, the student who is ahead of others, always comes first in any race. On the other hand, Gopal, his friend, never comes first, but he never quits. He is trying and may be on one golden day he will come first.

Thus, in picture reading one has to see both the abstract and concrete aspect of a picture. In fact, one picture can be interpreted in many ways. But while reading a picture, one should be relevant and unbiased.

In Figure 7, there are 15 pictures for reading. Try to extract meaningful information from each of them.

(Fig. 7—Picture Reading)

CHAPTER 30

THE ENGLISH TENSE

The Concept

Tense vs. Time: The form of the verb showing time is called tense. As there is no verb form to express future action, it is not tense. It is time. The time of an action, on the other hand, is the particular point when it happens. It is infinite. It can be past, present or future. It has nothing to do with the language. It can be indicated by words such as: yesterday, tomorrow, 5 years ago, in 1983, now, etc. (endless possibilities)

Tense is quite different. It is an inflectional (changing functions of words with changeable endings) form of a verb used in certain cases. It is part of the language. In other words, in English, a verb form is always in the present or the past tense (Example: go-present, went-past). There is no other possibility.

There are three forms of the main verb :

V1—present (go),
V2—past (went),
V3—past participle (gone).

Helping Verb: Helping verbs help the main verbs in making tense (Primary). They also add some special meaning to the main verbs (Modal)

THE STRUCTURE OF TENSE

TENSE / TIME	STRUCTURE	EXAMPLE	H. VERBS
Present Tense			
1. Simple	S + V1 OR S + do/does + V1	I go.(I do go)	do, <u>does</u>
2. Progressive	S + is/am/are + V1 + 'ing'	I am going.	<u>is</u>, am, are
3. Perfect	S + has/have + V3	I have gone.	have, <u>has</u>
4. Perfect Progressive	S + has/have + been +V1 + 'ing'	I have been going.	have been/has been
Past Tense			
5. Simple	S + V2 OR S + did + V1	I went. / I did go.	did
6. Progressive	S + was/were + V1 + 'ing'	I was going.	<u>was</u>(I), were
7. Perfect	S + had + V3	I had gone.	had
8. Perfect Progressive	S + had been + V1 + 'ing'	I had been going.	had been
Future Time			
9. Simple	S + shall/will + V1	I shall go.	shall, will
10. Progressive	S + shall / will + be + V1 + 'ing'	I shall be going.	shall be / will be
11. Perfect	S + shall / will + have + V3	I shall have gone.	shall have / will have
12. Perfect Progressive	S + shall have been / will have been + V1 +'ing'	I shall have been going.	shall have been / will have been.

N.B.: The underlined helping verbs are used for third person singular number subject. There are three classes of personal pronouns. The first person (Singular—I / Plural—we) refers to the person(s) speaking; the second person (Singular—you / Plural—you) refers to the person(s) spoken to; the third person (Singular—he, she, it, etc./ Plural—they, people, etc.) refers to the person(s) or thing(s) spoken about. Again a noun can be Singular (speaking about one person or thing) or Plural (speaking about more than one person or thing).

USES OF TENSE

1. **The Simple Present Tense is used:**
    (a) To express a habitual action; as, He drinks coffee every morning.
    (b) To express general truths; as, The sun rises in the east.
    (c) To introduce quotation; as, Keats says, "A thing of beauty is a joy forever."
    (d) As a broadcast commentaries on sporting events, instead of the Present Continuous, to describe activities in progress where there is

stress on the succession of happenings rather than on duration; as, The player falls down and the umpire crosses towards the player.

(e) In case of non-conclusive verbs like see, love, hate, etc; as, "I see an aeroplane.", not "I am seeing an aeroplane."

2. **The Present Continuous Tense is used:**

   (a) For an action going on at the time of speaking; as, She is singing. (now)

   (b) For a temporary action which may not be actually happening at the time of speaking; as, I am reading "Vikram Seth". (But I am not reading this moment.)

   (c) For an action that is planned or arranged to take place in the near future as, I am going to the cinema tonight.

   (d) The following verbs on account of their meaning, are not normally used in the continuous form:

   (i) Verbs of Perception, e.g. see, hear, smell, notice, recognize, etc. (ii) Verbs of Appearing, e.g. appear, look, seem, etc. (iii) Verbs of Emotion, e.g. want, wish, desire, feel, like, love, hate, hope 'prefer, etc. (iv) Verbs of Thinking, e.g. think, suppose, believe, remember, forget, know, understand, mean, mind, etc. (v) Have (possess), own, possess, belong to, contain, consist of, etc.

3. **The Present Perfect Tense is used:**

   (a) To indicate completed activities in the immediate past; as, He has just gone out.

   (b) To express past actions whose time is not given and not definite; as, Mr. Ravi has left for Japan.

   (c) To describe past events when we think more of their effect in the present than of the action itself; as, Aditya has eaten all the biscuits. (i.e. There are not any left for you.)

   (d) To denote an action beginning at some time in the past and continuing up to the present moment; as, I have known him for a long time.

   (e) The following adverb and adverb phrases can be used with the present perfect tense: just, never, ever, often, so far, till now etc. This tense is never used with adverbs of past time; as, He has gone to Mumbai yesterday (wrong). In such cases the simple past should be used; as, He went to Mumbai yesterday.

4. The Present Perfect Continuous Tense is used:

For an action, which began at some time in the past and is still continuing; as, He has been sleeping for five hours. (and is still sleeping)

5. The Simple Past Tense is used:
   (a) To indicate an action completed in the past. It often occurs with adverbs or adverb phrases of the past time; as, The man died yesterday.
   (b) Without an adverb of time. In such cases the time may be either implied or indicated by the context; as, I learnt Hindi in Kanpur.
   (c) For past habits; as, He studied many hours every day.

6. The Past Continuous Tense is used:
   (a) To denote some an action going on at some time in the past. The time of the action may or may not be indicated; as, The light went out while I was reading.
   (b) For persistent habits in the past (with always, continually etc.); as, He was always grumbling.

7. The Past Perfect Tense is used:
   (a) To describe an action completed before certain moment in the past; as, I met him in 2000. I had seen him last five years before.
   (b) To describe which action happened earlier when there are two actions of the past; as, I had written the letter before he arrived.

8. The Past Perfect Continuous Tense is used:
   For an action that began before a certain point in the past and continued up to that time; as, At that time he had been writing a novel for two months.

9. The Simple Future Time is used:
   (a) For an action that has till to take place; as, I shall see him tomorrow.
   (b) For immediate decision; as,
       Hari: My calculator is not working.
       Ravi: O.K. I shall repair it.

10. The Future Continuous Time is used:

(a) To represent an action as going on at some time in future; as, I shall be reading the paper then.

(b) For future events that are planned; as, I shall be staying here till Sunday.

11. The Future Perfect Time is used:

To indicate the completion of an action by a certain future time; as I shall have written my exercise by that time.

12. The Future Perfect Progressive Time is used:

To indicate an action represented as being in progress over a period of time that will end in future; as, By next May we shall have been living here for four years.

Exercise:

Choose the correct verb form from those in brackets:

1. The earth_____round the sun. (move, moves, moved)
2. My friends_____the Prime Minister yesterday. (see, have seen, saw)
3. I_____him only one letter up to now. (sent, have sent, send)
4. She_____worried about something. (looks, looking, is looking)
5. It started to rain while we_____tennis. (are playing, were playing, had played)
6. He_____fast when the accident happened. (is driving, was driving, drove)
7. He_____asleep while he was driving. (falls, fell, has fallen)
8. I'm sure I_____him at the party last night. (saw, have seen, had seen)
9. He_____a mill in this town. (have, has, is having)
10. He_____here for the last five years. (worked, is working, has been working)
11. He thanked me for what I_____. (have done, had done, have been doing)
12. I_____a strange noise. (hear, am hearing, have been hearing)
13. I_____him for a long time. (know, have known, am knowing)
14. We_____, English for five years. (study, am studying, have been studying)
15. Don't disturb me. I_____my homework. (do, did, am doing)
16. Abdul_____to be a doctor. (wants, wanting, is wanting)

17. The soup_____good. (taste, tastes, is tasting)
18. He_____TV most evenings. (watches, is watch, is watching)
19. He_____out five minutes ago. (has gone, had gone, went)
20. When he lived in Hyderabad, he_____to the cinema once a week. (goes, went, was going)
21. The baby_____all morning. (cries, has been crying)
22. I_____Rahim at the zoo. (saw, have seen, had seen)
23. I_____Kumar this week. (haven't seen, didn't see, am not seeing)
24. This paper_____twice weekly. (is appearing, appearing, appears)
25. Ashok fell off the ladder when he_____the roof. (is mending, was mending, mended)

"Nothing is improbable until it moves into past tense."

– George Ade

CHAPTER 31

TWENTY COMMON SENTENCE PATTERNS

Pattern 1: Subject + Verb

This is the simplest of verb patterns. The subject is followed by an intransitive verb, which expresses complete sense without the help of any other words.

	Subject	Verb
1.	Birds	fly.
2.	Fire	burns.

Pattern 2: Subject + Verb + Subject Complement

The complement usually consists of a noun (examples 1&2), a pronoun (3 & 4), or an adjective (5, 6, 7 & 8).

	Subject	Verb	Subject Complement
1.	This	is	a pen.
2.	His brother	became	a soldier.
3.	It	is	I (me).
4.	That book	is	mine.
5.	Gopal	looks	sad.
6.	My father	grew	angry.
7.	The children	kept	quiet.
8.	The milk	has turned	sour.

Pattern 3: Subject + Verb + Direct Object

	Subject	Verb	Direct Object
1.	I	know	his address.
2.	The boy	has lost	his pen.

Pattern 4: Subject + Verb + Indirect Object + Direct Object

	Subject	Verb	Indirect Object	Direct Object
1.	I	lent	her	my pen.
2.	—	Show	me	your hands.

Pattern 5: Subject + Verb + Direct Object + Preposition + Prepl. Object

	Subject	Verb	Direct Object	Preposition	Prepositional object
1.	I	lent	my pen	to	a friend of mine.
2.	The teacher	gave	homework	to	all of us.

Many verbs can be used both in Pattern 4 and in Pattern 5. Pattern 5 is preferred when the direct object is less important or when the indirect object is longer than the direct object.

Pattern 6: Subject + Verb + Noun/Pronoun + Adjective

	Subject	Verb	Noun/ Pronoun	Adjective
1.	The boy	pushed	the door	open.
2.	The smith	beat	it	flat.

Verbs used: get, keep, beat, drive, make, paint, leave, turn, find, like, wish, etc.

Pattern 7: Subject + Verb + Preposition + Prepositional Object

	Subject	Verb	Preposition	Prepositional Object
1.	We	are waiting	for	Suresh.
2.	He	agreed	to	our proposal.

Pattern 8: Subject + Verb + to-infinitive (as Object of the Verb)

	Subject	Verb	to-infinitive, etc. (Object of the Verb)
1.	She	wants	to go.
2.	I	forgot	to post the letter.

Verbs used: like, love, prefer, begin, start, agree, try, attempt, choose, continue, intend, propose, desire, wish, want, hate, dislike, hope, expect, promise, refuse, fear, remember, forget, offer, learn, etc.

Pattern 9: Subject + Verb + Noun/Pronoun + to-infinitive

	Subject	Verb	Noun/ Pronoun	to-infinitive, etc.
1.	I	would like	you	to stay.
2.	We	asked	him	logo.

Verbs used: ask, tell, order, command, persuade, encourage, urge, want, wish, request, intend, expect, force, tempt, teach, invite, help, warn, like, love, hate, allow, permit, remind, cause, mean, etc.

Pattern 10: Subject + Verb + Gerund

Subject	Verb	Gerund, etc.
1. She	began	singing.
2. He	has finished	talking.

In this pattern the gerund is the object of the verb.

Verbs used: begin, start, love, like, hate, stop, finish, enjoy, prefer, fear, remember, forget, mind, miss, suggest, practise, try, understand, keep, help, advise, admit, avoid, consider, delay, deny, etc.

Pattern 11: Subject + Verb + Noun/Pronoun + Present Participle

Subject	Verb	Noun/ Pronoun	Present Participle
1. I	saw	him	crossing the bridge.
2. We	smell	something	burning.

Verbs used: see, hear, smell, feel, watch, notice, find, observe, listen, get, catch, keep, leave, set, start, etc.

Pattern 12: Subject + Verb + Noun/Pronoun + Plain Infinitive

Subject	Verb	Noun/Pronoun	Plain Infinitive, etc.
1. I	saw	him	go out.
2. —	Let	me	go.

Verbs used: see, watch, notice, observe, hear, listen, feel, make, help, bid, etc.

Pattern 13: Subject + Verb + Noun/Pronoun + Past Participle

Subject	Verb	Noun/ Pronoun	Past Participle
1. I	heard	my name	called.
2. I	want	this letter	typed.

Verbs used: see, hear, find, feel, want, wish like, make, prefer, get, have, etc.

Pattern 14: Subject + Verb + Noun/Pronoun + (to be +) Complement

The complement may be an adjective, adjective phrase or noun.

	Subject	Verb	Noun/ Pronoun	(to be +) Complement
1.	I	consider	the plan	(to be) unwise.
2.	The court	appointed	her	guardian of the orphan.

Verbs used: appoint, choose, elect, make call, name, nominate, crown, christen, etc.

Pattern 15: Subject + Verb + that-clause (Object of the Verb)

	Subject	Verb	that-clause (Object of the Verb)
1.	I	suppose	(that) he is not at home.
2.	I	expect	(that) it will rain.

That is often omitted, especially after say, think, suppose, hope, expect, etc.
Verbs used: say, think, suppose, imagine, know, believe, admit, confess, declare, suggest, complain, hope, expect, fear, feel, hear, intend, notice, propose, etc.

Pattern 16: Subject + Verb + Noun/Pronoun + that-clause

	Subject	Verb	Noun/Pronoun	that-clause
1.	He	told	me	(that) he was coming.
2.	I	warned	him	that they were thieves.

Pattern 17: Subject + Verb + Interrogative + Clause

	Subject	Verb	Interrogative + Clause
1.	I	asked	where he was going.
2.	Nobody	knows	when he will arrive.

Verbs used: say, ask, wonder, know believe, imagine, decide, discuss, understand, show, reveal, find out suggest, tell (especially in the interrogative and negative), etc.

Pattern 18: Subject + Verb + Noun/Pronoun + Interrogative + Clause

	Subject	Verb	Noun/ Pronoun	Interrogative + Clause
1.	She	asked	me	when you had gone.
2.	—	(Please) advise	me	what I should do.

Verbs used: tell, ask, show, teach, advise, inform, etc.

Pattern 19: Subject + Verb + Interrogative + to-infinitive

Subject	Verb	Interrogative + to-infinitive, etc.
1. I	don't know	how to do it.
2. I	wonder	where to spend the week-end.

Verbs used: know, understand wonder, remember, forget, decide, settle, find out, enquire, see, explain, guess, learn, consider, etc.

Pattern 20: Subject + Verb + Noun/Pronoun + Interrogative + to-infinitive

Subject	Verb	Noun/ Pronoun	Interrogative + to-infinitive
1. I	shall show	you	how to operate it.
2. —	(Please) advise	me	what to do.

"Grammar is the logic of speech, even as logic is the grammar of reason."

– Richard Chenevix Trench

CHAPTER 32

GRAMMAR-BASED CONVERSATIONS

Conversation 1: Introduction (Student and Director of the Course)
Grammar Function: Yes-No Questions

Student	:	Good morning, sir
Director	:	Good morning. What can I do for you?
Student	:	I'm Srinivas. I want to learn how to speak English fluently.
Director	:	That's a good idea. But why?
Student	:	For better communication.
Director	:	Very good. Let me see how well you speak. I'll ask you a few questions. Where do you stay?
Student	:	At College Square.
Director	:	How far is it from here?
Student	:	About one kilometer.
Director	:	Do you have a telephone?
Student	:	Yes, we have.
Director	:	No, you should say, 'We do'. If I ask you 'Have you a telephone?', then you say, 'We have'. Well, how old are you?
Student	:	I'm eighteen.
Director	:	Good. What's your father?
Student	:	He is a Professor of Botany.
Director	:	Are you a student?
Student	:	Yes, I am. I'm doing B.C.A.
Director	:	In which college?
Student	:	In Ravenshaw Junior College.
Director	:	For how long have you been learning English?
Student	:	For more than twelve years.
Director	:	Twelve years! And yet you think you can't speak well?

Student	:	You see sir; I am fairly good at writing in English. I have studied grammar. I got fairly high grades in the exams. I must say that it was largely by memorizing and reproducing what I memorized.
Director	:	It's true. One rarely opens his mouth to express his thoughts and feelings. But in your case, you are doing fairly well.
Student	:	Thank you, sir.
Director	:	First you need to practise the sounds of words and accent the syllables properly.
Student	:	Syllables? What is a syllable, sir?
Director	:	When we speak, we divide the words into syllables and pronounce them. A syllable is a unit of one vowel sound with a consonant before or after it. Take the word 'pen'. There are three sounds p-e-n. The vowel sound is central to the syllable. The consonant sounds are placed before and after the vowel sound. The word 'pen' has one syllable. The word 'always' has two syllables.
Student	:	What is accent, sir?
Director	:	Some syllables are more prominent than the others. Such prominent syllables are said to receive the accent or stress. While pronouncing them, we place more emphasis on them. In the word 'always', the first syllable 'al'—gets the stress. And then you should follow correct intonation.
Student	:	Intonation? What is it, sir?
Director	:	Intonation is the rise and fall of the pitch of the voice in speaking. For instance, when you put a Yes-No question, you use the rising intonation. Do you get it? Is it clear? When you make a statement, you use the falling intonation. I get it. It is clear.
Student	:	Yes, sir.
Director	:	And you should familiarize yourself with appropriate expressions and use them as the situation demands. This course aims at engaging you in several speech activities and thus helps you to learn the skills so that you can speak fluently, accurately and appropriately.
Student	:	Thank you for your guidance. I'll follow the guidelines and practise the conversations.
Director	:	You can't do that all alone. Choose a companion to converse with.

Student	:	I will do so, sir. Thank you very much.
Director	:	All the best, young man!

Conversation 2: Telephoning (Latha, Secretary and Director)

Grammar Function: WH—Questions

Latha	:	Hello. Is that 9437303774?
Secretary	:	Yes. Ravenshaw Helpline. May I help you?
Latha	:	I'd like to speak to the Director.
Secretary	:	May I know who's calling?
Latha	:	This is Latha Jain.
Secretary	:	Please hold on . . .
Director	:	Hello. This is Janardan Mishra, Director of Ravenshaw Helpline
Latha	:	Good morning. My name is Latha. I'am a student. I have seen your advertisement about a new course in Spoken English.
Director	:	You are right; the English Language Speaking Course.
Latha	:	What's special about it, sir?
Director	:	We have designed it in such a way that the learner gets a lot of practice in speaking fluently and accurately.
Latha	:	I see. What's the duration of the course?
Director	:	It's an eight-week course and each session lasts for two hours.
Latha	:	Right. How much do you charge for the course?
Director	:	We charge one thousand rupees, which can be paid in two installments.
Latha	:	When are you starting it?
Director	:	On 18th September.
Latha	:	How can I enroll myself?
Director	:	You can come on 15th for enrolment between 10 a.m. and 5p.m
Latha	:	Thank you very much for all the information. I'll see you on the 15th.
Director	:	I'm looking forward to meeting you. You're welcome.

Conversation 3: Enrolling for a Course (Student and Secretary)

Grammar Function: Question Tag

Sec.	:	Good morning, Can I help you?
Student	:	I'd like to enroll for the Spoken English Course.
Sec.	:	Certainly. What's your first name please?
Student	:	Arpita

Sec.	:	Could you spell that for me?
Student	:	Yes, it's A.R.P.I.T.A.
Sec.	:	Thank you and what's your surname?
Student	:	Panda. That's spelled P.A.N.D.A.
Sec.	:	Thank you. Where are you from Ms. Arpita?
Student	:	Cuttack.
Sec.	:	I see. So, your mother tongue is Odia, isn't it?
Student	:	Yes, that's right.
Sec.	:	How old are you?
Student	:	18
Sec.	:	Are you going to pay the entire fee now or do you want to pay it in installment?
Student	:	I'll pay the entire fee now.
Sec.	:	Thank you . . . Here's the receipt. Okay, the timings and days are Monday through Friday from 6 p.m. to 8 p.m. Classes begin on the 18ᵗʰ of this month.
Student	:	Thank you very much.
Sec.	:	You're welcome.

Conversation 4: Courtesy (Pravat and Lisa)

Grammar Function: Daily Expressions

Pravat	:	Excuse me, can I sit here?
Lisa	:	Of course, it's my pleasure.
Pravat	:	How do you do?
Lisa	:	How do you do?
Private	:	I'm Pravat Pattanaik, and you?
Lisa	:	This is Lisa. Mohapatra. I am the sister of the bride.
Private	:	Glad to meet you Miss Lisa.
Lisa	:	Thank you. How's everything?
Private	:	Well, I'm sorry to say that there are not enough chairs to sit on and chit chat.
Lisa	:	No, definitely not. As you know this is a party with buffet. Should we go for putting so many chairs?
Private	:	That's all right. I do apologies. In fact, I was not complaining.
Lisa	:	Don't worry. Forget it. Would you like some tea?
Private	:	Not just now, thank you.
Lisa	:	I suggest you to go for a walk, shall we?
Private	:	Yes, why not?
Lisa	:	Will you wait a minute please? I have a call.

Private	:	All right.
Lisa	:	(after attending the call) Now it's all over. Let's go.

Conversation 5: Making Purchases (Customer and Shopkeeper)
Grammar Function: Nouns

Sk.	:	Good morning. Would you like some help?
Customer	:	Yes, please. I'd like to have a look at pens.
Sk.	:	Right. What kind?
Customer	:	Umm . . . Fountain pens.
Sk.	:	Well, we have a wide variety of fountain pens to choose from. Here you go.
Customer	:	I really like that maroon one.
Sk.	:	Yes, it's a top of the range pen. It comes quite cheap too at 44 rupees.
Customer	:	Really? That's quite a bargain. I'll take it.
Sk.	:	Anything else I can help you with?
Customer	:	A bottle of black ink please.
Sk.	:	Any particular company?
Customer	:	Do you have Chelpark?
Sk.	:	Yes, we do. That's 11 rupees.
Customer	:	Do you have document paper? I mean paper for computer printouts.
Sk.	:	Yes. Any particular brand?
Customer	:	I prefer the Millennium Copier.
Sk.	:	Which size?
Customer	:	A4. How much does a bundle cost?
Sk.	:	A bundle of 500 sheets costs 132 rupees.
Customer	:	I want two bundles . . . I'm afraid I don't have that much cash. Do you accept cheques?
Sk.	:	Yes, we do.
Customer	:	Here is the cheque. Thank you.
Sk.	:	That's my pleasure.

Conversation 6: Meeting at a Party (Sanjay and Gopal)
Grammar Function: Pronouns

Sanjay	:	Excuse me. Haven't we met before somewhere? Was it at the wedding reception of Arvind?
Gopal	:	Exactly. Aren't you Mr. Sanjay?
Sanjay	:	Yes, I am. You are Mr. Gopal, if I remember right. How are you?

Gopal	:	I am fine. Thank you. So we meet again. I remember you brought two big bouquets to greet the couple.
Sanjay	:	Gopal, meet my wife Sandhya.
Gopal	:	Hello madam, this is Gopal.
Sandhya	:	I'm Sandhya. It seems that I have seen you somewhere.
Gopal	:	You have met me? What are you telling?
Sandhya	:	Yes, I myself. By the way what was your college?
Gopal	:	Ravenshaw College.
Sandhya	:	Right, mine also.
Gopal	:	Which year did you pass graduation?
Sandhya	:	In 1997. Did you pass in the same year?
Gopal	:	Right. I might have seen you in the campus. I am sorry. I have not introduced my wife to both of you.
Radha	:	It's OK. No more formalities. Let's meet the couple and then we can be free to talk.
Sanjay	:	Yes, this is high time to meet the newly wedded couple.
Gopal	:	OK, let's move.

Conversation 7: Arranging a Party (Prem and Renu)

Grammar Function: Adjectives

Prem	:	Renu dear, get me a glass of water please. It's so hot.
Renu	:	Here you are! Yes, it's very warm and sultry today.
Prem	:	True. I wish it would rain . . . Well, on my way back, I went to the baker's and ordered a big chocolate cake.
Renu	:	We've hardly three days left to organize Anu's Birthday Party.
Prem	:	She's so excited about it.
Renu	:	Your dad called saying they're coming tomorrow.
Prem	:	Will they bring Sumana with them? Anu is so eager to meet her.
Prem	:	Yes, Archana too.
Renu	:	Lovely . . . Come on. Who else shall we invite? We must have Indu.
Prem	:	Who's Indu?
Renu	:	Oh, you know her. She's Anu's friend at school.
Prem	:	OK. How about Ravi and Jyothsna ?
Renu	:	Yes, I like them a lot.
Prem	:	What about Rahul?
Renu	:	Who's that?

Prem	:	Oh Renu. You're so forgetful. He's the man who returned from Nairobi a couple of months ago; big, bearded, and funny.
Prem	:	Ah! Yes. Sure. He tells very interesting anecdotes.
Renu	:	How about inviting Swaroop Rani who taught you classical music?
Prem	:	Oh, I forgot. Then let's invite Sundari and her husband. They are our neighbours. So helpful!
Renu	:	OK. How many are there now? Let me see. There are ten, eleven, . . . fourteen.
Prem	:	Including you and me?
Renu	:	Yes.
Prem	:	That's that. Now some tea?
Renu	:	That's a very good idea.

Conversation 8: Stealing a Cell (Police and Thief)

Grammar Function: Verbs

Police	:	Hello, hello . . . come here.
Thief	:	What happened sir?
Police	:	You don't know?
Thief	:	No sir, you just called me.
Police	:	Why did I call you?
Thief	:	(shouting) That is your business. Why are you disturbing me?
Police	:	Oh! I am disturbing you. You are not disturbing others?
Thief	:	What do you mean?
Police	:	I mean your mobile.
Thief	:	Don't talk nonsense. What is your problem with my mobile?
Police	:	My problem is I have got a complaint against you. You have stolen somebody's mobile. Can I see your mobile?
Thief	:	Listen sir, you might have been misguided. I am a gentleman.
Police	:	You listen gentleman, show your mobile.
Thief	:	But who are you?
Police	:	I am police sub-inspector Rakesh Dash.
Thief	:	Ohhhh! Sorry sir, in fact I have no mobile with me now.
Police	:	But what is that in your pocket?
Thief	:	That is my friend's mobile.
Police	:	What is your friend's name?
Thief	:	Suresh . . . , no no Bijay . . .
Police	:	Why are you trembling?
Thief	:	Please sir, forgive me. I shall share this with you.

Police	:	What! You are trying to bribe me?
Thief	:	No sir, it's not exactly bribe. We can manage it between us.
Police	:	OK, give me the mobile and come to my residence at OMP in the evening.
Thief	:	Thank you sir.

Conversation 9: Interviewing (Politician and Interviewer)

Grammar Function: Adverbs

Interviewer	:	Good morning sir. I'm from City Heights, a leading English Monthly.
Politician	:	Good morning. Please sit down and make yourself comfortable.
Interviewer	:	I've come to take your interview to publish it in our next issue.
Politician	:	But first, tell me one thing. What do you want to interview me for?
Interviewer	:	You see, sir, we publish a column called "A Day in the Life of . . ." which gives our readers some information about the personal lives of people who are in the limelight.
Politician	:	OK. fine, carry on.
Interviewer	:	Could you describe to me your daily routine, starting from the time you wake up?
Politician	:	Well, normally I get up around 7. Then I practise yoga and meditation for 45 minutes. It helps me keep a cool head.
Interviewer	:	Oh, that's a very healthy way of starting the day.
Politician	:	Then I have my bath and take breakfast between 8 and 8.30.
Interviewer	:	Do you start your work right away?
Politician	:	Usually I do. But more often than not, I'm interrupted by telephone calls, which seem to be never-ending.
Interviewer	:	That's to be expected, considering youth popularity.
Politician	:	My morning hours stretch from 9 to 12.30 when I take care of some of the serious matters that need my attention.
Interviewer	:	What time do you have your lunch?
Politician	:	Around 1 p.m. Then if there is nothing urgent, I take a nap till about 3 to refresh myself.
Interviewer	:	How are your evenings spent?
Politician	:	I generally have my tea at 3.30. Then I have some functions, meetings, inaugurations or felicitations to attend. Otherwise, I stay at home and catch up with the news or spend some time with my family.
Interviewer	:	You must be invited to many parties.

Politician   : Yes, I am. But unless they are very important, you see . . . I don't spend nights partying, I prefer to have an early supper around 8.30., followed by some T.V. viewing. Then I am off to bed by 9.30. I believe in the adage (saying), "Early to bed and early to rise makes a man healthy, wealthy and wise"

Interviewer : Oh, that you are, sir. I mean healthy, wealthy and wise! Thank you very much for sparing your valuable time.

Politician   : Oh, not at all. Goodbye.

Interviewer : Goodbye.

Conversation 10: Booking Hotel Rooms (Receptionist and Kartik)

Grammar Function: Prepositions

Receptionist : Good morning. Hotel Ambassador, Delhi.

Kartik   : Good morning. I'm speaking from Mumbai. We're coming to Delhi on an excursion. I'd like to book two double rooms, please.

Receptionist : Fine. Oh, just a moment. I'll get the register. Ok then When do you want to check in? What date is it?

Kartik   : We're going to arrive there on Friday, the 5th of May. We'll be staying till Monday, the 8th of May.

Receptionist : That seems to be okay. 5th to 8th May, you said.

Kartik   : Exactly. We want to have two rooms.

Receptionist : Yes, we have two nice double rooms overlooking the pool.

Kartik   : That sounds nice.

Receptionist : Your name, sir?

Kartik   : Kartik. K:A:R:T:I:K.

Receptionist : Your surname, sir?

Kartik   : Desai. D:E:S:A:I.

Receptionist : OK. Thanks.

Kartik   : I'd like to know the cost of one double room per night, please.

Receptionist : Yes. Well, a double room per night is one thousand three hundred rupees which includes breakfast.

Kartik   : How reasonable! Thank you very much. Bye. Bye.

Receptionist : Look forward to seeing you, sir.

Conversation 11: Ordering Food (Kartik, Pallavi, Sharma, Bindu and Waiter)

Grammar Function: Conjunctions

Kartik   :   Could we have a table for four?

Waiter	:	There's a nice table right there by the window.
Kartik	:	May we have the menu right away?
Waiter	:	Here you are, sir.
Kartik	:	Thank you. Hmm . . . What shall we have?
Pallavi	:	I'd prefer starting off with some fruit juice and then have some snacks. I'll try grape juice and the local speciality, Maddur Vada.
Bindu	:	I'd like to have Masala Dosa and hot coffee.
Sharma	:	Well, I'm famished. Nothing short of a square meal would satisfy me. I'd prefer a South Indian Special Thali. What about you Kartik?
Kartik	:	I think I shall try the North Indian Thali and then have a cup of chocolate ice-cream. So that's that. Let's order.
Pallavi	:	Waiter . . . A plate of Masala Dosa and hot coffee; a South Indian Special Thali; a North Indian Thali followed by a cup of chocolate ice-cream; and a glass of grape juice and a plate of Maddur Vada.
Waiter	:	Right. A plate of Masala Dosa and hot coffee; a South Indian Special Thali; a North Indian Thali and a cup of chocolate ice-cream; and a glass of grape juice and a plate of Maddur Vada.
Pallavi	:	Okay. [later]
Kartik	:	Waiter, get the bill please.
Waiter	:	Here you are, sir.

Conversation 12: Accident (Sanjaya and Gopal)

Grammar Function: Interjections

Sanjaya	:	Hello! What are you doing here?
Gopal	:	Oh! Here is an accident.
Sanjaya	:	Alas! The man is dead.
Gopal	:	Ah me! You see, how much blood is there!
Sanjaya	:	Ah! Here comes the police.
Gopal	:	Well! let's go.
Sanjaya	:	OK.

Conversation 13: Identifying People (Sunder and Prem)

Grammar Function: Present Simple

| Sunder | : | Hello, Prem. How are you? |
| Prem | : | Hi, Sundar. I'm fine. Thank you. And you? |

Sunder	:	I'm all right. You had gone to Puri for your sister's marriage. When did you come back?
Prem	:	Yesterday. We had a wonderful time there. Everything went on well. I mean all the arrangements, the accommodation and above all the Darshan of Lord Jagannath.
Sunder	:	I'm sure your sister is greatly delighted.
Prem	:	Yes, she is. Would you like to look at the photoes ?
Sunder	:	Yes, I'd love to.
Prem	:	Do you have time?
Sunder	:	Yes, I do. I love family photoes.
Prem	:	Here's the album. The man in the middle with a garland is my sister's husband. He is a businessman.
Sunder	:	Looks smart. Who's to the left of your brother-in-law?
Prem	:	That's his father, Mr. Rajagopal, a retired judge.
Sunder	:	The one on his left?
Prem	:	His second son, Rahul. He's studying medicine.
Sunder	:	Who's to the right of your sister?
Prem	:	That's her mother-in-law. Next to her is her mother. An old woman who keeps you engaged with her lively talk.
Sunder	:	I don't see you here.
Prem	:	It's their family with my sister.
Sunder	:	Let me see some more photoes. Ah, here you are. This is your family with the bridegroom, I suppose.
Prem	:	That's right.
Sunder	:	I guess I had better go now.
Prem	:	I've got to be going now too.
Sunder	:	In that case, I'll be seeing you.
Prem	:	So long. See you later.

Conversation 14: Making Acquaintances (Radhika, Neetu and Veena)
Grammar Function: Present Continuous

Radhika	:	Hello. I haven't seen you around. You must be new.
Neetu	:	Yes, I am.
Radhika	:	I'm Radhika. What's your name?
Neetu	:	Neetu. (They shake hands)
Radhika	:	So what course are you doing, Neetu?
Neetu	:	I've joined BBA—I. What about you?

Radhika	:	I'm doing the same course as you do but I'm in BBA—IInd year. How do you find the college?
Neetu	:	I'd say I like it. The lecturers seem very helpful and knowledgeable. And the students are friendly.
Radhika	:	Yes, that's the impression I had when I joined the college. Which school were you in?
Neetu	:	I attended St. Joseph's High School.

(Veena joins them)

Veena	:	Hello.
Radhika	:	Neetu, meet Veena, one of my close friends.
Veena	:	Hello, Neetu. Nice to meet you!
Radhika	:	She's doing BBA—I.
Veena	:	Oh, really?
Neetu	:	Yes. I guess you're doing BBA—II too.
Veena	:	Guessed right.
Neetu	:	Do you think we can catch a bite to eat? I'm starving. I haven't had breakfast.
Radhika	:	Nervous? Your first day of college. Sure. Let's order something.
Veena	:	I recommend the sandwiches. They're fine.
Radhika	:	OK then. Let's try them out.

[They place an order for sandwiches. Veena pays. They finish eating. They start walking back to the classrooms.]

Veena	:	It was really nice meeting you, Neetu.
Neetu	:	Yes. Thank you both for making my first day here so pleasant.
Radhika	:	Not at all a problem, Neetu. We'll see you tomorrow. Bye!
Neetu	:	Thanks again. See you tomorrow.
Veena	:	Bye!

Conversation 15: Asking for Directions (Kartik, Pallavi, Sharma, Bindu and the Travel Agent)

Grammar Function: Perfect Tense

T. Agent	:	Good evening.
Sharma	:	Good evening.
T. Agent	:	I think you enjoyed your sightseeing today.

Sharma	:	It was most enjoyable though it tired us a little. Your directions helped us to cover a lot of places. Thank you.
T. Agent	:	I'm sure you'll have an equally enjoyable time tomorrow.
Kartik	:	Please tell us which places to see tomorrow.
T. Agent	:	I presume you've booked the taxi for tomorrow.
Pallavi	:	Yes, we have.
T. Agent	:	That's fine. After breakfast you'll leave for Srirangapatnam, a place of great historical importance.
Bindu	:	Is it the same place shown in the TV serial on Tippu Sultan?
T. Agent	:	Exactly. It was once the capital of Tippu Sultan, "The Tiger of Mysore". Now it is largely in a ruined state, recalling the battles fought and the lost glory. There are several places of interest like Tippu's Palace, Daria Daulat Bagh, the Gumbuz, and a big temple of Sri Ranganatha.
Bindu	:	I think there is a river near that place.
T. Agent	:	Ah, sure. It's an island town surrounded by the river Kaveri.
Kartik	:	Where will we go from there?
T. Agent	:	A visit to Ranganthittu is a must. It's a bird sanctuary, hardly three kilometers from Srirangapatnam.
Pallavi	:	A bird sanctuary?
T. Agent	:	Yes. It keeps you absorbed in watching a host of migratory birds.
Kartik	:	OK. Then what?
T. Agent	:	Lunch and rest for a while. Then you could go straight to the Brindavan Gardens. You'll feel enchanted when there is illumination.
Pallavi	:	What an interesting programme we have for tomorrow! Thank you very much.
T. Agent	:	That's all right. Wish you a very pleasant day tomorrow. Goodbye.
All	:	Bye . . . Bye . . .

Conversation 16: Complaining (Customer, Receptionist and Sanjay)
Grammar Function: Simple Past

Receptionist	:	Good day. "Star Lamps". May I help you?
Customer	:	Good morning. My name is Ramesh Sharma. I bought a lamp from your store recently but I found that it's not working.

Receptionist	:	I see. Would you please hold the line while I connect you to the Complaints and Suggestions Section?
Customer	:	Thank you.
Sanjay	:	Hello, Mr. Sharma. This is Sanjay. I'm in charge of Complaints and Suggestions.
Customer	:	Yes, this is Ramesh Sharma. I bought a lamp from your store two days ago and it does not seem to work.
Sanjay	:	Do you have the receipt?
Customer	:	Yes, I do.
Sanjay	:	Can you please give me the code of the lamp?
Customer	:	It is FX 43029.
Sanjay	:	OK. Thank you. Now please tell me what exactly, the problem seems to be.
Customer	:	Well, when I turn the lamp switch on, it takes several, may be ten seconds, to light up.
Sanjay	:	So, is the problem the length of time it takes to light up?
Customer	:	That's part of the problem. When it eventually does light up, the light is very dim.
Sanjay	:	Aah! I see. There seems to be a loose connection. Why don't you bring the lamp and the receipt in? We will replace it.
Customer	:	Okay. I'll bring it in tomorrow around noon. Thank you very much for the help.
Sanjay	:	Sorry for the faulty lamp. Don't worry. You'll have a lamp in excellent working condition tomorrow. Bye.
Customer	:	That's all right. Bye.

Conversation 17: Making an Appointment (Secretary and Vimal)

Grammar Function: Article

Secretary	:	Hello. Dr. Sukumar's Office, can I help you?
Vimal	:	Good morning. I'd like to make an appointment with Dr. Sukumar on Wednesday, please.
Secretary	:	Who's speaking please?
Vimal	:	Vimal.
Secretary	:	Yes, Mr. Vimal, Wednesday is all right. But it will have to be in the afternoon. Will 4.30 do?
Vimal	:	That'll be fine. I'd like to know if there are facilities for scanning, X-Ray and clinical tests.
Secretary	:	Yes, there are. You can get all the tests done here itself. You need not go round different places.

Vimal	:	That'll make things easier. Thank you very much.
Secretary	:	You're welcome.

Conversation 18: At the Chemist's (Customer and Attendant)
Grammar Function: Modals

Customer	:	Hello.
Att.	:	Hello. Can I help you?
Customer	:	Yes, please. Can you make up this prescription?
Att.	:	Let me look at the whole prescription. I want to make sure that we have all the drugs. Yes. I'll take just five minutes to make it up. Just have your seat over there for a moment. Here you are.
Customer	:	I would also like some Vicks cough drops.
Att.	:	How many?
Customer	:	umm . . . 10 please.
Att.	:	10 Vicks cough drops.
Customer	:	Can I have a look at that Pond's Face-Wash?
Att.	:	Certainly.
Customer	:	Is this effective?
Att.	:	Yes, very much. It helps in reducing pimples and it reduces oiliness.
Customer	:	How much is this?
Att.	:	50 rupees.
Customer	:	Oh, that's quite expensive.
Att.	:	But it's very effective.
Customer	:	Please give me the bill for the medicines and cough drops.
Att.	:	OK. 53 rupees plus 10 rupees. That'll be 63 Rupees.
Customer	:	Here's a hundred.
Att.	:	Do you happen to have 3 rupees change?
Customer	:	Let me check. Yes, I do.
Att.	:	Here's your change.
Customer	:	Thank you.

Conversation 19: Renting a Flat (Owner and Enquirer)
Grammar Function: Conditionals

Owner	:	Hello, this is 6541278
Enquirer	:	Hello. Is that Mr. Mehta?
Owner	:	Yes, speaking.

Enquirer	:	I'm Mr. Vasudev. I've just seen the advertisement in today's paper. I'm calling to enquire about the furnished flat you have to rent. Is it still available?
Owner	:	Yes, it is. Would you like to know something about it?
Enquirer	:	I would. Could you give me the address of the flat?
Owner	:	It's number 309, Shahjahan Enclave, Defence Colony, New Delhi.
Enquirer	:	Okay. How big is the flat?
Owner	:	It's big enough for a family of four or five. There are two good-size bedrooms.
Enquirer	:	Is there running water from taps?
Owner	:	Twenty-four hours. Besides, drinking water is available from the corporation every day.
Enquirer	:	How much is the rent?
Owner	:	It's ten thousand rupees a month. The electricity is extra.
Enquirer	:	Do I have to pay anything for the maintenance of the flat?
Owner	:	Yes, you do. Five hundred rupees extra per month.
Enquirer	:	If I do decide to rent the flat, when will I be able to move in?
Owner	:	It will be available from the beginning of June.
Enquirer	:	Thank you very much. I'll be in touch.
Owner	:	You can come and have a look if you wish.
Enquirer	:	Yes, I'd like that.
Owner	:	Just give me a call before you decide to, Mr. Vasudev.
Enquirer	:	Of course, I'll do that. Thank you very much.

Conversation 20: At the Beauty Parlour (Customer and Hairstylist)

Grammar Function: Infinitives and Gerunds

Customer	:	Hello.
Hs.	:	Hello. Come right in.
Customer	:	I'd like to get a haircut please.
Hs.	:	Sure. What kind of haircut do you want?
Customer	:	Well, actually, I am not sure. I was hoping that you'd advise me on what hairstyle would suit my face.
Hs.	:	That's not a problem. Let me have a good look at you. Hmm . . . You have an oval face with a square jaw.
Customer	:	Yes, that's true. I want something that draws attention away from my jaw.
Hs.	:	I have a few pictures here. These styles suit oval faces like yours. Have a look at them and decide which one you want.

Customer	:	Okay. Give me a few minutes.
Hs.	:	Take your own time.
Customer	:	[A few minutes later] Excuse me, I've decided on this one.
Hs.	:	It'll suit you very well. Good choice. Would you like me to shampoo your hair?
Customer	:	Yes, please. It's a bit greasy.
Hs.	:	Oh, I love this new me. Thank you.
Hs.	:	You're welcome.
Customer	:	My husband will be very surprised.
Hs.	:	I'm sure pleasantly.
Customer	:	How much is it?
Hs.	:	That'll be 50 rupees.
Customer	:	There you go. Thank you very much. See you soon.
Hs.	:	You're welcome. Have a nice day.

Conversation 21: Planning an Excursion (Pallavi, Kartik, Sharma and Deepak)
Grammar Function: Reporting

Pallavi	:	It's getting hotter day by day. Unbearable. How much vacation time do you get, dear?
Kartik	:	Only two weeks this year, Pallavi.
Pallavi	:	Where shall we plan to go?
Kartik	:	How about going to Mysore and Ooty?
Pallavi	:	Oh, a great idea. Don't you think it'll be nice if some of our friends join us?
Kartik	:	Shall we ask Sharma and Deepak if they are interested?
Pallavi	:	The other day Mrs. Sharma asked me whether we were taking vacation.
Kartik	:	Let me try. [He telephones Mr. Sharma] Hello, Sharma.
Sharma	:	Hi, Kartik. What's new?
Kartik	:	We're planning to go to Mysore and Ooty on vacation. How about joining us?
Sharma	:	Really? We'd be delighted to join you. When do you propose to start?
Kartik	:	I think in a week's time. Please come in the evening. We'll work out the details. Meanwhile, I'll find out if Mr. and Mrs. Deepak are also willing to come with us.
Sharma	:	Please do. All right, then. See you in the evening.
Kartik	:	OK, Bye. [Telephones Deepak] Hello, Deepak. Have you made plans to go anywhere for your vacation?

Deepak	:	Are you planning to go anywhere?
Kartik	:	Yes, we have plans of going to Mysore and Ooty. Sharma and his wife will join us. How about you?
Deepak	:	Thank you for asking me, but I can't make it. My brother is coming from the States.
Kartik	:	What a pity that you can't come. Have a nice time with your brother.
Deepak	:	Thank you for the invitation, Kartik. Bye.
Kartik	:	Pallavi, Deepak can't make it. But Sharma says OK . . . Now something to drink? Tea?
Pallavi	:	No. no. Not tea in this hot weather. I'll bring a soft drink.
Kartik	:	That would be great! Thanks, Pallavi.

Conversation 22: The Playground (Anil and Sunil)

Grammar Function: Making Comparisons

Anil	:	Good morning Sunil. How are you?
Sunil	:	Good morning. I'm fine. As you know I have been suffering from cold for the last two weeks. Well, now I feel better than before.
Anil	:	That's fine. Oh, just a moment. I'll get the register for you. So you want to be a member of our cricket club?
Sunil	:	Sure. This club is a very popular club of this area and you are also providing more facilities than any other local clubs.
Anil	:	Any idea of the membership fees? That is also cheaper than other clubs.
Sunil	:	That's so nice of you.
Anil	:	That's my pleasure. But, remember one thing. You have to be sincere here.
Sunil	:	Sure. There is no problem with that.
Anil	:	Have you told your father about this?
Sunil	:	No.
Anil	:	Why?
Sunil	:	But I'll inform him quite soon.
Anil	:	OK. Thanks.
Sunil	:	I'd like to know the exact amount that I have to pay now.
Anil	:	Well, it's two hundred rupees now to register your name. Besides, every month you have to pay fifty rupees only.
Sunil	:	OK, thanks for your cooperation. Here is my money for the registration.

Anil   :   Thanks a lot.

Conversation 23: At the Library (Library Assistant and Suresh)
Grammar Function: Voices

L. A.   :   Good afternoon. What can I do for you, sir?

Suresh   :   Good afternoon. I'd like to apply for a membership of this library.

L. A.   :   May I know your name and occupation?

Suresh   :   Certainly. I'm Suresh. I'm a research scholar.

L. A.   :   What's your area of interest, sir?

Suresh   :   Education.

L. A.   :   We have an excellent collection of books on Education.

Suresh   :   How do I enroll myself as a member?

L. A.   :   Here's the application form. Please fill it in. You have to be introduced by a person who is a member of this library.

Suresh   :   But I don't know anyone who is a member.

L. A.   :   I see. Can you get it countersigned by the Head of the Institution where you are doing research?

Suresh   :   Well, that's not a problem. What's the membership fee?

L. A.   :   Three hundred rupees annually.

Suresh   :   How many books can I borrow at a time?

L. A.   :   Four books and one journal.

Suresh   :   How long can I keep them?

L. A.   :   Three weeks.

Suresh   :   I suppose you collect a fine for late-returning of books.

L. A.   :   Yes, we do. One rupee per book per day.

Suresh   :   Oh. Do you have a card catalogue?

L. A.   :   No, sir. It's computerized. You can check the authors and titles on the computer.

Suresh   :   I see. Is there a microfilm section?

L. A.   :   Yes, sir. There is provision for video-viewing also.

Suresh   :   Are you open the whole week?

L. A.   :   Unfortunately not, sir. We're open from Tuesday to Saturday. The timings are 10.30 a.m. to 7.30 p.m.

Suresh   :   That'll be convenient for me. OK. I'll bring the application form tomorrow. Thanks a lot.

L. A.   :   You're welcome.

Conversation 24: At the Bookseller's (Owner and Customer)

Grammar Function: Agreeing and Disagreeing

Owner	:	Good evening. Can I help you?
Customer	:	Yes. Good evening. Umm . . . I am looking for a few books.
Owner	:	What kind of books?
Customer	:	Well, mainly children's story books.
Owner	:	Okay, Do you have any particular title in mind?
Customer	:	Yes, I do. Like *Cinderilla* and *Of Mice and Men*.
Owner	:	Yes, we have those titles. I'll just get them for you.
Customer	:	Thank you. Do you have *The Magic Faraway Tree*?
Owner	:	Umm . . . Do you know who the author is?
Customer	:	I think it's written by Enid Blyton.
Owner	:	Oh yes. We have a whole lot of Enid Blyton's books. She's very popular with children.
Customer	:	I quite like her books too.
Owner	:	Me too. She writes in a very lively style,
Customer	:	Oh yes, I'd also like a copy of *Alice in Wonderland*.
Owner	:	Certainly. The hardback editions or soft back?
Customer	:	I prefer hardback editions
Owner	:	Will there be anything else?
Customer	:	That's all for the moment.
Owner	:	Your children will have a wonderful time reading all these classics.
Customer	:	Actually these are Christmas presents for my nieces and nephews.
Owner	:	What wonderful presents to give!
Customer	:	I think children don't read as much as they should, nowadays.
Owner	:	I wouldn't agree more.
Customer	:	Thank you very much for all the help. Can I have the bill, please?
Owner	:	Of course. That'll be 203 rupees.
Customer	:	There you go. Thank you very much.
Owner	:	You're welcome. Bye . . . bye . . .
Customer	:	Bye.

Conversation 25: Counselling (Student and Counsellor)

Grammar Function: Relative and Adverb Clauses

Student	:	Good morning, madam.
Clr.	:	Good morning. Please sit down. Now tell me. What can I do for you?

Student	:	Actually I'm going through a very confused phase, madam.
Clr.	:	That's why you are sitting in front of me, OK? Tell me what your problem is?
Student	:	Right from my childhood, I've nurtured a hope of entering the Indian Civil Service.
Clr.	:	Excellent! So what's bothering you?
Student	:	You see I don't have any information about how to go about it. I'm completely at sea.
Clr.	:	Well, in this age of IT boom and quick money, there's a huge and varied market. Still, the Services are a tough act to follow. Many young men and women take these exams in search of the power and glory that go with the IAS and IPS.
Student	:	What are the other Services which can be opted for?
Clr.	:	There are about 25 others in the Central category—Indian Audit and Accounts Service, Indian Postal Service, and Indian Revenue Service, to name a few.
Student	:	I see. What's the procedure for entry into these Services?
Clr.	:	Well, there's a combined competitive examination, which is held in two parts—the Preliminary Exam and the Main Exam. The Prelims are usually held on the second Sunday of June for which you have to send in an application.
Student	:	Where can I get hold of an application?
Clr.	:	It's published in The Employment News on the third Sunday of December usually.
Student	:	How many papers are there in the Prelims?
Clr.	:	Two objective, multiple choice type papers. One is an Aptitude paper and the other is of General Studies.
Student	:	I see. Suppose I qualify in the Prelims, what's the next step?
Clr.	:	Then you have to sit for Mains. It's usually held around November / December each year. There are two language papers—One in English and the other in an optional Indian language. Passing in these two is obligatory. Then you have one compulsory Essay paper, four papers in General Studies, and two papers in one optional subject you opt for. All these papers are subjective.
Student	:	Phew! That's a lot.
Clr.	:	Wait. There's more. After you qualify in the Mains, you're called for an Interview or Personality Test. This is the final stage of selection. This is really the acid test which either

takes you into the glamorous world of Civil Services or simply rejects you.

Student : So that's what it takes to be a bureaucrat! No wonder then that only a few hundreds qualify each year out of the hundreds of thousands who take the exam.

Clr. : I couldn't agree more. It's indeed a nerve-wracking and heartbreaking experience to go through each stage. So, are you ready to put in all your efforts?

Student : You bet, I am. In fact, all this information has made me even more determined to reach my goal. I've to prove to my parents and to myself that I've the mettle and not just a dream.

Clr. : That's what is needed, Sravan. You should have the right kind of inspiration and you should be prepared to put in long hours of hard work.

Student : Well, thank you very much, madam. I'm very grateful to you for being so patient with me and showing me a path.

Clr. : That's all right. All the very best, Sravan. Bye.

Student : Thanks again. Bye.

Conversation 26: Facing an Interview (Prasad, Receptionist and Manager HRD)

Grammar Function: All the Parts of Speech

Prasad : Good Morning. I'd like to meet the Manager HRD please. I've an interview at 11.

Receptionist : Your name, please.

Prasad : I'm Prasad.

Receptionist : Please take a seat. (telephones the Manager) Mr. Prasad, please go to Room No. 5.

Prasad : Thank you. (enters Room No. 5) Good morning, sir.

Manager : Good morning. Please sit down.

Prasad : Thank you.

Manager : You're an M.A. in English Literature. Was it only about English Literature?

Prasad : No, sir. I studied the History of English Language, Phonetics, Linguistics and a bit of American Literature also.

Manager : That's fine. That must have helped you to strengthen your communication skills.

Prasad : Yes, indeed.

Manager	: Do you know computing?
Prasad	: Yes, a little. I've basic knowledge of using a computer.
Manager	: That's good. You seem to have some experience in writing articles.
Prasad	: Yes. They were published in some reputed newspapers and magazines.
Manager	: Well. Mr. Prasad, what, in your view, is a good piece of writing? I mean what are the characteristics of good writing?
Prasad	: I think any composition should be well organized. There should be unity and coherence. I mean all the parts of an essay must be logically connected.
Manager	: You're right. But in the case of web writing, you should be able to aggregate content and make it comprehensive.
Prasad	: I suppose the writer should have the skill of summarizing and editing.
Manager	: And presenting in a concise, palatable way. Content writing is a new medium. Anything that is presented should be precise, succinct and grab the attention of the reader.
Prasad	: I understand. I'm fairly good at summarizing and reporting. Without being flowery or fanciful in style, I should make it crisp and exciting.
Manager	: I think you're absolutely right. Content writing is a new exciting territory. This is the time to actualize your potential.
Prasad	: I should be greatly pleased if you could give me an opportunity to explore and succeed.
Manager	: Let me see how you go about doing it. Can you prepare a short write-up on what we have been talking about—the web content writing?
Prasad	: That I'll do, sir, if you give me some time.
Manager	: Okay. Meet me at 4 in the evening with the script.
Prasad	: Thank you very much.
Manager	: See you later. Bye for now.
Prasad	: Good bye, sir.

Conversation 27: Group Discussion (A, B, C and D)

Grammar Function: All the Parts of Speech

A	: Oh, I'm stung by the spelling bee again and again.
B	: What's the matter?

A   :   The problem I'm facing is I never come to spell some of the words correctly—words with silent letters, magic 'e' and double letters. For instance, why should 'ie' in believe become 'ei' in receive when there is no change in pronunciation?

C   :   You have hit the nail on the head. What an odd language! English spelling seems to be arbitrary and idiosyncratic.

B   :   There is no correlation between speech and spelling.

D   :   The reason is obvious. There are as many as forty four speech sounds in English, whereas there are only twenty six letters in the alphabet to represent these sounds. There is no one-to-one relationship.

A   :   On the other hand, in our languages, we pronounce words as we write them and spell them as we pronounce.

B   :   But in English sometimes the same letter is pronounced differently. For instance, the letter 'a' is pronounced differently in 'at', 'any', 'all' and 'apple'.

C   :   The sound 'f' is spelt differently—with 'ph', 'gh', and 'f'.

D   :   Give me an example of a word with 'gh' pronounced as 'f'.

C   :   Umm . . . take 'tough' for example.

A   :   I think something should be done to simplify spelling. The Americans have done it to some extent as in color, cheek and program.

C   :   It was Webster, I think, who undertook the task of spelling reform in America.

D   :   Well, several attempts were made to reform spelling. Way back in 1768, Benjamin Franklin developed a phonetic alphabet to bring about correlation between speech and spelling.

B   :   Bernard Shaw also showed interest in this.

D   :   Now English has got the status of a 'Global Language'. It is being used increasingly all over the world. There may be variations in pronunciation, but the spelling in the written form is well established. To substitute the alphabetical system with a phonetic system may not be easy.

C   :   May not be feasible either. Printing all the books in phonetic script will be a very costly affair.

B   :   Yet some reform is very necessary. Some kind of simplification and uniformity may be attempted.

D   :   In fact, some changes are in sight. English is made the official language of the European Union. They have set up a Commission to bring about spelling reform. The British Government has given the green signal for improvement in spelling. It's a five-year plan. So you get another variety of English called "Euro-English".

A   :   That's welcome news. Perhaps winds of change may reach India also. Let's wait and see.

B   :   It remains to be seen how soon it will be. Do you know Bernard Shaw's joke on English spelling?

A   :   No, please narrate it.

B   :   At an eating party, Shaw announced, 'I don't eat 'ghoti'. 'Ghoti'-that word was never heard before. The others asked him what it meant. He said, 'Fish', and explained like this. 'Gh' is pronounced 'f' in rough, 'o' in women is pronounced 'i' and 'ti' in station is pronounced 'sh'. So 'ghoti' means fish.

All   :   Ha Ha Ha . . .

"Social criticism begins with grammar and the re-establishing of meanings."

– Octavio Paz

NOTES, UPDATE AND COMMENTS

The author will highly appreciate and gracefully acknowledge any comments, suggestions, recommendations, additions and modifications for further edition at the following address:

Janardan Mishra
Shyampur, Tulasipur, Jajpur, Odisha, India, PIN—755 025
Voice: 09437303774, 09668704368
e-mail: janardanmishra1976@gmail.com

REFERENCES

Alam, Qaiser Z. *English Language Teaching in India: Problems and Issues*. New Delhi: Atlantic Publishers and Distributors, 1988. Print.

McGrath, E. H. *Basic Managerial Skills for All*. New Delhi: Prentice-Hall of India, 2003. Print.

Mathew, Rama. *CBSE-ELT Curriculum Implementation Study*. Rep. Hyderabad: CIEFL, 1997. Print.

Materials for the Teaching of English. 2 block. Hyderabad: EFLU, 2007. Print. Types of Syllabi and Materials.

Curriculum and Instruction. 4 block. New Delhi: IGNOU, 2009. Print. Curriculum Planning.

Meghanathan, Rama. "English Language Education in Rural Schools of India: The Situation, the Policy and the Curriculum." Weblog post. *Http://www.teachingenglish.org.uk/blogs/*. British Council, 30 Oct. 2009. Web.

India. *The National Curriculum Framework*. New Delhi: NCERT, 2005. Print.

India. *Position Paper: National Focus Group on Teaching of English*. New Delhi: NCERT, 2006. Print.

Mohan, Krishna, and Meera Banerji. *Developing Communication Skills*. New Delhi: Macmillan, 2005. Print.

Bansal, R.K., and Harrison J.B. *Spoken English*. Hyderabad: Orient Longman, 2006. Print.

Prabhu, N. S. *Second Language Pedagogy*. Oxford: Oxford University Press, 1987. Print.

Adinarayana, L. *Spoken English*. 1st ed. Hyderabad: Neelkamal Publications, 2003. Print.

Willis, J. *A Framework for Task-Based Learning*. Harlow: Longman, 1996. Print.